PLAYS

BY

W. S. MAUGHAM

By W. SOMERSET MAUGHAM

LIZA OF LAMBETH
MRS. CRADDOCK
THE MERRY-GO-ROUND
THE EXPLORER
THE MAGICIAN
THE MOON & SIXPENCE
OF HUMAN BONDAGE
THE TREMBLING OF A LEAF
ON A CHINESE SCREEN
THE PAINTED VEIL
THE CASUARINA TREE
ASHENDEN
THE GENTLEMAN IN THE PARLOUR
CAKES AND ALE
    OR, THE SKELETON IN THE CUPBOARD
FIRST PERSON SINGULAR
THE NARROW CORNER
AH KING

Plays

JACK STRAW
LADY FREDERICK
THE EXPLORER
MRS. DOT
PENELOPE
THE TENTH MAN
SMITH
LANDED GENTRY
A MAN OF HONOUR
THE UNKNOWN
THE CIRCLE
CÆSAR'S WIFE
EAST OF SUEZ
THE LAND OF PROMISE
OUR BETTERS
THE UNATTAINABLE
HOME AND BEAUTY
LOAVES AND FISHES
THE LETTER
THE CONSTANT WIFE
THE SACRED FLAME
THE BREADWINNER
FOR SERVICES RENDERED
SHEPPEY

WILLIAM HEINEMANN LTD.

PLAYS

by

W. SOMERSET MAUGHAM

VOLUME VI.

THE UNKNOWN
FOR SERVICES RENDERED
SHEPPEY

LONDON
WILLIAM HEINEMANN LTD

THREE PLAYS IN ONE VOL.
FIRST PUBLISHED 1934

PRINTED
IN GREAT BRITAIN
AT THE WINDMILL PRESS

PREFACE

With the three pieces in this volume I conclude the edition of such of my plays as I have desired for one reason or another to reprint. When *For Services Rendered* was about to be produced and I mentioned to an interviewer that it was the last play but one that I proposed to write, I was much surprised to find that this matter, which I supposed of concern only to myself, aroused nearly as much interest as though a well-known prize-fighter had announced his intention of retiring from the ring. For a week, from dawn till dewy eve, I received in my parlour a succession of gentlemen of the Press from all parts of the world; they came from the furthest Hebrides, they came from Sydney, Australia and from Toronto, Canada, they came from Buenos Ayres (known to us film fans for its connection with the White Slave Traffic) and from Buda Pesth in Hungary, celebrated for Tzigane orchestras and the aperient water of Hunyadi János; and, if I may express myself in the vernacular, I spilt the beans. I was rung up from the offices of great newspapers that till then had never communicated with me but to ask me what I ate for breakfast or what was my opinion of the Modern Girl and invited, sometimes for nothing and sometimes for fifteen, twenty or even thirty guineas, my bitter tale to tell. I could not but wish that I had kept my own counsel or that I had sworn my first interviewer to secrecy. I found it very boring to repeat the same thing a dozen times to a dozen interviewers. Nor were they anxious that I should; each wanted an exclusive story. Some time ago an ingenious person induced a number of authors to write a story on a plot that he provided and the readers were expected to be amused by seeing how different authors dealt with the same idea. I had to make all the different stories on the same plot myself.

What I had to say really was very simple. For some years I had had in mind the four plays with which I proposed to finish my career as a practising dramatist. I was prepared to write them only on this account, for I did not think any of them was likely to succeed and I knew how difficult it was for a dramatist to recover a popularity that he had lost. I was much surprised that *The Sacred Flame* and *The Bread-winner* had a considerable success. I expected nothing of *For Services Rendered.* During the rehearsals of this piece I amused myself by devising the way in which it might have been written to achieve popularity. Any dramatist will see how easily the changes could have been made. The characters had only to be sentimentalised a little to affect their behaviour at the crucial moments of the play and everything might have ended happily. The audience could have walked out of the theatre feeling that war was a very unfortunate business, but that notwithstanding God was in his heaven and all was right with the world; there was nothing to fash oneself about and haddock *à la crème* and a dance would finish the evening very nicely. But it would not have been the play I wished to write.

Before going on I should like to say a few words about *The Unknown*, the first play printed in this volume. It was produced immediately after the war, and the circumstances of the time helped it to a certain success. I could not anticipate it, for in performance it turned out to have an error of construction that I had not seen. I took up again in it an idea I had used many years before in a forgotten novel called *The Hero* and the drama I saw in my mind's eye lay in the conflict between two persons who loved one another and were divided by the simple piety of the one and the lost faith of the other. But to my surprise it appeared in re-presentation that the drama lay in the arguments on one side and the other, and not at all in the personal relations of the characters. The result was that the play came to an end with the second act; the third consequently was meaningless and there was no trick or device I could think of that could make it significant.

Sheppey puzzled a good many of the critics. Some of them, strangely ignorant of the principles of the drama, reproached me because I had set a problem and had not solved it. The dramatist takes a situation and wrings out of it all the dramatic value he can. *Sheppey* does not set out to be a problem play; I should describe it as a sardonic comedy. It is this none the less because the action is placed in Camberwell rather than in Mayfair, and the dramatic conflict depends on the hero's attempt to act up to some of the precepts of Christianity rather than on the complications ensuing on his having gone to bed with another man's wife. When I wrote it I was aware that the last scene might displease. It seemed to me to be in the same vein of comedy as the rest of the play, and I did not think I was asking an audience to accept too much when I set before them an hallucination of Sheppey's disordered brain. But it would be foolish not to recognise that they were as puzzled as the critics. I am conscious that I am no longer in touch with the public that patronises the theatre. This happens in the end to most dramatists and they are wise to accept the warning. It is high time for them then to retire.

I do so with relief. For some years I have found it increasingly irksome to confine myself within the necessary limits of dramatic convention. With a greater knowledge of men, with the toleration and perhaps wisdom that the passing years have brought me, I have found it difficult to draw characters as decided and precise as the stage demands. The first rule of drama is to stick to your point, but when your experience is wide every idea that comes to you has so many ramifications that the temptation to follow them is tedious to resist. In the preface to the fifth volume of these plays I have hinted how tiresome I find this representative dialogue that enables you to represent so little. The dialogue of the present day is a sort of spoken shorthand by means of which the listener must guess at the thoughts

and emotions of the persons of the play. When you consider
the complexity of human nature it is hard to resist the
feeling that the characters themselves that can be represented
on the stage have little more substance than mathematical
symbols. Everything must be taken from them but what is
useful to get on with your play. Nor, if you have any
independence of temper, can you reconcile yourself to the
interposition between you and your audience of the actors
and the producer. You cannot have that intimate relation
there is between the writer of a book and his reader. The
placing of a play on the stage is a business of its own and
there are few dramatists, unless they have been actors, who
can do it satisfactorily. But the producer very naturally
looks upon a play as a means to exercise his own creative
activity, and it is very seldom that he has the artistic integ-
rity to confine himself to a faithful interpretation. It may
be a better play that he produces than the author wrote, but
it is a different one. A bad, a vain producer can do terrible
things. Because he is not a man of many ideas he attaches
the greatest importance to any he has. Every dramatist has
suffered from the bits of business a producer has invented
and insists on keeping at whatever cost of probability or of
dramatic effect. It is often said that a good actor can bring
out of a character far more than the author ever put in it, and
this is doubtless true, though it is more often the case that a
bad actor brings out far less; but I do not know that this is a
matter on which the author must necessarily congratulate
himself. I have seen the greatest actress in England give a
magnificent performance of Hedda Gabler, but I think it
would have driven Ibsen to distraction. She put so much
into the part that he had never thought of that the character
he had drawn was entirely obliterated. I should not like
these remarks to be taken as a mark of ingratitude to the
actors and actresses who have acted in my plays. To take
only the plays in this volume, I can say that I have never
seen such a moving performance as that of Miss Haidee
Wright in *The Unknown*, and that of Miss Flora Robson in

For Services Rendered. My earlier plays owed much of their
success to the exquisite comedy of Miss Marie Tempest and
to the great and versatile gifts of Miss Irene Vanbrugh. I
have spoken in a previous preface of Miss Fay Compton. I
know how much I am indebted to Miss Gladys Cooper. She
is as beautiful now as when she first went on the stage, and
she has become an actress of extraordinary variety, emotional
force and sensitiveness. She can play nothing without
distinction.

I have written nearly thirty plays. There is no subject,
however hackneyed, calf-love, jealousy, the ill-assorted
marriage, the relation between fathers and sons, that the
writer cannot deal with as though it had never been dealt
with before but there is no subject that he can deal with
more than once with profit and there are some that his own
idiosyncrasies for ever debar him from. The material is
inexhaustible, but the writer can only deal with it so far as
his personality reaches, and eventually, though the mine
remains as rich as ever for others, for him it is worked out.
It seems to me also that play-writing is a young man's job.
A play demands actuality. Though its theme may be of
permanent value, it seems essential to dress it in the mode of
the moment. Not only must the dramatist follow the
changes of habit, observing for example how the automatic
telephone has displaced the old-fashioned one and the
phonograph the piano, but he must be alive to the changes
of convention, the changes in vocabulary and the changes in
the ephemeral thoughts that influence the motives and
actions of people. All this the young writer does instinctively,
because he is part of the change himself, but the older
dramatist only with labour. It is difficult for him to take any
interest in these trivial matters; nor does it seem very
fitting that he should. I do not know whether it is more
tedious to see a play written now in the manner of a genera-
tion back or whether it is more painful to see one written by
an elderly man determined to be up to date.

Most ideas that come to the writer come to him in terms

of the medium he is in the habit of using; if he is a dramatist in play form; if a novelist or a short story writer as novels or short stories. If he is all three they come in the medium in which he is interested at the time. Speaking for myself I know that when I was interested in play-writing I would get ideas for half-a-dozen plays a year; and then, when I was engaged in writing short stories, ideas used to occur to me in that form. The fact that so many of them have been turned into plays, successful or otherwise, seems to show that they might just as easily have come to me as plays in the first case. I think there are very few ideas that can be treated only in one way. If one came to me that clamoured to be written as a play I suppose I should write it, but with the last play in this volume I end my career as a professional dramatist.

I step on the shelf, but from it cast an enquiring eye on the future of the theatre. I hope the reader will not accuse me of stupid egotism if I hazard the suggestion that the form of drama that I have known is destined to end very soon, and of course I do not mean for any such foolish reason as that I have ceased to write. Realistic drama in prose is a form of art, though a minor one, and a minor art, responding to a particular state in civilisation, is likely to perish with a change in that state. The history of prose drama is short. It seems to have sprung into life here and there, during the sixteenth century, in rude farces like those played by Tabarin in a booth to attract customers for his quack medicines. In Spain it quickly achieved uncommon merit in the racy plays of Lope de Rueda, but was killed by the greater attractiveness to the public of verse. It was raised to a form of art by Molière, flourished with his reflected light in the comedies of the Restoration, and was practised with elegance by Marivaux and Beaumarchais in the France of the eighteenth century; it throve with increasing luxuriance in France during the next hundred years, and was cultivated by a long series of men of talent. It reached its utmost height in the solid work of Ibsen. It seems to me

that Ibsen brought the realistic prose drama to such perfection as it is capable of, and in the process killed it. His
plays seem stagy enough now; *When We Dead Awaken*,
which many good judges think an important work, is a
piece of theatrical clap-trap that you cannot believe in for a
moment; but it was his influence that finally stripped the
drama of those elements of recreation which, in my opinion,
are essential to it. The dramatists have wilfully cast aside the
ornaments that made their plays an entertainment for the
eye and ear. The desire for verisimilitude has resulted in an
intolerable dullness. Realism, where realism is out of place,
has forced the dramatists in order to hold the attention of
their audience to resort to themes outside the normal run of
life, and so is responsible for the plays of murder and
detection that give, with all their absurdities, the opportunity
for thrilling incident. An intelligent Chinese going the
round of the theatres in London would think that murder
and theft were habitually practised in the middle-class
households of this country.

The great dramatists of the past sacrificed truth of
characterisation and probability of incident to situation,
which (to my mind, rightly) they considered the essence of
drama. But the interest of the present day is in the analysis
of character. I think this is something new, and points to a
change of civilisation, and this, as I suggested just now,
entails the death of a form of art that was sustained by it.
The characters of the older fiction were static; Balzac and
Dickens told you all about their persons when they first
brought them before your notice, and they remained un-
altered, whatever happened to them and however long a
period elapsed, till their authors had finished with them.
This view of human nature evidently suited the prepos-
sessions of the time, and it was perfectly convenient to the
playwright. It enabled him to make his characters con-
sistent and distinct. But the characters of fiction now are
diverse and unstable. It has been found that the novelist
can get all the excitement of a tale of adventure by the

gradual disclosure of a person's character; in other cases he
is concerned to show the changes in it that are occasioned
by lapse of time and the circumstances of life. He examines,
sometimes naïvely, sometimes subtly, the contradictions of
human nature, and his readers are ready to take an interest in
the complexity of the man in the street. All this is very
difficult for the dramatist to deal with, and he has discarded
the two devices, the soliloquy and the aside, by which he
might have achieved at least some success. The burden is
thrown upon the actors to translate into flesh and blood the
conventional hieroglyphs which are all the dramatist can
provide them with. It is too great a burden. The spectator
no longer believes in the persons that are set before him.

But my melancholic prognosis applies only to the modern
realistic prose drama. I do not mean of course that the
drama can die. Its long history shows that like music,
painting, architecture and poetry it responds to a permanent need of the human race. But when a form of art has
reached what perfection it is capable of and then decays
there is nothing to do but return to its origins. You have an
example in sculpture at the present day which is finding a
new inspiration in the wood-carving of the negroes and in
the stone work of the Mayan and Peruvian craftsmen.
The early drama amused the eye with spectacle and dancing
and the ear with verse and music. I think the modern
playwright would do well to call in these allied arts to his
help. I do not suppose blank verse can ever be used again,
but I do not see why a quick, running metre like that used
by the old Spanish dramatists, though with less frequent
rhymes, should not be acceptable. A long tirade in verse, as
everyone knows who has seen a play of Racine, has apart
from the sense, by its volume of rhythmical sound, a very
high dramatic value. I do not see why music should not be
used, as in the old melodramas, to prepare a mood or
emphasise an emotion. There is no need to remark on the
diverting effect of beautiful scenes and gay costumes or on
the agreeableness of good dancing. An ingenious dramatist

should be able to make all these an integral part of his play. With such pleasant means of recreation he might render acceptable to the public that drama of the soul which in my last preface I suggested was the natural development forced upon him by the success of the cinema.

But I would not condemn the dramatist to occupy himself only with high and serious matters. Comedy also has its claims. It has been greatly hampered by the demand for verisimilitude. My good fortune has brought me in contact with most of the celebrated wits of my day; and I have noticed that they sparkle but intermittently; no one in private life shines so continuously as a witty character should in a play, he is never so pointed, finished and apt; the conversation of a comedy is artificial in its essence, and to take pains to make it resemble the conversation of real life is absurd. The aim of comedy is not to represent life, but amusingly to comment on it. There is no valid reason why farce should not enter into it. In practice it is almost impossible to hold the attention of an audience for two hours and a half with pure comedy. But when the humours grow broad the critics shake their heads and, mildly or acrimoniously, regret the introduction of horse-play. I think they make a mistake. Comedy, depending as it does on wit, appeals only to the intellect; that is not enough: farce appeals to the belly. The great comic writers of the past felt no fear of it, and I would have the comic writers of the future feel no fear of it either, but use it, as freely as Aristophanes and Molière, whenever it suits their purpose. They must not mind if the very superior look down their noses. They can always console themselves with the recollection that Walter Pater laughed consumedly at *The Magistrate*.

CHARACTERS

Colonel Wharton
Major Wharton (John)
Mrs. Wharton
Mrs. Littlewood
Rev. Norman Poole
Mrs. Poole
Sylvia Bullough
Dr. Macfarlane
Kate
Cook

The action of the play takes place at the Manor House, Stour, in the County of Kent.

THE UNKNOWN

THE FIRST ACT

The drawing-room at the Manor House, COLONEL WHARTON'S residence. It is a simple room, somewhat heavily furnished in an old-fashioned style; there is nothing in it which is in the least artistic; but the furniture is comfortable, and neither new nor shabby. On the papered walls are the Academy pictures of forty years ago. There are a great many framed photographs of men in uniform, and here and there a bunch of simple flowers in a vase. The only things in the room which are at all exotic are silver ornaments from Indian bazaars and flimsy Indian fabrics, used as cloths on the occasional tables and as drapery on the piano.

At the back are French windows leading into the garden; and this, with its lawn and trees, is seen through them. It is summer, and the windows are open. Morning.

MRS. WHARTON *is sitting in the corner of the sofa, knitting a khaki comforter. She is a slight, tall woman of five-and-fifty; she has deliberate features, with kind eyes and a gentle look; her dark hair is getting very grey; it is simply done; and her dress, too, is simple; it is not at all new and was never fashionable.*

KATE, *a middle-aged maid-servant, in a print dress, a cap and apron, comes in.*

KATE: If you please, ma'am, the butcher's called.

MRS. WHARTON: Oh! I arranged with Cook that we should have cold roast beef again for luncheon to-day, Kate. Tell the butcher to bring two and a half pounds of the best end of the neck for to-night, and tell him to pick me out a really nice piece, Kate. It's so long since the Major has had any good English meat.

5

KATE: Very good, ma'am.

MRS. WHARTON: And he might send in a couple of kidneys. The Colonel and Major Wharton enjoyed the kidneys that they had for breakfast yesterday so much.

KATE: Very good, ma'am. If you please, ma'am, the gardener hasn't sent in a very big basket of peas. Cook says it won't look much for three.

MRS. WHARTON: Oh, well, it doesn't matter as long as there are enough for the gentlemen. I'll just pretend to take some.

KATE: Very good, ma'am.

> [*As she is going,* COLONEL WHARTON *enters from the garden with a basket of cherries. He is a thin old man, much older than his wife, with white hair; but though very frail he still carries himself erectly. His face is bronzed by long exposure to tropical suns, but even so it is the face of a sick man. He wears a light tweed suit which hangs about him loosely, as though he had shrunk since it was made for him. He has a round tweed hat of the same material.*

COLONEL WHARTON: Has the paper come yet, Kate?

KATE: Yes, sir. I'll bring it.

> [*Exit* KATE.

COLONEL WHARTON: I've brought you in some cherries, Evelyn. They're the only ripe ones I could find.

MRS. WHARTON: Oh, that is nice. I hope you're not tired.

COLONEL WHARTON: Great Scott, I'm not such a crock that it can tire me to pick a few cherries. If I'd been able to find a ladder I'd have got you double the number.

MRS. WHARTON: Oh, my dear, you'd better let the gardener get them. I don't approve of your skipping up and down ladders.

COLONEL WHARTON: The gardener's just as old as I am and not nearly so active. Hasn't John come in yet? He said he was only going to the post.

MRS. WHARTON: Perhaps he went in to see Sylvia on the way back.

COLONEL WHARTON: I shouldn't have thought she wanted to be bothered with him in the morning.

MRS. WHARTON: George!

COLONEL WHARTON: Yes, dear.

MRS. WHARTON: It seems so extraordinary to hear you say: "Hasn't John come in yet? He said he was only going to the post." It makes me rather want to cry.

COLONEL WHARTON: It's been a long time, Evelyn. It's been a bad time for both of us, my dear. But worse for you.

MRS. WHARTON: I tried not to be troublesome, George.

COLONEL WHARTON: Dear child, aren't I there to share your troubles with you?

MRS. WHARTON: It seems so natural that he should come in any minute, it seems as though he'd never been away— and yet somehow I can't quite believe it. It seems incredible that he should really be back.

COLONEL WHARTON: [*Patting her hand.*] My dear Evelyn!

> [KATE *brings in the paper and gives it to the* COLONEL. *She goes out.*]

COLONEL WHARTON: Thank you. [*While he puts on his spectacles.*] It's a blessing to be able to read the births, deaths, and marriages like a gentleman instead of turning before anything else to the casualties.

MRS. WHARTON: I hope before long that we shall be composing a little announcement for that column.

COLONEL WHARTON: Have they settled a day yet, those young people?

MRS. WHARTON: I don't know. John hasn't said anything, and I didn't see Sylvia yesterday except for a moment after church.

COLONEL WHARTON: Evelyn dear, the gardener tells me he

hasn't got much in the way of peas ready for to-night, so I've told him to send in a few carrots for me; I think they're probably better for my digestion.

MRS. WHARTON: Nonsense, George. You know how much you like peas, and I'm not very fond of them. I was hoping there'd only be enough for two so that I shouldn't have to eat any.

COLONEL WHARTON: Evelyn, where do you expect to go when you die if you tell such stories?

MRS. WHARTON: Now, George, don't be obstinate. You might give in to me sometimes. They're the first peas out of the garden and I should like you to eat them.

COLONEL WHARTON: No, my dear, I'd like to see you eat them. I'm an invalid, and I must have my own way.

MRS. WHARTON: You tyrant! You haven't seen Dr. Macfarlane this morning? I'm so anxious.

COLONEL WHARTON: You old fusser! No sooner have you stopped worrying over your boy than you start worrying over me.

MRS. WHARTON: Even though you won't let me call my soul my own, I don't want to lose you just yet.

COLONEL WHARTON: Don't be alarmed. I shall live to plague you for another twenty years.

[KATE *comes in*.

KATE: If you please, ma'am, Mrs. Poole has called.

MRS. WHARTON: Why haven't you shown her in?

KATE: She wouldn't come in, ma'am. She said she was passing and she just stopped to enquire how you were.

COLONEL WHARTON: Tell her to come in, Kate. What's she making all this fuss about?

KATE: Very well, sir.

[*Exit*.

MRS. WHARTON: I expect she wants to hear all about John.

COLONEL WHARTON: If she'll wait a minute she'll have the chance of seeing the young fellow himself.

> [KATE *comes in, followed by* MRS. POOLE. *The visitor is a thin, rather dour person of middle age, brisk in her movements, competent and firm. She is a woman who knows her own mind and has no hesitation in speaking it. She is not unsympathetic. She wears a serviceable black coat and skirt and a black straw hat.*

KATE: Mrs. Poole.

> [*Exit.*

COLONEL WHARTON: What do you mean by trying to get away without showing yourself? Is this how you do your district visiting?

MRS. POOLE: [*Shaking hands with* MRS. WHARTON *and with the* COLONEL.] I wanted to come in, but I thought you mightn't wish to see me to-day, so I put it like that to make it easier for you to send me about my business.

MRS. WHARTON: We always wish to see you, my dear.

MRS. POOLE: If I had a son that I hadn't seen for four years and he'd been dangerously wounded, I think I'd want to keep him to myself for the first few days after he got home.

COLONEL WHARTON: Then you're not as unselfish a woman as Evelyn.

MRS. WHARTON: Or perhaps not nearly so vain.

MRS. POOLE: Did you go down to the station to meet him on Saturday?

MRS. WHARTON: The Colonel went. He wouldn't let me go because he said I'd make a fool of myself on the platform.

COLONEL WHARTON: I took Sylvia. I thought that was enough. I knew I could trust her to control herself.

MRS. POOLE: And when are they going to be married?

MRS. WHARTON: Oh, I hope very soon. It's been a long and anxious time for her.

MRS. POOLE: Can you bear to give him up when he's only just come back to you?

MRS. WHARTON: Oh, but it's not giving him up when he's marrying Sylvia. She's been like a daughter to us. D'you know, they've been engaged for seven years.

MRS. POOLE: I hope they'll be very happy. Sylvia certainly deserves to be.

COLONEL WHARTON: She's done cheerfully the most difficult thing anyone can do. All through the war when she was pining to be off and do her bit she stayed at home with a bed-ridden mother.

MRS. WHARTON: Poor Mrs. Bullough.

COLONEL WHARTON: Yes, but poor Sylvia too. It's easy enough to do your duty when duty is dangerous and exciting, but when you can do nothing—no one knows better than I what it is to sit still and look on when others are doing the things that are worth while. This war came ten years too late for me.

MRS. POOLE: That's what the Vicar has been saying ever since the war began. But after all your son has taken your place, and I think you can be proud of him.

COLONEL WHARTON: [*With intense satisfaction.*] The rascal with his Military Cross and his D.S.O.

MRS. POOLE: I'm so glad that his first day here was a Sunday.

MRS. WHARTON: You don't know what I felt when we knelt down side by side in church. I was very grateful.

MRS. POOLE: I know. I could see it in your face and the Colonel's.

COLONEL WHARTON: God has vouchsafed us a great mercy.

MRS. POOLE: The Vicar was dreadfully disappointed that he didn't stay for Holy Communion. You know that he looks upon that as the essential part of the service.

MRS. WHARTON: I think we were a little disappointed, too. We were so surprised when John walked out.

MRS. POOLE: Did he say why he had?

MRS. WHARTON: No. I talked it over with the Colonel. We didn't quite know what to do. I don't know whether to mention it or not.

MRS. POOLE: I do hope he'll stay next Sunday.

MRS. WHARTON: He was always a very regular communicant.

COLONEL WHARTON: I don't see why you shouldn't say something to him about it, Evelyn.

MRS. WHARTON: I will if you like.

> [*There is the sound of a laugh in the garden.*

Why, here he is. And Sylvia.

> [SYLVIA BULLOUGH *and* JOHN WHARTON *come in. She is no longer quite young. She has a pleasant, friendly look rather than beauty, and she suggests the homely virtues of a girl very well brought up in a nice English family; she gives the impression of a practical, competent, and sensible woman. She will make a good wife and an excellent mother. She is very simply dressed in light summery things, and she wears a straw hat. She is carrying a string bag, in which are a number of household purchases.* JOHN WHARTON *is in mufti. He is a man of thirty.*

SYLVIA: Good morning, everybody!

MRS. WHARTON: My dear, how nice of you to come in.

JOHN: She didn't want to, but I made her.

> [SYLVIA *kisses* MRS. WHARTON *and shakes hands with* MRS. POOLE, *then she kisses the* COLONEL.

SYLVIA: [*Gaily.*] That's a deliberate lie, John.

MRS. WHARTON: This is my son, Mrs. Poole.

JOHN: [*Shaking hands with her.*] I daresay you suspected it.

MRS. POOLE: I had a good look at you in church, you know.

JOHN: Is that how vicars' wives behave themselves?

MRS. POOLE: They allow themselves a little licence when young people come home on leave.

COLONEL WHARTON: Did you meet in the village?

JOHN: Not exactly. I saw Sylvia darting into Mrs. Gann's shop, evidently to avoid me. . . .

SYLVIA: [*Interrupting.*] I don't know how you imagined I could see you out of the back of my head.

JOHN: So I ran like a hare, and caught her in the very act of buying two pounds of vermicelli.

SYLVIA: To say nothing of a tin of sardines and a packet of mustard.

JOHN: Now take off your hat, Sylvia. You mustn't hide the best feature you've got.

SYLVIA: [*Taking it off.*] I hope you don't think I shall go on doing exactly what you tell me a minute after the war's over.

JOHN: I haven't noticed any startling alacrity to do what I tell you as it is.

SYLVIA: You ungrateful fellow! When have I hesitated to carry out your slightest wish?

MRS. WHARTON: He's only been back forty-eight hours, poor dear.

JOHN: Didn't I go down to you on my bended knees in the middle of the road and ask you to come for a walk with me?

SYLVIA: Oh, well, I wanted to see your father. I was anxious to hear what the specialist had said.

JOHN: [*Surprised.*] Have you been seeing a specialist, father? Aren't you well?

COLONEL WHARTON: Perfectly. It was only to satisfy your poor mother.

JOHN: But why didn't you tell me? Is anything the matter with him, mother?

MRS. WHARTON: My dear, your father wouldn't let me tell you anything about it when you came. He didn't want you to be worried. And I thought myself it might just as well keep till to-day.

COLONEL WHARTON: The fact is I haven't been quite up to the mark lately, and Dr. Macfarlane thought I'd better see a specialist. So I went into Canterbury on Saturday and saw Dr. Keller.

MRS. POOLE: Yes, I heard you'd been to see him. They say he's very clever.

JOHN: What did he say?

COLONEL WHARTON: Well, you know what these doctor fellows are. He wouldn't say much to me. He said he'd write to Macfarlane.

JOHN: Well?

COLONEL WHARTON: I suppose Macfarlane got the letter this morning. He'll probably be round presently.

MRS. POOLE: I saw him going along the Bleane Road in his dog-cart about an hour ago. You might ask him who it was he was going to see.

JOHN: Are you feeling ill, father?

COLONEL WHARTON: No. I shouldn't have dreamed of going to a specialist, only your mother was worrying.

SYLVIA: Don't put all the blame on her. I was, too.

JOHN: [*Going over to him and putting his arm in his.*] Poor old father, you mustn't be ill.

COLONEL WHARTON: Oh, I'm not going to die just yet, you know.

JOHN: I should jolly well think not. Wait till you're a hundred and two, and then we'll begin talking about it.

> [*The Vicar of Stour, the* REV. NORMAN POOLE, *appears at the window. He is a tall, thin man, bald, dressed in a short black coat, with a black straw hat. He is energetic, breezy, and cheerful. He likes to show that,*

*although a clergyman, he is a man; and he affects a
rather professional joviality.* MR. *and* MRS. POOLE
*have that physical resemblance which you sometimes see
in married people. You wonder if they married
because they were so much alike, or if it is marriage
which has created the similarity.*

VICAR: Hulloa, hulloa, hulloa! May I come in?

MRS. WHARTON: [*Smiling.*] Of course. How do you do?

COLONEL WHARTON: My dear Vicar!

VICAR: [*Entering.*] I suppose I ought to have gone round to
the front door, and rung the bell like a gentleman. My
dear Dorothy, when will you teach me how to behave?

MRS. POOLE: I've long given up the attempt.

VICAR: I thought I'd look in and say how-do-you-do to the
wounded hero.

MRS. WHARTON: My son. The Vicar.

VICAR: Welcome! I passed you in the village just now. I
had half a mind to come up and wring your hand, but I
thought you'd say, who the deuce is this clerical gent?

JOHN: How do you do?

VICAR: An authentic hero. And he speaks just like you and
me. The world's a strange place, my masters. Well,
what d'you think of Blighty?

JOHN: I'm very glad to be home again. I thought I never
should get back.

VICAR: You've not been home since the beginning of the
war, have you?

JOHN: No, you see I was in India when it broke out. What
with Gallipoli and one thing and another, I was done
out of my leave every time.

VICAR: Well, it's a long lane that has no turning. But I
understand that you've picked up some bits and pieces
here and there. The Military Cross and the D.S.O., isn't
it?

MRS. POOLE: You must be a very proud man.

VICAR: How did you win them?

JOHN: Oh, I don't know. Playing about generally.

MRS. WHARTON: I don't think you'll get very much more than that out of John.

VICAR: [*To* JOHN.] You lucky beggar! You've had your chance and you were able to take it. That's where I should have been, where my heart was, with the brave lads at the front. And my confounded chest has kept me chained to this little tin-pot parish.

MRS. POOLE: My husband suffers from his lungs.

JOHN: I'm sorry to hear that.

VICAR: Yes, the Great White Peril. They say its ravages are terrible. That's why I came here, you know; I was in charge of the parish of St. Jude's, Stoke Newington, when I crocked up. I tried to get them to let me go when the war broke out, but they wouldn't hear of it.

MRS. WHARTON: They also serve who only stand and wait.

VICAR: I know, I know. It's this confounded energy of mine. I'm a crock, and I've just had to make the best of it. I'm on the shelf. The future is in the hands of you brave lads who've been through the fire. I suppose you went to sleep during my sermon yesterday.

JOHN: Not at all. I listened to it very attentively.

VICAR: I shouldn't blame you if you had. That's about all I've been able to do during the war, to preach. And, upon my word, I sometimes wonder what good I've done.

MRS. WHARTON: You've been a great help to us all.

VICAR: For my part I don't deplore the war. Our Lord said: "Think not that I come to send peace on earth: I came not to send peace, but a sword." The Christian Church has lived by her sword. Every advance which this world of ours has known in liberty, in justice, in enlightenment, has been won for it by the sword of Jesus Christ.

COLONEL WHARTON: I wish all parsons were as broad-minded. I know what war is. I was in Egypt and in South Africa. I've been through half a dozen wars in India. I have no use for slop and sentimentality. My own belief is that war is necessary to a nation. It brings out all a man's best qualities.

VICAR: There I heartily agree with you. It is the great school of character. Amid the clash of arms the great Christian virtues shine forth with an immortal lustre. Courage, self-sacrifice, charity, self-reliance. No one knew before the war what a pinnacle of heroism was within the power of our brave lads at the front.

MRS. POOLE: What do you think about it, Major Wharton?

JOHN: [Smiling.] I? I think it's a lovely day. I have three weeks' leave, and the war is a long way off.

VICAR: [With a chuckle.] A very good answer. I've been saying the obvious, I know that just as well as you do, but you know, sometimes the obvious has to be said, and when it has, I think a man should have the courage to say it. Now, my dear, let's be off.

MRS. POOLE: I don't know what Mrs. Wharton will think of us for inflicting ourselves on her like this.

VICAR: We're all friends here, I hope and trust. If we weren't welcome, Mrs. Wharton only had to say so. To my mind the afternoon call is a convention more honoured in the breach than the observance.

MRS. WHARTON: It's been very good of you to come.

[There is a general shaking of hands.

VICAR: [To JOHN.] Well, good-bye, young fellow. I've tried to show you that I'm by way of being rather broad-minded as parsons go. It wouldn't shock me in the least to hear you say "damn" or "blast." I'm often inclined to use a bit of strong language myself. I asked you just now if you'd gone to sleep during my sermon. I wouldn't have turned a hair if you had.

JOHN: It's very kind of you to say so. I may avail myself of your suggestion on some future occasion.

VICAR: On a future occasion, perhaps—shall we say next Sunday?—I hope you won't leave the House of God without partaking in the greatest of all the Sacraments of our Church. Don't forget that the Almighty has in His mercy brought you in safety through great and terrible peril. That's all I wanted to say to you. Good-bye, God bless you.

JOHN: Good-bye.

VICAR: [*Shaking hands with* MRS. WHARTON.] Good-bye. These parsons, what a nuisance they make of themselves, don't they?

MRS. WHARTON: I wanted to ask you if you'd seen poor Mrs. Littlewood since her return.

VICAR: No, she didn't come to church yesterday. And of course, Sunday's my busy day—I'm the only man in the parish who works seven days a week—so I haven't had a chance to see her yet, poor soul.

SYLVIA: She came down by the 6.35 on Saturday. She was in the same train as John, but I wasn't bothering much about anyone else just then, and I didn't speak to her.

COLONEL WHARTON: I wish we could do something for her.

MRS. WHARTON: [*Explaining to* JOHN.] She was telegraphed for last week to go to Ned at Boulogne. He died on Tuesday.

JOHN: [*With astonishment.*] Ned! But he was only a kid.

MRS. WHARTON: Oh, he'd grown up since you were home. He was nearly nineteen.

MRS. POOLE: Both her sons are gone now. She's quite alone.

MRS. WHARTON: We must all be very kind to her. It will be

terrible for her in that big house all by herself. I wish you'd spoken to her on Saturday, George.

COLONEL WHARTON: I felt rather shy about it. After all, we've had rather an anxious time over that young scamp there. If anything had happened to him—well, I should have had Evelyn, but she, poor soul, has nobody.

SYLVIA: I ought to have gone to see her yesterday.

MRS. WHARTON: She must be absolutely prostrated with grief.

VICAR: I wonder if she'd like to come and stay at the Vicarage. I can't bear to think of her all alone.

MRS. POOLE: That's a splendid idea, Norman, and just like you. I'll ask her at once. I'll be glad to do what I can for her.

SYLVIA: Of course one ought to try and find something to occupy her mind.

VICAR: Happily she has always been a deeply religious woman. When all's said and done, in grief like that there's only one unfailing refuge.

> [KATE *enters, followed by* MRS. LITTLEWOOD. *She is a little elderly woman. She is not dressed in mourning, but in the clothes she may be expected to have been wearing before her bereavement.*

KATE: Mrs. Littlewood.

> [*Exit* KATE.

MRS. WHARTON: [*Rising and going to meet her.*] My dear friend, how very glad I am to see you.

MRS. LITTLEWOOD: How do you do? [*She smiles brightly at the assembled company.*] Oh, John, have you come back? [*To* MRS. WHARTON.] I came to ask if you and the Colonel would come and play bridge this afternoon.

MRS. WHARTON: Bridge!

> [*They all look at her with surprise, but no one says anything.*

Mrs. Littlewood: I was going to ask Dr. Macfarlane to make a fourth, but perhaps John will come.

Mrs. Wharton: [*With embarrassment.*] It's very kind of you, but the Colonel hasn't been very well lately. I don't think he feels like going out, and I shouldn't like to leave him.

Mrs. Littlewood: Oh, I'm sorry.

Mrs. Wharton: Won't you sit down?

Mrs. Littlewood: Thank you very much. I won't stay. I'll go round to the Wilkinsons and see if they'll play.

Vicar: I hope you weren't very tired by your journey.

Mrs. Littlewood: I wasn't tired at all.

Mrs. Poole: We thought you were, because we didn't see you in church.

Mrs. Littlewood: No, I didn't come. I thought it would bore me.

[*There is a moment's silence.*

Mrs. Wharton: Did you—did you come straight through from France?

Mrs. Littlewood: No. I stayed a couple of nights in London.

Mrs. Wharton: [*With pity in her voice.*] All alone?

Mrs. Littlewood: No. I picked up a very nice woman in the hotel, and we went out together. We went to the Gaiety one night and the next we went to the Empire. Do you know that I'd never seen George Robey before?

Mrs. Poole: Who is George Robey?

Vicar: I believe he's a comedian.

Mrs. Littlewood: [*Very pleasantly.*] How long are you here for, John?

John: I have three weeks' leave.

Mrs. Littlewood: We must all make much of you. I'll give a tennis party for you, shall I?

SYLVIA: Oh, Mrs. Littlewood, I'm sure you don't want to give parties just now.

MRS. LITTLEWOOD: I'd love to. It's so seldom one gets an excuse for one in a place like this.

MRS. WHARTON: [*Taking her hand.*] My dear, I want you to know how deeply we all sympathise with you in you great loss.

MRS. LITTLEWOOD: [*Patting* MRS. WHARTON'S *hand, and then releasing her own.*] That's very kind of you. [*To* SYLVIA *and* JOHN.] Would Wednesday suit you young people? I'll have both courts marked out.

SYLVIA: [*Desperately.*] I couldn't come, Mrs. Littlewood, I couldn't come.

MRS. LITTLEWOOD: Why on earth not?

SYLVIA: [*Controlling herself to civility.*] I'm engaged that day.

COLONEL WHARTON: John has so short a time at home. I think he and Sylvia have a feeling that they don't want to go to parties.

VICAR: [*Deliberately.*] I hope you got over to France in time to find your son alive.

> [MRS. LITTLEWOOD *gives him a rapid glance, stops a moment as though to collect herself, then answers almost indifferently.*

MRS. LITTLEWOOD: No, he was dead, poor child. [*To* MRS. WHARTON.] Good-bye, my dear, I'm sorry you can't come and play bridge this afternoon. I suppose I shall have to send you a wedding-present. John.

JOHN: I suppose you will.

MRS. LITTLEWOOD: [*With a smile at the rest of the company.*] Good-bye.

> [*She goes out. They are left in amazement.*

MRS. POOLE: Is she absolutely heartless?

COLONEL WHARTON: I always thought she was devoted to her sons.

SYLVIA: And Ned was her favourite.

MRS. POOLE: She wasn't wearing mourning.

SYLVIA: Isn't she going to, do you suppose?

MRS. WHARTON: I can't understand it. She adored those boys.

MRS. POOLE: I didn't ask her to come and stay at the Vicarage, Norman.

VICAR: I don't think we'd better till the situation's a little clearer. She gives one the impression of not caring two straws for Ned's death. She must be as hard as nails.

MRS. WHARTON: No, she isn't that. I've known her for thirty-five years. D'you think she's mad?

COLONEL WHARTON: We'd better say a word to Macfarlane when he comes, Evelyn.

VICAR: I was never so taken aback in my life as when she said she didn't come to church because she thought she'd be bored.

MRS. POOLE: Norman, I must go. I've got a lot of things to do at home.

VICAR: Come along then. We'll just walk out through the garden.

> [*There are farewells, rather distracted by the queer incident that has just occurred, and the* VICAR *and* MRS. POOLE *go out. The* COLONEL *accompanies them to the door.*

SYLVIA: You're very silent, John.

JOHN: I was thinking about Mrs. Littlewood. She doesn't give me the impression of being either callous or mad.

SYLVIA: What does she mean, then?

JOHN: [*Reflectively.*] I don't know. [*With a shrug of the shoulders, throwing off his mood.*] And at the moment I don't very much care. Come and sit down and be a comfort to a wounded hero.

SYLVIA: Idiot!

MRS. WHARTON: Will you stay to luncheon, Sylvia dear?

SYLVIA: No, I think I ought to get back to mother.

JOHN: Before you go let's tell them what we've been talking about.

COLONEL WHARTON: I don't think it's very hard to guess.

JOHN: I want Sylvia to marry me as soon as ever it's possible.

MRS. WHARTON: Of course.

JOHN: If we look nippy we can get a special licence and be married on Thursday. We don't want to go far for our honeymoon, because I have such a short time. And my suggestion is London.

SYLVIA: What do you think, Mrs. Wharton?

MRS. WHARTON: Well, my dear, I think that whatever you and John decide will be quite right.

SYLVIA: He's only just come back to you. I can't bear to take him away immediately. Wouldn't you prefer us to wait a little longer?

MRS. WHARTON: My dear, we've always decided that you should be married the moment he came back. We've been quite prepared to lose him. And perhaps after a few days, if the Colonel's well enough, you wouldn't mind if we came up to London, too. We'd try not to be in your way.

SYLVIA: [*Going down on her knees beside* MRS. WHARTON *and kissing her*.] Oh, my dear, you're so kind to me. I don't know how I can ever thank you for all your kindness.

MRS. WHARTON: It's been a weary, anxious time for all of us. I know how unhappy you've been sometimes. I want you to have him now. He's a good boy, and I think he'll make you happy.

SYLVIA: [*Getting up and giving* JOHN *her hand*.] I'm sure he will. I'll try to make you a good wife, John.

JOHN: I expect you'll be quite good enough for the likes of me. Then it's to be Thursday next.

SYLVIA: [*With a smile.*] It is.

> [*He draws her to him and kisses her. She very nearly breaks down.*

SYLVIA: I've wanted you for so long, John, so dreadfully long.

JOHN: For goodness' sake don't cry.

SYLVIA: [*Breaking away from him, with a chuckle.*] You brute, John! I hate you.

MRS. WHARTON: Did you like the Vicar, John?

JOHN: He seemed all right.

COLONEL WHARTON: He's a first-rate fellow. He had a very good living in London at one time, and he resigned and took one in the East End instead.

JOHN: Really?

COLONEL WHARTON: He said he wasn't ordained to drink China tea with elderly women of means. [*With a chuckle.*] He says very good things sometimes.

MRS. WHARTON: They were perfectly wonderful in the East End. They wanted to live in exactly the same way as their parishioners, so they did without a servant, and did all their housework, even their washing, themselves.

JOHN: It sounds hateful, but of course it really was heroic.

MRS. WHARTON: D'you remember what he said to you about Holy Communion? Your father and I were a little disappointed that you didn't stay for it yesterday.

JOHN: I'm sorry for that, mother dear.

MRS. WHARTON: It would have been such a great pleasure to both of us if we could all three have received it together.

JOHN: Dear mother. . . . If you're really going home to luncheon, Sylvia, I'll walk back with you.

MRS. WHARTON: The Vicar has a Communion service on Wednesday morning. Would you come then? It'll be the last opportunity before your marriage.

JOHN: Oh, my dear, you're not going to ask me to get up in the middle of the night? After all, one of the pleasures of coming home is to lie in bed in the morning. I don't know how I ever tear myself out of those lavender-scented sheets.

MRS. WHARTON: Dear John, won't you come to please us?

JOHN: [*Still trying to pass it off lightly.*] Oh, my dear mother, d'you think it's really necessary?

MRS. WHARTON: I should like it so much, my dear. You know, it means a great deal to us.

JOHN: [*More gravely.*] Don't you think one should go to a ceremony like that in a certain frame of mind?

COLONEL WHARTON: [*Good-humouredly.*] Come, my boy, you're not going to refuse the first request your mother has made you since you came back?

JOHN: I'm awfully sorry, mother. I beg you not to insist.

MRS. WHARTON: I don't quite know what you mean. It's not like you to be obstinate. . . . Won't you come, John?

JOHN: No, mother.

COLONEL WHARTON: Why not?

JOHN: I've been away a long time. There are some things one can't help, you know. I've been through very terrible experiences.

MRS. WHARTON: [*Aghast.*] Do you mean to say you've lost your—faith?

JOHN: I'm awfully sorry to give you pain, dear.

SYLVIA: [*Her eyes fixed on him.*] You've not answered your mother's question, John.

JOHN: If you want a direct answer, I'm afraid it must be—yes.

MRS. WHARTON: [*Overcome.*] Oh, John!

SYLVIA: But you came to church yesterday.

JOHN: That was just a formal ceremony. I assisted passively, as a Jew might assist at the wedding of one of his Christian friends.

SYLVIA: You stood when we stood, and knelt down, and seemed to pray.

JOHN: I would do that if I were in a Roman Catholic church. That seemed to me only good manners. [*With a smile.*] Do you think it was very deceitful?

SYLVIA: I don't quite see why you should strain at a gnat.

JOHN: I don't. It's the camel I can't swallow. I knew it would distress you if I refused to come to church. I didn't want to seem a prig. But the other seems to me different. When I'm asked to take an active part in a ceremony that means nothing to me it's quite another matter. I'd rather not tell a deliberate lie. And surely from your point of view it would be blasphemous.

MRS. WHARTON: [*Occupied with her own thoughts.*] How dreadful!

JOHN: [*Going up to her and putting his arm round her.*] Don't be unhappy, mother. I can't help feeling as I do. After all, these are matters that only concern oneself.

SYLVIA: [*Reflecting.*] Are they?

JOHN: Surely. [*To his mother.*] I would rather not have told you. I knew how much you'd take it to heart. But I was obliged to. And perhaps it's better as it is. I hated the thought of deceiving you and father. Now let's put it out of our minds.

COLONEL WHARTON: John, have you forgotten that in three weeks you'll be going back to the Front? Sooner or later you'll find yourself once more in the fighting line. Have you asked yourself what it will be like to face death without the help of Almighty God?

JOHN: It's always difficult to face death.

COLONEL WHARTON: You wouldn't be the first who found

it easy to stand alone when all was going well and found it a very different thing in danger or illness.

JOHN: [*With a smile.*] When the devil was sick, the devil a monk would be.

SYLVIA: Archie, Mrs. Littlewood's elder boy, was badly wounded on the Somme. His battalion had to retreat and somehow or other he wasn't picked up. He lay in the corner of a wood for three days and kept himself alive on a beet that he pulled out of the field. Heaven knows, I don't want anything like that to happen to you, but are you sure your courage wouldn't fail you then? Are you sure you wouldn't call on God instinctively to help you?

JOHN: And if I did, what of it? That wouldn't be me, that mangled, bleeding, starved, delirious thing. It's me now that speaks, now that I'm well and conscious and strong. It's the real me now. I disclaim and disown anything I may feel or say when I'm tortured with pain and sickness. It would give my real self just as little as a prisoner on the rack gives the truth.

SYLVIA: [*Looking at him fixedly.*] You're afraid of something like that happening, aren't you?

JOHN: Yes, I shouldn't like my body to play me a dirty trick when I hadn't the presence of mind to look after it.

COLONEL WHARTON: Have you ever been in real danger since you—since you began to think like this?

JOHN: Yes. Once I was in a trench the Germans had enfiladed. They'd got the line exactly. The shells fell one after another, first at the end of the trench, and then they came slowly down. One could calculate almost mathematically when the shell must come that would blow one to smithereens.

MRS. WHARTON: [*With a little gasp of terror.*] Oh, John, don't!

JOHN: [*Smiling.*] Well, something went wrong, or else I certainly shouldn't be here now.

COLONEL WHARTON: Do you mean to say you weren't frightened?

JOHN: Frightened isn't the word for it. Talk of getting the wind up: it was a perfect hurricane. I felt as though I were shrinking up so that my clothes suddenly hung about me like sacks. And against my will a prayer came to my lips. From long habit, I suppose, they tried to form themselves into an appeal to God to turn the shell away. I had to fight with myself. I had to keep saying to myself: "Don't be a fool. Don't be a damned fool."

MRS. WHARTON: And you resisted? It was the voice of God speaking to you. The prayer was said in your heart, and He in His mercy heard it. Doesn't that prove to you that you're wrong? At that moment you believed, even though you struggled not to. Your whole soul cried out its belief in God.

JOHN: No, not my soul: my fear of death.

COLONEL WHARTON: I've been in battle, too. In South Africa and in the Soudan we were in some pretty tight places now and then. When I went into action I commended my soul to God, and now that I'm an old man I can say that I never knew fear.

JOHN: I don't think I'm particularly brave. Before an attack I've often had to light a cigarette to hide the trembling of my lips.

COLONEL WHARTON: The Christian doesn't fear death. His whole life is but a preparation for that awful moment. To him it is the shining gateway to life everlasting.

JOHN: I should be sorry to think that life was nothing but a preparation for death. To my mind death is very unimportant. I think a man does best to put it out of his thoughts. He should live as though life were endless. Life is the thing that matters.

SYLVIA: Doesn't that suggest a very base materialism?

JOHN: No, because you can't make the most of life unless you're willing to risk it, and it's the risk that makes the difference. It's the most precious thing a man has, but it's valueless unless he's prepared to stake it.

SYLVIA: What do you think it can be worth while to risk life for?

JOHN: Almost anything. Honour or love. A song, a thought. [*After a moment's reflection, with a smile.*] A five-barred gate.

SYLVIA: Isn't that rather illogical?

JOHN: Perhaps. I don't put it very well. I think what I mean is that life in itself has no value. It's what you put in it that gives it worth.

COLONEL WHARTON: Why do you think you've come safely through the perils and dangers of the war? John, do you know that every day your mother and Sylvia and I prayed that God might see fit to spare you?

JOHN: [*With sudden energy.*] Were you the only ones? Why didn't He see fit to spare the others?

SYLVIA: Who are we to question the inscrutable designs of the Omnipotent?

COLONEL WHARTON: [*Answering his son.*] I don't know what you mean by that. In war somebody's got to be killed. When a commander gives battle he knows pretty accurately what his losses are going to be before he starts.

[JOHN *gives a slight shrug of the shoulders. He recovers his equanimity.*

JOHN: If you don't mind my saying so, I think we'd much better not start arguing. Arguments never bring one much forrader, do they?

MRS. WHARTON: [*Gently.*] But we want to understand, John. You were always such a pious boy.

JOHN: [*Smiling.*] Oh, mother, that's rather a terrible thing to say to anybody.

MRS. WHARTON: [*With an answering smile.*] Oh, I didn't mean it like that. On the contrary, you were rather troublesome. Sometimes you were very headstrong and obstinate.

JOHN: That's better.

MRS. WHARTON: We tried to bring you up to fear God. It used to make me happy sometimes to see how simple and touching your faith was. You used to pray to God for all sorts of absurd things, to make a lot of runs in a cricket match or to pass an exam. that you hadn't worked for.

JOHN: Yes, I remember.

MRS. WHARTON: If you've lost your faith, we know it can't be as so many lose it, on purpose, because they've given themselves over to sensuality, and dare not believe in a God whom every action of their lives insults. If you'll only tell us everything, perhaps we can help you.

JOHN: My dear, you'd much better let the matter rest. I should only have to say things that would hurt you all.

MRS. WHARTON: We're willing to take the risk of that. We know you wouldn't hurt us intentionally. Perhaps they're only difficulties that we might be able to explain. And if we're not clever enough perhaps the Vicar can.

[JOHN *shakes his head without speaking.*

SYLVIA: Don't you want to believe in God, John?

JOHN: No.

[*There is a moment's pause.* KATE *comes in to announce* DR. MACFARLANE. *This is a rather eccentric old man, with long white hair, small, with rosy cheeks. He is an old-fashioned country doctor, and wears rather shabby black clothes and carries a rusty silk hat in his hand. There is in him something of the gentleman farmer and something of the apothecary of a former day.*

KATE: Dr. Macfarlane.

[*Exit.*

MRS. WHARTON: Oh! I'd forgotten for the moment. [*With a smile of welcome.*] We've been expecting you.

DR. MACFARLANE: [*Shaking hands with the two ladies.*] I've been busy this morning. [*To* JOHN.] And how are you, John?

JOHN: Sitting up and taking nourishment, thank you.

DR. MACFARLANE: You look none the worse for all your adventures. A little older, perhaps.

MRS. WHARTON: Oh, of course, you've not seen John before.

DR. MACFARLANE: No. My wife saw him yesterday in church, but unfortunately I couldn't go. I had to see a patient.

JOHN: The same patient?

DR. MACFARLANE: I beg your pardon.

JOHN: You've had to see a patient at about eleven every Sunday morning for the last twenty-five years. I was wondering if it was the same one.

DR. MACFARLANE: If it is, I certainly deserve praise for keeping the undertakers at bay so long. [*Going up to the* COLONEL.] And how are you feeling to-day, Colonel?

COLONEL WHARTON: Oh, I'm feeling pretty well, thank you. Have you had a letter from that fellow in Canterbury?

DR. MACFARLANE: Yes.

COLONEL WHARTON: Well, what does he say?

DR. MACFARLANE: You military gentlemen, you want to go so fast.

MRS. WHARTON: Have you brought the letter with you?

DR. MACFARLANE: It's very technical. Saving your presence, I don't think any of you would make head or tail of it. Now, Mrs. Wharton, my dear, shall you and I go for a little stroll in your beautiful garden, and we'll have a talk about this old tyrant.

COLONEL WHARTON: What's the object of that? Evelyn will only tell me everything you've said the moment you're gone. She's never been able to keep anything from me in her life.

DR. MACFARLANE: You must have patience with me. I'm an old man, and I like to do things in my own way.

COLONEL WHARTON: Well, *I'm* no chicken, and I'm not going to stand any of your nonsense. Tell us straight out what the doctor says and be damned to you. I beg your pardon, my dear, but I have to talk to the old fool in the only way he understands.

DR. MACFARLANE: Very rough, isn't he?

JOHN: The gentlest pirate who ever cut a throat.

COLONEL WHARTON: You know, you're a transparent old fraud, Doctor. The moment you came in I saw you had some bad news for me. You were expecting to find Evelyn alone.

DR. MACFARLANE: This is the hour at which all self-respecting retired colonels are reading *The Times* in their study.

MRS. WHARTON: What does Dr. Keller say?

COLONEL WHARTON: I suppose he wants an operation. It's a nuisance but, with God's help, I can go through with it.

DR. MACFARLANE: Well, I suppose you'd have to know sooner or later. Let these young people clear out and we'll talk it all over quietly.

COLONEL WHARTON: Nonsense. John is my son and Sylvia is almost my daughter. What concerns me concerns

them, I fancy. Why, you couldn't make more fuss if
I'd only got a month to live.

DR. MACFARLANE: [*Hesitating.*] Do you want me to tell
you the whole thing now—just like this?

COLONEL WHARTON: Yes. You don't think I'm afraid to
hear the worst. Whatever it is, I hope I have the pluck
to bear it like a Christian and a gentleman.

> [*There is a pause.*

DR. MACFARLANE: You're quite right. I have bad news for
you. Dr. Keller confirms my diagnosis. I was pretty
sure of it, but I didn't want to believe it. I thought I
might be mistaken . . . I'm afraid you're very ill indeed.
You must be extremely careful.

MRS. WHARTON: George!

COLONEL WHARTON: Come, come, my dear, don't get in a
state. And does he recommend an operation?

DR. MACFARLANE: No.

COLONEL WHARTON: [*Startled.*] Do you mean to say that
. . . But I don't feel so bad as all that. Now and then
I have attacks of pain, but then . . . you don't mean
to say you think I'm going to die? For God's sake tell
me the truth.

DR. MACFARLANE: My dear old friend!

COLONEL WHARTON: You mean I've got a fatal disease.
Can—can nothing be done?

DR. MACFARLANE: I don't know about that. There's always
something that can be done.

COLONEL WHARTON: But a cure, I mean. Can't I be cured?

DR. MACFARLANE: If you want the truth really, then I'm
afraid I can hold out no hope of that.

COLONEL WHARTON: How long d'you give me? [*Trying to
laugh.*] I suppose you're not going to grudge me a year
or two?

DR. MACFARLANE: [*Pretending to take it lightly.*] Oh, you can be quite sure we'll keep you alive as long as we can.

JOHN: You've got a wonderful physique, father. My own impression is that you'll make fools of the doctors and live for another twenty years.

DR. MACFARLANE: Medicine isn't an exact science like surgery. It's a doctor's duty to tell a patient the truth when he asks for it, but if I were a patient I would always take it with a grain of salt.

> [*The* COLONEL *looks at him suspiciously.*

COLONEL WHARTON: You're keeping something from me. If it was only that, why did you want to see Evelyn alone?

DR. MACFARLANE: Well, some people are very nervous about themselves. I wasn't quite sure if you'd better know or not. I thought I'd talk it over with her.

COLONEL WHARTON: Am I in immediate danger of death? For God's sake tell me. It would be cruel to leave me in ignorance.

MRS. WHARTON: Please answer quite frankly, doctor.

DR. MACFARLANE: [*After a pause.*] I think if you have any arrangements to make, it would be wise if you made them soon.

COLONEL WHARTON: Then it's not a question of a year or two even? Is it months or weeks?

DR. MACFARLANE: I don't know. No one can tell.

COLONEL WHARTON: You're treating me like a child. [*With sudden rage.*] Confound you, sir, I order you to tell me.

DR. MACFARLANE: It may be at any time.

COLONEL WHARTON: [*With a sudden cry of terror.*] Evelyn! Evelyn!

MRS. WHARTON: Oh, my dear! My dear husband!
> [*She takes him in her arms as though to protect him.*

DR. MACFARLANE: Why did you force me to tell you?

COLONEL WHARTON: [*In a terrified whisper.*] Oh, Evelyn! Evelyn!

D

MRS. WHARTON: [*To the others.*] Please go.

JOHN: [*To* SYLVIA.] Come. They want to be alone. Dr. Macfarlane, will you come into the garden for a few minutes?

DR. MACFARLANE: Of course I will. Of course.

> [*They go out.* COLONEL *and* MRS. WHARTON *are left alone. For a moment they are silent.*]

MRS. WHARTON: Perhaps it isn't true, my dear.

COLONEL WHARTON: It's true. I know it's true now.

MRS. WHARTON: Oh, it's so hard. I wish it were I instead. I'd be so glad to take your place, darling.

COLONEL WHARTON: We've been so happy together, Evelyn.

MRS. WHARTON: We have very much to be grateful for.

COLONEL WHARTON: Oh, Evelyn, what shall I do?

MRS. WHARTON: Oh, my dear, I'm so sorry for you. I'm so dreadfully sorry . . . I think you're very brave. If I'd been told like that I—I should have broken down.

COLONEL WHARTON: It was so unexpected.

MRS. WHARTON: [*Trying to comfort him.*] I'm thankful that your faith has always been so bright and clear. What a comfort that is now, darling, what an immense consolation! [*She draws him more closely to her.*] You're throwing aside these poor rags of mortality to put on a heavenly raiment. It is what we've always kept in our minds, isn't it? that this brief life is only a place of passage to the mansions of our dear Father. [*She feels the dismay in his heart and she strives to give him courage.*] You've never hesitated at the call of an earthly leader. You're a good soldier; it's a Heavenly Leader that's calling you now. Christ is holding out His loving arms to you.

COLONEL WHARTON: Evelyn—I don't want to die.

END OF THE FIRST ACT

THE SECOND ACT

The Scene is the same as in the preceding Act.
Two days have passed. It is Wednesday afternoon.

MRS. WHARTON *is sitting by a little table, looking reflectively in front of her. On the table is a work-basket, and by the side of this a baby's shirt that she is making. A fire is alight in the grate. After a minute,* JOHN *comes in. She looks up at him with a pleasant smile. He goes to her and puts his hand on her shoulder. She gently pats his hand.*

JOHN: Are you idling, mother? It's not often I catch you giving the devil an opportunity.

MRS. WHARTON: Isn't it wicked of me?

JOHN: What is this you're up to? What in Heaven's name are you making a baby's shirt for? Hang it all, I'm not married yet.

MRS. WHARTON: [*Pretending to be a little shocked.*] Don't be naughty, John. It's for poor Annie Black's baby.

JOHN: Who's she?

MRS. WHARTON: She was engaged to Edward Driffield, the carpenter's second man, and they were going to be married next time he came home on leave. He's been killed, and she's expecting a baby.

JOHN: Poor thing.

MRS. WHARTON: The Pooles are looking after her. You see, she had nowhere to go, and they didn't want her to have to go to the Workhouse, so Mrs. Poole has taken her in at the Vicarage. And I said I'd make all the baby's things.

JOHN: [*Affectionately.*] You're a nice old mother.

MRS. WHARTON: Don't you think it was good of the Pooles?

JOHN: Yes, charming.

MRS. WHARTON: They're coming here this afternoon, John. I wanted the Vicar to see your father. . . . I haven't told your father they're coming.

JOHN: Haven't you?

MRS. WHARTON: He's rather sensitive just now. It's quite natural, isn't it? And I didn't know exactly how he'd take it. I thought if Mrs. Poole came too it would look as though it were just a friendly visit. And perhaps the Vicar will have an opportunity to say a few words to your father.

JOHN: [*Smiling.*] I take it that you want me to help you to leave them alone together.

MRS. WHARTON: I hate doing anything underhand, John, but I think it would help your father so much if he could have a little private talk with the Vicar.

JOHN: Why didn't you suggest it to him?

MRS. WHARTON: I didn't like to. I was afraid he'd be vexed. I thought he'd suggest it himself.

JOHN: [*Very tenderly.*] Don't distress yourself, mother.

MRS. WHARTON: I'm trying not to think of it, John. My only hope is that the end may come without suffering.

JOHN: I wasn't thinking of that.

MRS. WHARTON: [*After a moment's pause.*] I don't know what you mean, John.

JOHN: Yes, you do. You only have to look in father's face.

MRS. WHARTON: I really don't understand. [*Almost vehemently.*] You're wrong, John. He suffers much more pain than you think. That's what gives him that look.

JOHN: [*Gravely.*] It's fear that's in his face, mother, the fear of death. You know it just as well as I do.

MRS. WHARTON: [*With dismay.*] I was so hoping that no one would know but me. It tears my heart. And I can do nothing. And he's so strange. Sometimes he looks at me almost as though I were his enemy.

JOHN: He doesn't want to die, does he? At the bottom of his heart is envy because you can go on living.

MRS. WHARTON: Have you noticed that? I tried not to see it.

JOHN: Don't be angry with him or disappointed. You know, it's a hard thing to die for all of us. Generally one's vitality is lowered so that life seems rather a burden, and it's not very hard then to make a seemly end. But poor father's got something much more difficult to face.

MRS. WHARTON: He's been supported all his life by his confidence in the great truths of our religion. Oh, John, it's so dreadful that just at this moment, when he must put them all to the test, he should falter. It's almost a betrayal of the God who loves him.

JOHN: My dear, you can't imagine that God won't understand? What do these last weeks matter beside a life that has been cheerful and innocent, devout, unselfish, and dutiful? We were talking about it the other day, don't you remember? And I claimed that a man should be judged by what he believed and did in the heyday of his strength, and not by what was wrung from him in a moment of anguish. Pray that God may give my father courage and resignation.

MRS. WHARTON: How can you ask me to pray, John, when you don't believe in God?

JOHN: Pray all the same, my dear, and for me too.

MRS. WHARTON: I don't suppose I shall survive your father very long, dear. Husbands and wives who've been so much to one another as we have don't often make a very good job of separation. I'm so glad to think that you'll have Sylvia.

JOHN: Sylvia's a good girl, isn't she?

MRS. WHARTON: When you were away I was dreadfully

anxious on my own account, of course, but I was anxious on hers too. She's had a very hard time with her mother, and there's been dreadfully little money, only their pensions; if anything had happened to you, when her mother died she would have had practically nothing. You've been engaged so long and she's not very young any more. It's not likely that anyone else would have wanted to marry her.

JOHN: Mother darling, you're being terribly sentimental now.

MRS. WHARTON: [*With comic indignation.*] I'm not, John. You don't know what it is for a penniless woman to be quite alone in the world when she's lost her youth.

JOHN: Yes, I do. But the tears needn't come into your eyes, because Sylvia and I are going to be married and her future is quite adequately provided for.

MRS. WHARTON: She's the only girl I've ever known that I could bear to think of your marrying.

JOHN: Well, as she's the only girl I ever knew that I could bear to marry, we're both quite satisfied.

[KATE *enters, followed by* MRS. LITTLEWOOD.

KATE: Mrs. Littlewood.

[*Exit* KATE.

MRS. LITTLEWOOD: [*Kissing* MRS. WHARTON.] How do you do?

MRS. WHARTON: How are you, my dear?

MRS. LITTLEWOOD: [*To* JOHN.] I brought you a wedding present, John.

[*She hands him a small case in which is a pearl pin.*

JOHN: Oh, I say, that is splendid of you. Just look, mother. Isn't it a ripper?

MRS. LITTLEWOOD: It was Archie's, you know. He always used to be so proud of it.

JOHN: It's awfully good of you to give me something that belonged to him.

Mrs. Wharton: That is nice of you, Charlotte.

Mrs. Littlewood: Nonsense. It wasn't any use to me any more. I thought it much better that John should have it than that it should lie in a safe. They tell me pearls go yellow if they're not worn.

Mrs. Wharton: John, dear, go and smoke a cigarette in the garden. I want to have a chat with Mrs. Littlewood.

John: All right, mother.

[*He goes out.*

Mrs. Littlewood: Do you know that I'm thinking of letting my house? I only kept it so that the boys should have a home to come to when they had a holiday, and now that they're both dead, I think I shall find it more amusing to live in London. I shall join a bridge club.

Mrs. Wharton: Charlotte, what does it mean? Why do you talk like that?

Mrs. Littlewood: My dear, why shouldn't I join a bridge club? [*With a smile.*] At my age it's surely quite respectable.

Mrs. Wharton: I'm bewildered. Don't you want me to talk of your boys?

Mrs. Littlewood: [*Dryly.*] If you feel you really must pour out your sympathy, you may, but I don't know that I particularly want it.

Mrs. Wharton: No one can understand you. You've behaved so strangely since you came back from France . . . I think it was dreadful of you to go to the theatre when the poor lad was hardly cold in his grave. You seem to think of nothing but bridge.

Mrs. Littlewood: I suppose different people take things in different ways.

Mrs. Wharton: I wonder if you're quite in your right mind.

Mrs. Littlewood: [*Somewhat amused.*] Yes, I saw you wondered that.

MRS. WHARTON: If you only knew how eager I am to help you. But you won't let me come near you. We've known one another for more than thirty years, Charlotte. Why do you put up a stone wall between us?

MRS. LITTLEWOOD: [*Gently, as though she were talking to a child.*] My dear, don't worry your kind heart. If I wanted your help I would come to you at once. But I don't. I really don't.

[MRS. WHARTON *hears her husband's step on the stairs.*

MRS. WHARTON: Here is George. [*Going to the window.*] You can come in when you want to, John.

[*The* COLONEL *comes into the room. His face is a little whiter than it was two days ago, and there is in his eyes every now and then a haunted look.*

MRS. WHARTON: Charlotte Littlewood is here, George.

COLONEL WHARTON: So I see. How do you do?

MRS. LITTLEWOOD: You're not looking quite up to the mark to-day, Colonel.

COLONEL WHARTON: That's a cheering thing to say to a man. I'm feeling pretty well.

MRS. WHARTON: I was thinking he was looking much better the last day or two.

COLONEL WHARTON: I presume it's not on my account that you've lit the fire on a day like this.

MRS. WHARTON: No, I feel a little chilly. You always forget that I'm not as young as I was, George.

[*The* COLONEL *sits down in an armchair and* MRS. WHARTON *takes a couple of cushions.*

MRS. WHARTON: Let me put them behind you, darling.

COLONEL WHARTON: For goodness' sake don't fuss me, Evelyn. If I want cushions I'm perfectly capable of getting them for myself.

[JOHN *enters with* SYLVIA *and hears the last two speeches.*

JOHN: Come, come, father, you mustn't spoil mother. She's waited on us both for thirty years. Don't let her get into bad habits at her time of life.

MRS. WHARTON: Oh, Sylvia, we didn't expect to see you to-day. You said you'd be too busy.

SYLVIA: I felt I must just look in and see how you all were.
   [*The* COLONEL *gives her a suspicious look. She kisses* MRS. WHARTON *and* MRS. LITTLEWOOD *and the* COLONEL.

JOHN: [*Showing* SYLVIA *the pearl pin.*] Look what Mrs. Littlewood has given me. Makes it worth while being married, doesn't it?

SYLVIA: Oh, how lovely!

MRS. LITTLEWOOD: You'll find a little present waiting for you when you get home.

SYLVIA: How exciting! I shall run all the way back.

MRS. WHARTON: Now you're here you'd better stay to tea, darling.

SYLVIA: I really can't. I've got so much to do at home.

JOHN: Nonsense. You've got nothing to do at all. We're not going to dream of letting you go.

SYLVIA: Remember that you'll have me always from to-morrow on. Don't you think you could well spare me to-day?

JOHN: No.

SYLVIA: Tiresome creature. Though I must say it's rather pleasing.

COLONEL WHARTON: I never saw two young people who were so thoroughly satisfied with one another as you are.

JOHN: [*Putting his arm round* SYLVIA's *waist.*] But I'm not in the least satisfied with Sylvia. I should like her to have jet-black hair and eyes like sloes.

SYLVIA: What are sloes, idiot?

JOHN: I don't know, but I've read about them from my youth up.

SYLVIA: Oh, Colonel, d'you know that on my way here through the fields, I actually saw a rabbit?

JOHN: I hear there's absolutely nothing on the place now, father.

COLONEL WHARTON: No, the vermin's been allowed to increase so. There are one or two cock pheasants round the house and that's about all. I don't know what next season—but after all, I needn't worry myself about next season. That'll be your trouble, John.

JOHN: I wish I had as much chance of getting a shot at those cock pheasants as you have.

COLONEL WHARTON: By George, I wish I were twenty years younger. I'd take my chance of being shot by a German. It's a bit better than dying like a rat in a trap.

[KATE *enters to announce the* VICAR *and* MRS. POOLE.

KATE: Mr. and Mrs. Poole.

[*Exit.*

MRS. WHARTON: How do you do?

[*There are general greetings. The* COLONEL *looks at them and from them to his wife, suspiciously. The* POOLES *are rather cold with* MRS. LITTLEWOOD.

COLONEL WHARTON: How do you do? It's good of you to have come. Sit down.

MRS. POOLE: Well, Sylvia, are you all ready for to-morrow?

SYLVIA: More or less.

MRS. POOLE: We thought you might intend to postpone the wedding for a few days.

COLONEL WHARTON: They've waited long enough. Why should they wish to do that?

SYLVIA: [*Hastily.*] I told Mrs. Poole yesterday that I didn't think I could possibly get everything arranged by to-morrow.

COLONEL WHARTON: I see that my wife has told you that I'm not very well.

MRS. POOLE: Oh, aren't you, Colonel? I'm so sorry to hear that.

VICAR: She told me this morning after Communion that you weren't quite up to the mark these days.

COLONEL WHARTON: I remember in Egypt, when a horse or a mule sickened, the vultures used to gather round out of an empty sky. Most remarkable.

MRS. WHARTON: George, what are you saying?

COLONEL WHARTON: [*With a bitter chuckle.*] Did Evelyn ask you to come and minister to me?

VICAR: It's not very unnatural that when I hear you're ill I should like to come and see you. And, of course, it does happen to be one of the duties of my office.

COLONEL WHARTON: I don't know why Evelyn should think I want to be molly-coddled out of the world like an old woman. I've faced death before. I don't suppose anyone wants to die before he must, but when my time comes I hope to face it like a gentleman and a soldier.

JOHN: Oh, that I should live to hear my own father talking through his hat. Don't you believe a word those rotten old doctors say. You'll live to bully your devoted family for another twenty years.

COLONEL WHARTON: Don't talk nonsense to me, John. You all treat me like a child. No one must cross me. I must be petted and spoilt and amused and humoured. God damn it, you never let me forget it for a minute.

MRS. WHARTON: Shall we go for a little turn in the garden? The sun is out now.

COLONEL WHARTON: If you like. I shall stay here. I'm chilly.

MRS. WHARTON: A stroll would do you good, George. The Vicar was asking how the new Buff Orpingtons were getting on.

COLONEL WHARTON: [*With a chuckle.*] You're very transparent, my poor Evelyn. When I want to have a chat with the Vicar I'll let him know.

MRS. LITTLEWOOD: [*Who has been watching the scene with some amusement.*] Why don't you have a game of piquet with me, Colonel?

COLONEL WHARTON: I haven't played piquet for years. I will with pleasure. Where are the cards, Evelyn?

MRS. WHARTON: I'll get them for you.

> [*She gets cards from a drawer, and puts them on the card table. The* COLONEL *sits down at the table and sorts the piquet cards out of the pack.*

VICAR: I called on you on Monday, Mrs. Littlewood.

MRS. LITTLEWOOD: So I heard.

VICAR: I was told you were not at home. As I walked away it was impossible for me not to see that you were in your garden.

MRS. LITTLEWOOD: It's inadequately protected from the road.

VICAR: I was rather hurt. I'm not aware that there's been anything in my behaviour since I came here to justify you in treating me with discourtesy. Our relations have always been more than cordial.

MRS. LITTLEWOOD: I didn't wish to see you.

VICAR: So much as that I had the intelligence to infer. But I felt it my duty not to allow pique to interfere with the due discharge of my office. I had various things to say to you which I thought you should hear, so yesterday I called again, and again was told you were out.

MRS. LITTLEWOOD: [*Coolly.*] I didn't wish to see you.

VICAR: May I ask why?

MRS. LITTLEWOOD: Well, I suppose you wanted to talk about my boy. I didn't think your conversation could give him back to me.

VICAR: Don't you think I could have helped you to bear your loss? I think I could have found in my heart words to persuade you to resignation. I might at least have offered you my sympathy.

MRS. LITTLEWOOD: I'm sorry to seem ungracious, but I don't want your sympathy.

VICAR: Your attitude amazes me.

MRS. POOLE: If we didn't all know how devoted you were to your sons, one might really think you were indifferent to their loss.

MRS. LITTLEWOOD: [*Reflectively.*] No, I'm not exactly indifferent.

VICAR: Since you won't see me alone, I must say things to you here and now which I should rather have kept for your private ear. I have a right to remonstrate with you because your behaviour is a scandal to my parish.

MRS. LITTLEWOOD: [*With a smile.*] Oh, I beg your pardon. I thought it was my welfare you were concerned with. If it's that of the parish, pray say anything you like.

VICAR: [*Flushing, but not to be put off.*] I think it was horrible to go to a music-hall on the very day you had returned from your son's grave in France. But that was in London, and you outraged nobody but yourself. What you do here is different. This is a very small place, and it's shameful that you should give parties and go about from house to house playing cards.

MRS. POOLE: It seems so heartless not to wear mourning.

JOHN: [*Rather flippantly, to prevent the conversation from growing too awkward.*] Why? I certainly should hate anyone to wear mourning for me.

VICAR: You give all and sundry the impression that you're perfectly callous. What influence do you think such a thing may have on these young fellows in the village who have to risk their lives with all the other brave lads at the Front? You take from them the comfort that we at home love them and if they fall will hold their memories gratefully in our hearts for ever.

MRS. LITTLEWOOD: I shouldn't have thought the eccentricity of one old woman could matter very much to anyone.

> [*She pauses and looks out into the open for a moment, and then makes up her mind to speak. She speaks quite quietly, almost to herself.*

When they sent for me and I went over to France I wasn't very anxious, because I knew that God, who had taken my eldest son, would leave my second. You see, he was the only one I had left. And when I got there and found he was dead—I suddenly felt that it didn't matter.

MRS. WHARTON: My dear, what do you mean? How can you say such a thing?

JOHN: Don't, mother. Let her go on.

MRS. LITTLEWOOD: I didn't feel that anything very much mattered. It's difficult to explain exactly what I mean. I feel that I have nothing more to do with the world and the world has nothing more to do with me. So far as I'm concerned it's a failure. You know I wasn't very happy in my married life, but I loved my two sons, and they made everything worth while, and now they're gone. Let others take up the—the adventure. I step aside.

MRS. WHARTON: You've suffered too much, my dear.

MRS. LITTLEWOOD: No, the strange thing is that I haven't suffered very much. Don't you know how sometimes one has a horrid dream and knows one's only dreaming all the time? [*To the* VICAR, *with the same good temper, almost amused.*] You're surprised that I should go to the theatre. Why? To me, it's no more unreal a spectacle than life. Life does seem to me just like a play now. I can't take it very seriously. I feel strangely detached. I have no ill-feeling for my fellow-creatures, but you don't seem very real to me or very important. Why shouldn't I play bridge with you?

VICAR: Oh, but, my dear, my dear, there's one reality that you can never escape from. There's God.

[*A flash passes behind the old woman's eyes. She rises and puts out her hand as though to ward off a blow.*

MRS. LITTLEWOOD: I don't think we'll talk about God if you please. I prefer to play piquet.

[*She sits down at the table at which the* COLONEL *has already taken his seat.*

COLONEL WHARTON: Do you play four hands or six to the game?

MRS. LITTLEWOOD: Four—and double the first and last. It makes it more exciting.

COLONEL WHARTON: Shall we cut for deal?

MRS. LITTLEWOOD: [*Cutting.*] You're not likely to beat that.

COLONEL WHARTON: I suppose in the Vicar's presence we daren't play for money?

MRS. LITTLEWOOD: We'll pretend he's not here. Will a shilling a hundred suit you?

COLONEL WHARTON: I don't think that'll break either of us.

[KATE *enters, followed by* DR. MACFARLANE.

KATE: Dr. Macfarlane.

[*Exit.*

DR. MACFARLANE: How d'you do?

MRS. WHARTON: [*Shaking hands with him.*] So nice of you to come in.

DR. MACFARLANE: How is the Colonel to-day?

COLONEL WHARTON: Playing piquet.

JOHN: You're coming to-morrow, aren't you, Doctor?

DR. MACFARLANE: Of course I am. I brought you both

into the world. I have almost a personal interest in
seeing you made one flesh.

VICAR: [*Jovially.*] It's many a long day since you've been
inside a church, Doctor.

DR. MACFARLANE: Since you clerical gentlemen left off
threatening me with eternal flames I feel justified in
following my own inclinations in the matter.

VICAR: [*Chaffing him.*] But we still believe in annihilation.

DR. MACFARLANE: I'm willing to take my chance of that.
It has no terrors for a man who's not had a holiday for
twenty years.

VICAR: You're not an irreligious man. I don't know why
you don't come to church.

DR. MACFARLANE: Shall I tell you? Because after repeated
experiment I've reached the conclusion that I'm not a
whit the better for it.

JOHN: You'll have to give him up, Vicar. He's a stubborn
old thing. He takes advantage of the fact that he's the
only doctor within ten miles who won't kill you so long
as he can make seven and sixpence a visit by keeping
you alive.

COLONEL WHARTON: Do you mean to say that our Church
doesn't believe any longer in eternal punishment?

JOHN: Oh, father, hell has always left me perfectly cold.
You and I are quite safe. You see, mother would never
be happy in Heaven without us, and God couldn't refuse
her anything she asked.

MRS. WHARTON: [*Affectionately.*] John, what nonsense you
talk.

MRS. POOLE: I sometimes think the modern Church has
been very rash in surrendering a belief which has the
authority of Our Lord himself. How many sinners have
been brought to repentance by the fear of everlasting
punishment!

JOHN: That rather suggests calling down fire from Heaven to light a cigar.

MRS. POOLE: That may be funny, but I don't see the point of it.

JOHN: [*Good-humouredly.*] Well, I should have thought it hardly required anything so tremendous as eternity to deal with human wickedness. I suppose sin is due to a man's character, which he can't help, or to his ignorance, for which he isn't to blame.

VICAR: In fact, to your mind sin is all moonshine.

JOHN: I think it a pity that Christianity has laid so much stress on it. We assert in church that we're miserable sinners, but I don't think we mean it, and what's more, I don't think we are.

MRS. POOLE: We are conceived in sin, and sin is part of our inheritance. Why did Christ die if not to atone for the sin of men?

JOHN: In war one gets to know very intimately all sorts of queer people. I don't suppose I shall ever know any men so well as I knew the men in my company. They were honest and brave and cheerful, unselfish, good fellows; perhaps they swore a good deal, and they got drunk if they had the chance, and they had the glad eye for a pretty girl. But do you think they were sinners for that? I don't.

VICAR: Look in your own heart and say if you are not conscious of grievous, terrible sin.

JOHN: Frankly, I'm not.

VICAR: Do you mean to say that you have nothing to reproach yourself with?

JOHN: I've done a certain number of things which I think were rather foolish, but I can't think of anything that I'm particularly ashamed of.

VICAR: Do you mean to tell me that you've always been perfectly chaste?

E

JOHN: I'm normal and healthy. I've been no more chaste than any other man of my age.

VICAR: And isn't that sin?

JOHN: I don't think so. I think it's human nature.

VICAR: We're arguing at cross-purposes. If when you say "white" you mean what the rest of the world calls "black," all words are futile.

JOHN: [*With a smile.*] The singular thing is that if I'd answered your question with a "yes," you would probably have thought me a liar or a fool.

VICAR: This terrible condition of humanity, which seems to cry out against the very idea either of man's dignity, or of God's justice, has but one explanation, and that is sin.

JOHN: You're referring to the war? It needs some explaining, doesn't it?

VICAR: Every Christian must have asked himself why God allows the infamous horror of war. I'm told the padres are constantly being asked by the brave lads at the Front why the Almighty allows it to continue. I can't blame anyone for being puzzled. I've wrestled with the question long and anxiously . . . I can't believe that God would leave His children to suffer without a clue to His intention.

MRS. POOLE: The ways of God are inscrutable. How can we tell what are the aims of the eternal? We only know that they are good.

JOHN: Meanwhile men are being killed like flies, their wives and mothers are left desolate, and their children fatherless.

VICAR: You mustn't forget exactly what is meant by "Almighty." It means not so much able to do all things as powerful over all things.

JOHN: Ah, the padre of my regiment told me that. I may be very stupid, but I think the distinction rather fine.

For the plain man the difficulty remains. Either God
can't stop the war even if He wants to, or He can stop
it and won't.

MRS. POOLE: In my opinion there can be no hesitation. It
is written: "Not a sparrow shall fall on the ground
without your Father."

VICAR: Remember that we have free will and God makes
use of our free will to punish us and to teach us and to
make us more worthy of His grace and mercy. Man,
born in sin, justly brought this long-drawn disaster on
himself as surely as Adam brought on himself the divine
punishment which we all inherit.

JOHN: If I saw two small boys fighting I'd separate them,
even though one was a lazy little beggar and the other
had stolen Farmer Giles' apples. I wouldn't sit by and
let them seriously hurt one another so that they should
be better boys in future.

MRS. POOLE: But you speak as though all this suffering must
be useless. We all know how suffering can purify and
elevate. I've seen it myself over and over again.

DR. MACFARLANE: People say that. They're generally
thinking of elderly ladies in comfortable circumstances
who with the aid of a very good doctor show a becoming
resignation in a chronic disease.

JOHN: I should like some of those people who talk about
the purifying influence of suffering to have a mouthful
of gas and see how they liked it.

VICAR: The war is terrible. Its cruelty is terrible. The
suffering it has caused is terrible. There is only one
explanation for it; and that is the loving kindness and
the infinite mercy of our heavenly Father.

JOHN: Can you bring yourself to believe that?

VICAR: We were given over to drunkenness and lust, to
selfishness and flippancy and pride. It needed this tremendous trial to purify us. It will be a nobler England

that comes out of the furnace. Oh, I pray to God that all this blood may wash our souls clean so that we may once more be found worthy in His sight.

MRS. POOLE: Amen.

JOHN: You must evidently know much more about it than I do. When the men in my company did things I thought were wrong I used to jolly them a bit. I fancy I got better results than if I'd bashed them on the head with a sledge-hammer.

VICAR: Sin began with the beginning of the human story and has continued through all its course. The motive of the divine redemption lies in the fact that men, though created for so lofty a purpose, have plunged so deep into sin and have so deeply defaced in themselves the image of God, that only the self-sacrificing act of God in redeeming them can raise them from ruin.

JOHN: I wish you'd been a company-commander and had seen how gaily a man can give his life for his friend.

VICAR: But I know, my dear boy, I know. And do you think God will be unmindful of their sacrifice? I pray and believe that they will find mercy in His sight. I am sure He is more ready to pardon than to punish. After all, our Lord came to call sinners to repentance, and who should know better than the Ministers of God that to err is human, to forgive, divine?

> [*The piquet players have played their game with a certain distraction, and during the last few speeches have made no more pretence of playing at all.* MRS. LITTLEWOOD *has listened attentively. Now she puts down her cards, gets up, and walks up to the* VICAR.

MRS. LITTLEWOOD: And who is going to forgive God?

MRS. WHARTON: [*With horror.*] Charlotte!

VICAR: [*With grave disapproval.*] Don't you think that is rather blasphemous?

MRS. LITTLEWOOD: [*Quietly and deliberately at first, but with ever-increasing excitement*.] Ever since I was a child I've served God with all my might, and with all my heart, and with all my soul. I've tried always to lead my life in accordance with His will. I never forgot that I was as nothing in His sight. I've been weak and sinful, but I've tried to do my duty.

MRS. WHARTON: Yes, dear, you've been an example to us all.

MRS. LITTLEWOOD: [*Taking no notice.*] Honestly, I've done everything I could that I thought was pleasing in His sight. I've praised Him and magnified His name. You've heard that my husband deserted me when I'd borne him two children, and I was left alone. I brought them up to be honest, upright and God-fearing men. When God took my eldest son I wept, but I turned to the Lord and said: "Thy will be done." He was a soldier, and he took his chance, and he died in a good cause.

VICAR: A great and a good cause.

MRS. LITTLEWOOD: But why did God take my second? He was the only one I had left, the only comfort of my old age, my only joy, the only thing I had to prevent me from seeing that my life had been wasted and it would have been better if I had never been born. I haven't deserved that. When a horse has served me long and faithfully till he's too old to work, I have the right to send him to the knacker's yard, but I don't, I put him out to grass. I wouldn't treat a dog as my Father has treated me. I've been cheated. You say that God will forgive us our sins, but who is going to forgive God? Not I. Never. Never!

    [*In a height of frenzy she rushes out into the garden. There is silence in the room.*

MRS. WHARTON: Don't be angry with her, Vicar. She's beside herself with grief.

VICAR: She'll come back. She's like a petulant child that has been thwarted for its good. It cries and stamps, but in a little while it throws itself into its mother's arms, and begs, all tears, for forgiveness.

MRS. POOLE: [*With a little sigh of relief.*] I knew you'd take it like that, Norman. You're so tolerant and broad-minded.

VICAR: I think I see my way to help her, poor soul.

JOHN: I wonder how. Your only explanation of evil is sin. I daresay you can get people to acknowledge that they've deserved their own suffering. But you'll never prevent them from being revolted at the suffering of others. Why is evil permitted in the world by an all-good God?

VICAR: I can hardly hope that any answer of mine will satisfy you. By God's grace I am a Christian. You are an atheist.

[*There is a moment's embarrassment.* JOHN *realises that his mother or* SYLVIA *has repeated what he has said.*

JOHN: That suggests a very dogmatic attitude. I don't see how anyone can positively assert that there is no God. It would be as reasonable as to assert that there's nothing on the other side of a wall that you can't look over.

VICAR: Do you believe in God?

JOHN: I don't think it's quite your business to ask me. [*With a smile.*] Wasn't it St. Paul who said: "Be not zealous overmuch."

VICAR: You can't be unaware that by certain statements of yours the other day you gave the greatest pain to those nearest and dearest to you.

SYLVIA: What you said made me very unhappy, John. I didn't know what to do. I went to the Vicar and asked his advice.

JOHN: Don't you think that a man's belief is his own affair? I don't want to interfere with other people's. Why can't they leave me quietly to mine?

SYLVIA: It can't be entirely your affair, John. You and I propose to be married to-morrow. It's only reasonable that I should know exactly how you stand in a matter that concerns me so closely.

JOHN: I hadn't thought of that. I daresay there's something in what you say. I'm willing to do my best to explain to you and to father and mother. But I really think we needn't drag strangers in.

MRS. WHARTON: I think it would be much better if you would talk with the Vicar, John. We don't pretend to be very clever, and it wouldn't mean much if you asked us questions that we couldn't answer.

VICAR: When you're ill you send for a doctor, he prescribes for you, and you get well.

JOHN: [*With a smile.*] What do you think of that, doctor?

DR. MACFARLANE: It is an idea that we do our little best to spread about the world.

VICAR: Anyhow, you take a doctor's advice and you don't argue with him. Why? Because he's an expert, and you presume that he knows his business. Why should the science of the immortal soul be a less complicated affair than the science of the perishable body?

MRS. WHARTON: Look upon us as very silly, old-fashioned people, and be kind to us. If various doubts are troubling you, put them frankly before the Vicar. Perhaps he can help you.

VICAR: [*Sincerely.*] Believe me, I'll do everything in my power.

MRS. WHARTON: And if he can convince you that you were wrong, I know you too well to dream that pride would stop you from confessing it. It would give us such heartfelt joy, my dear, if you could believe again as you did when you were a little child and used to say your prayers kneeling on my lap.

VICAR: I really think I can help you. Won't you forget that I'm a stranger and let me try?

DR. MACFARLANE: Perhaps you'd like me to leave you. I was only waiting till the Colonel had finished his game so that I might take him upstairs and have a look at him. But I can come back later.

JOHN: I don't mind your staying at all. [*To the* VICAR.] What is it you wish to ask me?

VICAR: Do you believe in the God in whose name you were baptized into the Church?

JOHN: No!

VICAR: That at all events is frank and honest. But aren't you a little out of date? One of the most gratifying occurrences of recent years has been the revival of belief among thoughtful men.

JOHN: I should have thought it was a revival of rhetoric rather than of religion. I'm not enormously impressed by the cultured journalist who uses God to balance a sentence or adorn a phrase.

VICAR: But it hasn't only been among educated men. Not the least remarkable thing about the war has been the return of our brave lads at the Front to the faith which so many of us thought they had forgotten. What is your explanation of that?

JOHN: Fear with the most part. Perplexity with the rest.

VICAR: Don't you think it very rash to reject a belief that all the ablest men in the world have held since the dawn of history?

JOHN: When you're dealing with a belief, neither the number nor the ability of those who hold it makes it a certainty. Only proof can do that.

MRS. POOLE: Are you quite sure that at the bottom of your heart it's not conceit that makes you think differently from the rest of us?

VICAR: No, my dear, let us not ascribe unworthy motives to our antagonist.

JOHN: [*Smiling.*] At all events, not yet.

VICAR: What makes you think that the existence of God can't be proved?

JOHN: I suppose at this time of day people wouldn't still be proving it if proof were possible.

VICAR: My dear fellow, the fact that there is no people on the face of the earth, however barbarous and degraded, without some belief in God, is the most conclusive proof you can want.

JOHN: What of? It's conclusive proof that the desire for His existence is universal. It's not proof that the desire is fulfilled.

VICAR: I see you have the usual Rationalistic arguments at your fingers' ends. Believe me, they're old friends, and if I've answered them once I've answered them a thousand times.

JOHN: And have you ever convinced anyone who wasn't convinced before?

VICAR: I can't make the blind to see, you know.

JOHN: I wonder that hasn't suggested to you a very obvious conclusion.

VICAR: What?

JOHN: Why, that arguments are futile. Think for a minute. You don't believe in God for any of the reasons that are given for His existence. You believe in Him because with all your heart you *feel* that He exists. No argument can ever touch that feeling. The heart is independent of logic and its rules.

VICAR: I daresay there's something in what you say.

JOHN: Well, it's the same with me. If you ask me why I don't believe in the existence of God I suppose I can give you a certain number of reasons, but the real one, the one that gives all the others their force, is that I feel it in my heart.

VICAR: What is the cause of your feeling?

JOHN: I'm sure you'll think it very insufficient. I had a friend and he was killed.

VICAR: I'm afraid one must be prepared to lose one's friends in a war like this.

JOHN: I daresay it's very silly and sentimental of me. One gets used to one's pals dying. Someone says to you: "So-and-So's knocked out." And you answer: "Is he really? Poor chap." And you don't think very much more about it. Robbie Harrison wasn't quite an ordinary man.

MRS. WHARTON: I was afraid you'd feel his death very much. You never mentioned it in your letters. I felt it was because you couldn't bear to speak of it.

JOHN: He was one of those lucky beggars who do everything a little better than anybody else. He was clever and awfully nice-looking and amusing. I never knew anyone who loved life so much as he did.

MRS. WHARTON: Yes, I remember his saying to me once: "Isn't it ripping to be alive?"

JOHN: But there was something more in him than that. He had one quality which was rather out of the ordinary. It's difficult to explain what it was like. It seemed to shine about him like a mellow light. It was like the jolly feeling of the country in May. And do you know what it was? Goodness. Just goodness. He was the sort of man that I should like to be.

MRS. WHARTON: He was a dear.

JOHN: I was awfully excited when war was declared. I was in India at the time. I moved heaven and earth to get out to the Front. I thought war the noblest sport in the world. I found it a dreary, muddy, dirty, stinking, bloody business. And I suppose Robbie's death was the last straw. It seemed so unjust. I don't know that it was grief so much that I felt as indignation. I was revolted by all the horror and pain and suffering.

MRS. POOLE: You must have seen some dreadful things.

JOHN: Perhaps it's Christianity that has shown us the possibility of a higher morality than Christianity teaches. I daresay I'm quite wrong. I can only tell you that all that's moral in my soul revolts at the thought of a God who can permit the monstrous iniquity of war. I can't believe that there is a God in heaven.

VICAR: But do you realise that if there isn't, the world is meaningless?

JOHN: That may be. But if there is it's infamous.

VICAR: What have you got to put in the place of religion? What answer can you give to the riddle of the universe?

JOHN: I may think your answer wrong and yet have no better one to put in its place.

VICAR: Have you nothing to tell us at all when we ask you why man is here and what is his destiny? You are like a rudderless ship in a stormy sea.

JOHN: I suppose the human race has arisen under the influence of conditions which are part of the earth's history, and under the influence of other conditions it will come to an end. I don't see that there is any more meaning in life than in the statement that two and two are four.

SYLVIA: [*With suppressed passion.*] Then you think that all our efforts and struggles, our pain and sorrow, our aims, are senseless?

JOHN: Do you remember our going to the Russian ballet before the war? I've never forgotten a certain gesture of one of the dancers. It was an attitude she held for an instant, in the air; it was the most lovely thing I ever saw in my life; you felt it could only have been achieved by infinite labour, and the fact that it was so fleeting, like

the shadow of a bird flying over a river, made it all the
more wonderful. I've often thought of it since, and it
has seemed to me a very good symbol of life.

SYLVIA: John, you can't be serious.

JOHN: I'll tell you what I mean. Life seems to me like a huge
jig-saw puzzle that doesn't make any picture, but if we
like we can make little patterns, as it were, out of the
pieces.

SYLVIA: What is the use of that?

JOHN: There's no use, and no need. It's merely something
we can do for our own satisfaction. Pain and sorrow are
some of the pieces that we have to deal with. By making
the most of all our faculties, by using all our oppor-
tunities, out of the manifold events of life, our deeds, our
feelings, our thoughts, we can make a design which is
intricate, dignified, and beautiful. And death at one
stroke completes and destroys it.

[*There is a moment's silence.*

MRS. POOLE: I wonder why you're coming to church
to-morrow to be married?

JOHN: [*With a smile.*] I think Sylvia would be outraged at
the thought of being married in a registry office.

MRS. POOLE: It's lucky for you the Vicar is broad-minded.
A stricter man might think it his duty to refuse the
blessing of the Church to an unbeliever.

MRS. WHARTON: [*Anxiously.*] Vicar, you're not thinking of
doing anything like that?

VICAR: I confess the question has crossed my mind.
[*Kindly.*] I don't think I can bring myself to expose such
good Christians as you and Sylvia to such a humiliation.

SYLVIA: You need not harass yourself, Vicar. I've decided
not to marry John.

JOHN: [*Aghast.*] Sylvia! Sylvia, you can't mean that!

SYLVIA: I was dreadfully troubled the other day when you

told us you'd lost your faith, but I hadn't the courage to say anything then. It came as such an awful shock.

JOHN: But you never made the least sign.

SYLVIA: I hadn't time to think it out, but I've been thinking hard ever since, day and night, and I've listened very carefully to what you've said to-day. I can't keep up the pretence any more. I've quite made up my mind. I won't marry you.

JOHN: But in God's name, why?

SYLVIA: You are not the John I loved and promised myself to. It's a different man that has come back from abroad. I have nothing in common with that man.

JOHN: Sylvia, you don't mean to say that you don't care for me any more because on certain matters I don't hold the same views as you?

SYLVIA: But those matters are the most important in the world. You talk as though it were a difference of opinion over the colour of our drawing-room curtains. You don't even understand me any more.

JOHN: How can I understand something that seems absolutely unreasonable to me?

SYLVIA: Do you think religion is something I take up with my Prayer-book when I go to church, and put away on a shelf when I get home again? John, God is a living presence that is always with me. I never at any moment lose the consciousness of that divine love which with infinite mercy tends and protects me.

JOHN: But, dear heart, you know me well enough. You know I would never hinder you in the exercise of your religion. I would always treat it with the utmost respect.

SYLVIA: How could we possibly be happy when all that to me is the reason and the beauty of life, to you is nothing but a lie?

JOHN: With tolerance on both sides, and, I hope, respect,

there's no reason why two people shouldn't live peaceably together no matter how different their views are.

SYLVIA: How can I be tolerant when I see you deep in error? Oh, it's more than error, it's sin. You've had your choice between light and darkness, and you've deliberately chosen darkness. You are a deserter. If words mean anything at all you are condemned.

JOHN: But, my dear, a man believes what he can. You don't seriously think that a merciful God is going to punish him because he's unable to believe something that he finds incredible?

SYLVIA: No one doubts that Our Lord will have mercy on those who have never had the chance of receiving His teaching. You've had the chance, and you've refused to take it. Do you forget the Parable of the Ten Talents? It is a terrible warning.

JOHN: After all, if I'm wrong I hurt nobody but myself.

SYLVIA: You forget what marriage is. It makes us one flesh. I am bidden to cleave to you and to follow you. How can I, when our souls must ever be separated by an unsurpassable abyss?

MRS. WHARTON: Sylvia, this is a dreadfully grave decision you're making. Be careful that you're acting rightly.

JOHN: Sylvia, you can't throw me over like this after we've been engaged for seven years. It's too heartless.

SYLVIA: I don't trust you. I have no hold over you. What have you to aim at beside the satisfaction of your own vulgar appetite? Sin means nothing to you.

JOHN: My dear, you don't suppose it's religion that makes a man decent? If he's kind and honest and truthful it's because it's his nature, not because he believes in God or fears hell.

SYLVIA: We're neither of us very young any more, there's no reason why we should make a mystery of natural things. If we married my greatest hope was that we should have children.

JOHN: It was mine too.

SYLVIA: Have you asked yourself how this would affect them? Which are they to be, Christians or Agnostics?

JOHN: My dear, I promise you I will not interfere with your teaching of them.

SYLVIA: Do you mean to say you will stand by while they are taught a pack of worthless lies?

JOHN: Your faith has been the faith of our people for hundreds of years. In the case of a difference of opinion I could not take it on myself to refuse children instruction in it. When they reach years of discretion they can judge for themselves.

SYLVIA: And supposing they ask you about things? The story of Our Saviour appeals to children, you know. It's very natural that they should put you questions. What will you answer?

JOHN: I don't think you could ask me to say what I thought untrue.

MRS. WHARTON: He could always refer them to you, Sylvia dear.

SYLVIA: You naturally wouldn't come to church. What sort of an example would you set your children in a matter of which I was impressing on them the enormous importance?

JOHN: [*With a smile.*] My dear, surely you're letting a lack of humour cloud a lively intelligence. Vast numbers of excellent churchmen don't go to church, and I'm not aware that their children are corrupted by it.

SYLVIA: [*Passionately.*] You don't understand. You'll never understand. It's a joke to you. It's all over and done with, John. Let me go. I beseech you to let me go.

COLONEL WHARTON: [*Half rising from his chair.*] I feel most awfully ill.

MRS. WHARTON: [*In alarm.*] George!

JOHN: [*Simultaneously.*] Father!

> [MRS. WHARTON, JOHN, *and the* DOCTOR *hurry towards him.*

DR. MACFARLANE: What's the matter?

MRS. WHARTON: George, are you in pain?

COLONEL WHARTON: Awful!

DR. MACFARLANE: You'd better lie down on the sofa.

COLONEL WHARTON: No, I'd rather go upstairs.

DR. MACFARLANE: Don't crowd round him.

COLONEL WHARTON: I feel as if I were going to die.

DR. MACFARLANE: Do you think you can manage to walk?

COLONEL WHARTON: Yes. Help me, Evelyn.

JOHN: Put your arm round my neck, father.

COLONEL WHARTON: No, it's all right. I can manage.

DR. MACFARLANE: We'll get you upstairs and put you to bed.

MRS. WHARTON: Come, darling, put all your weight on me.

DR. MACFARLANE: That's right. You needn't come, John. You'll only be in the way.

> [MRS. WHARTON *and the* DOCTOR *help the* COLONEL *out of the room.*

MRS. POOLE: We'd better go, Norman. [*To* JOHN.] I hope it's nothing very serious.

JOHN: I'm sure I hope not.

MRS. POOLE: Please don't bear us a grudge for any of the things Norman or I have said to you to-day. You know, I saw the letter your Colonel wrote to Mrs. Wharton when you were wounded, and I know how splendid you've been.

JOHN: Oh, nonsense!

VICAR: I'm afraid you may have to go through a good deal of distress in the near future. If you should change your mind in some of the things that we've talked about this afternoon no one would be more happy than myself.

JOHN: It's very good of you to say so, but I don't think it likely.

VICAR: One never knows by what paths the Most High will call His creatures to Himself. He is more cunning to save His children than they are to lose themselves. If you listen to the call, come to the Communion Table. I will ask no questions. It will be a joyful day for me if I am privileged to offer you the Blessed Sacrament of Our Lord and Saviour.

> [*He stretches out his hand and* JOHN *takes it.*

JOHN: Good-bye.

> [*The* VICAR *and* MRS. POOLE *go into the garden.* JOHN *turns to* SYLVIA.

JOHN: Is it the question that the Vicar put me when we were talking about sin that has upset you, Sylvia?

SYLVIA: No, I don't think it was very nice of him to put it. I never thought about the matter. I don't see why I should expect you to be better than other men.

JOHN: Did you really mean all you said just now?

SYLVIA: Every word.

> [*She takes off her engagement ring and hands it to him. He does not take it.*

JOHN: [*With deep emotion.*] Sylvia, I couldn't say it before all those people, it seemed too intimate and private a matter. Doesn't it mean anything to you that I love you? It's been so much to me in all I've gone through to think of you. You've been everything in the world to me. When I was cold and wet and hungry and miserable, I've thought of you, and it all grew bearable.

SYLVIA: I'm very sorry. I can't marry you.

JOHN: How can you be so cold and heartless? Sylvia, my dear, I love you! Won't you give it a chance?

> [*She looks at him steadily for a moment. She braces herself for the final effort.*

SYLVIA: But I don't love you any more, John.

> [*She hands him the ring again and he takes it silently.*

JOHN: It's not a very swagger one, is it? I was none too flush in those days and I didn't want to ask father to help me. I wanted to buy it out of my own money.

SYLVIA: I've worn it for seven years, John.

> [*He turns away from* SYLVIA *and walks over to the fireplace. When* SYLVIA *sees what he is going to do she makes a gesture as though to prevent him, but immediately controls herself. He stands looking at the fire for a moment, then throws the ring in; he watches what will happen to it.* SYLVIA *clutches her heart. She can hardly prevent the sobs which seem to tear her breast.*

SYLVIA: I think I'll be getting home. John—if your father or mother want me you can send, can't you?

JOHN: [*Looking over his shoulder.*] Of course. I'll let you know at once.

SYLVIA: [*In a natural voice.*] Good-bye, John.

JOHN: Good-bye, Sylvia.

> [*He turns back to look at the fire, and she walks slowly out of the room.*

END OF THE SECOND ACT

THE THIRD ACT

The Scene is the same as in the preceding Acts. It is early morning on the following Wednesday. The dead ashes of yesterday's fire are still in the grate. Not far away is heard the ringing of a church bell to call the faithful to the first service.

MRS. WHARTON *is standing by a table on which is a large basket of white flowers which she had just brought in from the garden. She picks up a rose, and with a faint smile gives it a little caress.* SYLVIA *comes in from the garden.*

SYLVIA: [*With surprise.*] Mrs. Wharton!

MRS. WHARTON: Oh, Sylvia, is it you?

SYLVIA: It startled me to see you there. I came in this way because I saw the door was open and your front-door bell's so noisy. I thought if the Colonel was asleep it might wake him.

MRS. WHARTON: It's early, isn't it?

SYLVIA: Yes, I'm on my way to the early service. I thought I'd look in just to ask how the Colonel was. But I didn't expect to see you. I thought Kate or Hannah might be about.

MRS. WHARTON: George is dead, Sylvia.

SYLVIA: [*In amazement.*] Mrs. Wharton!

MRS. WHARTON: He died quite peacefully about an hour ago. I've just been to gather some flowers to put in his room.

SYLVIA: Oh, Mrs. Wharton, I'm so sorry. I'm so dreadfully sorry for you.

MRS. WHARTON: [*Patting her hand.*] Thank you, my dear; you've been very kind to us during these days.

SYLVIA: Where is John?

67

MRS. WHARTON: I think he must have gone out for a walk. I went to his room a little while ago and he wasn't there. He wanted to sit up with me last night, but I wouldn't let him.

SYLVIA: But . . . but doesn't John know his father is dead?

MRS. WHARTON: No, not yet.

SYLVIA: Didn't you call him?

MRS. WHARTON: I had no idea the end was so near. George wanted to be alone with me, Sylvia. We'd been married for thirty-five years, you see. He was conscious almost to the last. He died quite suddenly, like a child going to sleep.

SYLVIA: It's such a terrible loss. You poor dear, you must be quite heart-broken.

MRS. WHARTON: It's a very great loss, but I'm not heart-broken. George is happy and at rest. We should be very poor Christians if the death of those we love made us unhappy. George has entered into eternal life.

SYLVIA: Oh, Mrs. Wharton, what a blessed thing it is to have a faith like yours.

MRS. WHARTON: My dear, a very wonderful thing happened last night. I can't feel grief for dear George's death because of the recollection of that. I feel so strange. I feel as though I were walking in an enchanted garden.

SYLVIA: I don't know what you mean.

MRS. WHARTON: Since that day when George refused to talk with the Vicar I never dared mention the subject. He was not himself. It made me so unhappy. And then last night, soon after Dr. Macfarlane went away, he asked of his own accord for Mr. Poole. The Vicar's a dear, kind man. He'd said to me that if ever George asked for him he'd come at once, at any hour of the day or night. So I sent for him. He gave George the Holy Sacrament. And Sylvia, a miracle happened.

SYLVIA: A miracle?

MRS. WHARTON: No sooner had the bread and the wine touched his lips than he was transfigured. All his—his anxiety left him, and he was once more his dear, good, brave self. He was quite happy to die. It was as though an unseen hand had pulled back a dark curtain of clouds and he saw before him, not night and a black coldness, but a path of golden sunshine that led straight to the arms of God.

SYLVIA: I'm so glad. I'm happy too now.

MRS. WHARTON: The Vicar read the prayers for the dying and then he left us. We talked of the past and of our reunion in a little while. And then he died.

SYLVIA: It's wonderful. Yes, it was a miracle.

MRS. WHARTON: All through my life I've been conscious of the hand of God shaping the destinies of man. I've never seen His loving mercy more plainly manifest.

[KATE *opens the door and stands on the threshold, but does not come into the room.*

KATE: The woman's come, ma'am.

MRS. WHARTON: Very well. I'm just coming.

[KATE *goes out and shuts the door behind her.* MRS. WHARTON *takes up her basket of flowers.*

MRS. WHARTON: John will be in immediately, Sylvia. He promised to come and relieve me at half-past eight, so that I might get something to eat. Will you see him?

SYLVIA: Yes, Mrs. Wharton, if you wish me to.

MRS. WHARTON: Will you tell him that his father is dead? I know you'll do it very gently.

SYLVIA: Oh, Mrs. Wharton, wouldn't you prefer to tell him yourself?

MRS. WHARTON: No.

SYLVIA: Very well.

MRS. WHARTON: You know he loves you, Sylvia. It would make me so happy if you two could arrive at some understanding. It seems such a pity that the happiness of both of you should be ruined.

SYLVIA: I would do anything in the world for John, but I can't sacrifice what is and must be dearer to me even than he.

MRS. WHARTON: Can't you teach him to believe?

SYLVIA: Oh, I wish I could. I pray for him night and day.

MRS. WHARTON: I wished afterwards that I'd asked him to be present when his father and I received the Communion. I think at that last solemn moment he might have been moved to receive it with us.

SYLVIA: D'you think. . . . Perhaps a miracle would have taken place in him, too. Perhaps he would have believed.

MRS. WHARTON: I must go upstairs.

[*An idea seizes* SYLVIA, *and she gives a strange little gasp. As* MRS. WHARTON *is about to leave the room she stops her with a sudden question.*

SYLVIA: Mrs. Wharton. . . . Mrs. Wharton, do you think the end can ever justify the means?

MRS. WHARTON: My dear, what an extraordinary question! It can never be right to do evil that good may come.

SYLVIA: Are you quite sure that that's so always? After all, no one would hesitate to tell a lie to save another's life.

MRS. WHARTON: Perhaps not. [*With a faint smile.*] We must thank God that we're not likely to be put in such a position. Why did you ask me that?

SYLVIA: I was wondering what one should do if one could only rescue somebody from terrible danger by committing a great sin. Do you think one ought to do it or not?

MRS. WHARTON: My dear, you haven't the right to offend God for the sake of anyone in the world.

SYLVIA: Not even for the sake of anyone you loved?

MRS. WHARTON: Surely not, my dear. And no one who

loved you would wish you for a moment to do a wicked thing for his sake.

SYLVIA: But take your own case, Mrs. Wharton; if you saw the Colonel or John in deadly peril wouldn't you risk your life to save them?

MRS. WHARTON: [*With a smile.*] Of course I should. I should be happy and thankful to have the opportunity. But that's not the same. I should only be risking my life, not my soul.

SYLVIA: [*Almost beside herself.*] But if their souls were in peril, wouldn't you risk your soul?

MRS. WHARTON: My dear, what do you mean? You seem so excited.

SYLVIA: [*Controlling herself with a great effort.*] I? You mustn't pay any attention to me. I haven't been sleeping very well the last three or four nights. I daresay I'm a little hysterical.

MRS. WHARTON: Wouldn't you prefer to go home, darling?

SYLVIA: No, I'd like to stay here if you don't mind. I'd like to see John.

MRS. WHARTON: Very well. I shan't be very long.

> [*She goes out. The church bell gives a hurried tinkle and then stops.* SYLVIA *walks up and down the room and stands still in front of a photograph of* JOHN *in his uniform. She takes it up and looks at it. Then putting it down she clasps her hands and raises her eyes. She is seen to be praying. She hears a sound in the garden, inclines her head to listen, and goes to the window. She hesitates a moment and then braces herself to a decision. She calls.*

SYLVIA: John!

> [*He comes, stops for a moment on the threshold, and then walks forward casually.*

JOHN: Good morning! You're very early.

SYLVIA: I looked in to ask how your father was.

JOHN: When I left him last night he was fairly comfortable. I'll go and find out from mother how he is.

SYLVIA: No, don't—don't disturb him.

JOHN: I'm going to take mother's place in a few minutes. I awoke early, so I went for a walk. . . . You've been very good and kind to all of us during these wretched days, Sylvia. I don't know what we should have done without you.

SYLVIA: I've been so dreadfully sorry. And you all had so much to bear. It wasn't only the thought that the poor dear couldn't—can't recover, but . . . it was so much worse than that.

JOHN: [*With a quick glance at her.*] I suppose it was inevitable that you should see it too. Somehow I hoped that only I and mother knew.

SYLVIA: Oh, John, you can't mind about me. I've loved your father as though he were my own. Nothing he did could make me love him less.

JOHN: He's afraid to die. It's dreadful to see his terror and to be able to do nothing to help him.

SYLVIA: Would you do anything to help him if you could?

JOHN: Of course.

SYLVIA: It's unfortunate that you found it necessary to say what you did about religion. He's always been a very simple man. He always accepted without question the faith in which he was brought up. Perhaps he's not quite so sure now.

JOHN: Nonsense, Sylvia. Father's faith is very much too steady for it to be unsettled by any opinions of mine.

SYLVIA: Ordinarily, I dare say. But he's ill, he's in terrible pain, he's not himself. I think perhaps it's a pity you didn't hold your tongue. It's so easy to create doubts and so hard to allay them.

JOHN: [*Much disturbed.*] That's an awful thought to have put into my head, Sylvia. I should never forgive myself if. . . .

SYLVIA: If you'd believed as we believe, he would have been supported, as it were, by all our faith. It would have made that terrible passage from this life to the life to come a little less terrible. You've failed him just when he needed you.

JOHN: [*Indignantly.*] Oh, Sylvia, how can you say anything so heartless?

SYLVIA: [*Coldly.*] It's true.

JOHN: Heaven knows, I know that death isn't easy. You can't think I'd be so inhuman as to do anything to make it more difficult?

SYLVIA: Except mortify your pride.

JOHN: [*Impatiently.*] What has pride got to do with it?

SYLVIA: There was pride in every word you said. Are you sure it's not pride of intellect that's responsible for your change of heart?

JOHN: [*Icily.*] Perhaps. How do you suggest I should mortify it?

SYLVIA: Well, you see, you can confess your error.

JOHN: I don't think it's an error.

SYLVIA: At least you can undo some of the harm you've done. Do you know what is chiefly tormenting your father? Your refusal to receive the Holy Communion. He keeps talking about it to your mother. He keeps harping on it. He's dreadfully distressed about it. If you received the Communion, John, it would give your father peace.

JOHN: Sylvia, how can I?

SYLVIA: All your life your father has done everything in the world for you. Nothing's been too good for you. You owe him all your happiness, everything you are and hope to be. Can't you do this one little thing for him?

JOHN: No, it's out of the question. I really can't. I'm awfully sorry.

SYLVIA: How can you be so hard? It's the last wish he'll ever have in the world. It's your last chance of showing your love for him. Oh, John, show a little mercy to his weakness!

JOHN: But, Sylvia, it would be blasphemous.

SYLVIA: What are you talking about? You don't believe. To you it's merely an idle ceremony. What can it matter to you if you go through a meaningless form?

JOHN: I've been a Christian too long. I have a hundred generations of Christianity behind me.

SYLVIA: You never hesitated at coming to church when we were going to be married.

JOHN: That was different.

SYLVIA: How? That was a sacrament, too. Are you afraid of a little bread and wine that a priest has said a few words over?

JOHN: Sylvia, don't torment me. I tell you I can't.

SYLVIA: [*Scornfully.*] I never imagined you would be superstitious. You're frightened. You feel just like people about sitting thirteen at table. Of course it's all nonsense, but there may be something in it.

JOHN: I don't know what I feel. I only know that I, an unbeliever, can't take part in a ceremony that was sacred to me when I believed.

SYLVIA: [*Bitterly.*] It's very natural. It only means that you love yourself better than anyone else. Why should one expect you to have pity for your father, or gratitude?

JOHN: Oh, Sylvia, where did you learn to say such cruel things? I can't, I tell you, I can't. If father were in his normal mind, neither he nor mother would wish me to do such a thing.

SYLVIA: But your mother does wish it. Oh, John, don't be

stubborn. For God's sake give yourself the opportunity. Your father's dying, John; you have no time
to lose. . . . John, the Communion Service has only
just begun. If you get on your bicycle you'll be there in
time. The other day the Vicar said if you presented
yourself at the Communion table he would not hesitate
to administer it.

>   [JOHN *looks steadily in front of him for a moment, then
>   makes up his mind; he stands up suddenly and without a
>   word goes out of the room.*

SYLVIA: [*In a whisper.*] O God, forgive me, forgive me,
forgive me!

>   [*The Curtain is lowered for one minute to denote the lapse of
>   half an hour. When it rises* SYLVIA *is standing at the
>   window, looking out into the garden.* MRS. LITTLE-
>   WOOD *enters.*

MRS. LITTLEWOOD: May I come in?

SYLVIA: Oh, Mrs. Littlewood, do!

MRS. LITTLEWOOD: I met Dr. Macfarlane just outside my
house, and he told me the Colonel was dead. I came with
him to see if I could be of any use.

SYLVIA: It's very kind of you. Is Dr. Macfarlane here?

MRS. LITTLEWOOD: Yes. He went upstairs. Where is
John?

SYLVIA: He'll be here directly.

>   [MRS. WHARTON *comes in, followed by* DR. MACFAR-
>   LANE. MRS. LITTLEWOOD *goes up to her and the two
>   old ladies kiss one another. For a moment they stand
>   clasped in one another's arms.*

MRS. LITTLEWOOD: My dear old friend!

MRS. WHARTON: It was dear of you to come, Charlotte. I
knew you'd feel for me.

DR. MACFARLANE: Now sit down, my dear Mrs. Wharton,
sit down and rest yourself.

>   [*He puts her into a chair and places a cushion behind her.*

MRS. WHARTON: Hasn't John come in yet?

SYLVIA: I'm sure he won't be long now. He should be here almost at once.

DR. MACFARLANE: Sylvia, my dear child, won't you go and get Mrs. Wharton a cup of tea? I think it would do her good.

SYLVIA: Certainly.

MRS. WHARTON: Oh, my dear, don't trouble.

SYLVIA: But it's no trouble. You know I love doing things for you.

[She goes out.

MRS. WHARTON: Everybody's so very kind in this world. It makes one feel humble. . . . George and I have been married for five-and-thirty years. He never said a cross word to me. He was always gentle and considerate. I daresay I was very troublesome now and then, but he was never impatient with me.

MRS. LITTLEWOOD: Is it true that John and Sylvia are not going to be married after all?

MRS. WHARTON: I'm afraid so.

MRS. LITTLEWOOD: Isn't it strange how people in this world seem to go out of their way to make themselves unhappy!

MRS. WHARTON: I've talked it over with Sylvia. Religion means so much to her. She wouldn't have minded if John had come back blind and crippled, she'd have devoted her life to him without a murmur.

DR. MACFARLANE: People always think they could put up with the faults we haven't got. Somehow or other it's always those we have that stick in their throats.

MRS. WHARTON: Oh, Doctor, don't say sarcastic things. You don't know how deeply Sylvia is suffering. But it's a matter of conscience. And I do see that one can't ask anyone to compromise with his soul.

DR. MACFARLANE: I have an idea our souls are like our manners, all the better when we don't think too much about them.

MRS. WHARTON: Sylvia's giving up a great deal. I don't know what's to become of her if she doesn't marry John. When her mother dies she'll only have thirty pounds a year.

> [SYLVIA *comes back with a cup of tea on a small tray and puts it on a table by* MRS. WHARTON'S *side.*

SYLVIA: Here is the tea, Mrs. Wharton.

MRS. WHARTON: Oh, thank you, my dear, so much. You do spoil me. . . . I can't imagine why John is so long. He's generally so very punctual.

SYLVIA: [*In a low voice.*] John came in, Mrs. Wharton.

MRS. WHARTON: Oh, then, you saw him?

SYLVIA: Yes.

MRS. WHARTON: Did you speak to him?

SYLVIA: Yes.

MRS. WHARTON: Why did he go out again? Where has he gone?

SYLVIA: He'll be back immediately.

DR. MACFARLANE: Drink your tea, dear lady, drink your tea.

> [SYLVIA *takes her place again at the window and looks into the garden. She takes no notice of the people in the room.*

MRS. WHARTON: I'm glad to have you two old friends with me now. The only thing that really seems to belong to me any more is the past, and you were both so much part of it.

DR. MACFARLANE: You came here immediately after your honeymoon. Is that really thirty-five years ago?

MRS. LITTLEWOOD: My mother and I were the first people

who called on you. I remember how stylish we thought you in your green velvet, Evelyn.

MRS. WHARTON: I remember it well. I had it dyed black its third year. I think the fashions were very much more ladylike in those days. A bustle did set off a woman's figure, there's no denying that.

DR. MACFARLANE: What waists you had and how tight you used to lace!

MRS. WHARTON: I often wonder if the young people ever enjoy themselves as much as we used to. Do you remember the picnics we used to have?

MRS. LITTLEWOOD: And now it's all as if it had never been, all our love and pain and joy and sorrow. We're just two funny old women, and it really wouldn't have mattered a row of pins if we'd never been born.

DR. MACFARLANE: I wonder, I wonder.

MRS. WHARTON: You've had the privilege of giving two sons to a noble cause. Wasn't it worth while to be born for that?

MRS. LITTLEWOOD: Sometimes I've asked myself if this world in which we're living now isn't hell. Perhaps all the unhappiness my husband caused me and the death of those two boys of mine is a punishment for sins that I committed in some other life in some other part of the universe.

MRS. WHARTON: Charlotte, sometimes you say things that frighten me. I'm haunted by the fear that you may destroy yourself.

MRS. LITTLEWOOD: I? No, why should I? I don't feel that life is important enough for me to give it a deliberate end. I don't trouble to kill the fly that walks over my ceiling.

DR. MACFARLANE: I've been curing or killing people for hard on fifty years, and it seems to me that I've seen innumerable generations enter upon the shifting scene,

act their little part, and pass away. Alas, who can deny
that in this world virtue is very often unrewarded and
vice unpunished? Happiness too rarely comes to the
good, and the prizes of this life go too frequently to the
undeserving. The rain falls on the just and on the
unjust alike, but the unjust generally have a stout
umbrella. It looks as though there were little justice in
the world, and chance seems to rule man and all his
circumstances.

MRS. WHARTON: But we know that all that is mere idle
seeming.

DR. MACFARLANE: Seeming perhaps, but why idle? Seeming
is all we know. The other day when you were talking I
held my tongue, because I thought you'd say I was a
silly old fool if I put my word in, but I've puzzled over
suffering and pain too. You see, in my trade we see so
much of them. It made me unhappy, and for long I
doubted the goodness of God, as you doubt it, dear
friend.

MRS. LITTLEWOOD: [*With a smile.*] I think you're preaching
at me, Doctor.

DR. MACFARLANE: Then it's the first time in my life.

MRS. LITTLEWOOD: Go on.

DR. MACFARLANE: I want to tell you how *I* found peace.
My explanation is as old as the hills, and I believe many
perfectly virtuous persons have been frizzled alive for
accepting it. Our good Vicar would say I was a heretic.
I can't help it. I can't see any other way of reconciling
the goodness of God with the existence of evil.

MRS. LITTLEWOOD: Well, what is it?

DR. MACFARLANE: I don't believe that God is all-powerful
and all-knowing. But I think He struggles against evil as
we do. I don't believe He means to chasten us by
suffering or to purify us by pain. I believe pain and
suffering are evil, and that He hates them, and would

crush them if He could. And I believe that in this age-
long struggle between God and evil we can help, all of
us, even the meanest; for in some way, I don't know how,
I believe that all our goodness adds to the strength of
God, and perhaps—who can tell?—will give Him such
power that at last He will be able utterly to destroy evil—
utterly, with its pain and suffering. [*With a smile.*]
When we're good, we're buying silver bullets for the
King of Heaven, and when we're bad, well, we're
trading with the enemy.

SYLVIA: [*Without looking round.*] John has just ridden back
on his bicycle.

DR. MACFARLANE: Come, Mrs. Littlewood, they don't want
us here just now.

MRS. LITTLEWOOD: [*Getting up.*] No, I'm sure you will
prefer to be alone with John.

MRS. WHARTON: It was very good of you to come. Good-
bye, my dear, and God bless you.

MRS. LITTLEWOOD: Good-bye.

> [*They kiss one another and* MRS. LITTLEWOOD *goes out.*

DR. MACFARLANE: [*Shaking hands with* MRS. WHARTON.] I
may look in later in the day to see how you are.

MRS. WHARTON: Oh, my dear doctor, I'm not in the least
ill, you know.

DR. MACFARLANE: Still, don't try to do too much. You're
not quite a young woman, you know. Good-bye,
Sylvia.

> [SYLVIA *does not answer.* DR. MACFARLANE *goes out.*
> SYLVIA *advances into the room and then turns and looks
> again at the door through which* JOHN *must come. She
> does all she can to control her great nervousness.*

MRS. WHARTON: Sylvia, is anything the matter?

SYLVIA: No. Why?

MRS. WHARTON: You seem so strange.

SYLVIA: [*Paying no attention to the remark.*] John is just coming.

MRS. WHARTON: You know, my dear, it seems to me that in this life most difficulties can be arranged if both parties are willing to give way a little.

SYLVIA: Sometimes it's impossible to give way, and then the only hope is—a miracle.

> [*She says the last word with a little smile to conceal the fact that she attaches the greatest importance to it.* JOHN *comes in. He is pale and looks extremely tired. He stops for a moment in surprise on seeing his mother. He goes over and kisses her.*

JOHN: Oh, mother, I thought you were upstairs. I'm afraid I'm very late.

MRS. WHARTON: It doesn't matter, my dear. How dreadfully white you look.

JOHN: I went for a walk this morning. I've had nothing to eat. I'm rather tired.

MRS. WHARTON: My dear, you frighten me, your face is all drawn and pinched.

JOHN: Oh, mother, don't worry about me. I shall be all right after breakfast. After all, it's quite enough to have one invalid on your hands.

> [MRS. WHARTON *looks at him in surprise.* SYLVIA *gives a nervous start, but immediately controls herself.*

SYLVIA: Have you been—where you said you were going?

JOHN: Yes.

> [SYLVIA *opens her mouth to speak, but stops; she gives* JOHN *a long, searching look; she realises that what she had hoped for has not taken place, and with a little gasp of misery turns away her head and sinks, dejected and exhausted, into a chair.* JOHN *has held her look with his and now turns to his mother.*

JOHN: Is father asleep?

MRS. WHARTON: [*With a little shiver.*] John!

G

JOHN: What's the matter?

MRS. WHARTON: I thought you knew. My dearest, your father's dead.

JOHN: Mother!

MRS. WHARTON: I asked Sylvia to break it to you. I thought. . . .

SYLVIA: [*In a dull voice.*] I didn't tell him when you asked me to, Mrs. Wharton.

JOHN: I don't understand. It seems impossible. He was well enough last night. When did he die?

MRS. WHARTON: At about seven this morning.

JOHN: But, mother dear, why didn't you call me?

MRS. WHARTON: I didn't expect it. We'd been talking and he said he was tired and he thought he could sleep a little. He dozed off quietly, and in a little while I saw he was dead.

JOHN: Oh, my poor mother, how will you bear your grief?

MRS. WHARTON: You know, it's so strange, I'm not in the least unhappy. I don't feel that he's left me. I feel him just as near to me as before. I don't know how to explain it to you. I think he's never been so much alive as now. Oh, John, I know that the soul is immortal.

JOHN: Darling, I'm so glad you're not unhappy. Your dear eyes are positively radiant.

MRS. WHARTON: If you only knew what I seem to see with them!

JOHN: Won't you take me up and let me see him?

MRS. WHARTON: I think the women are not done yet, John. I'll go up and see. I'll call you as soon as everything is ready.

JOHN: I'm sorry I've caused you so much pain since I came back, mother. I wish I could have avoided it.

MRS. WHARTON: [*She puts her arms round his neck, and he kisses her.*] My dear son!

[She goes out. JOHN *goes towards the window and looks out into the garden. For a moment* SYLVIA *does not dare to speak to him. At last she makes an effort.*

SYLVIA: [*Desperately.*] John, whatever you have to say to me, say it.

JOHN: [*With frigid politeness.*] I don't think I have anything in particular to say to you.

SYLVIA: I suppose you think I'm just a wicked liar.

JOHN: I ask you no questions. I make you no reproaches. What is the matter?

SYLVIA: Oh, John, after all we've been to one another it's brutal to talk to me like that. If you think I did wrong, say so.

JOHN: Why?

SYLVIA: You're cruel and hard. [*She goes up to him.*] John, you must listen to me.

JOHN: Well?

SYLVIA: Your mother asked me to tell you of your father's death. I concealed it from you. I told you a whole tissue of lies. I traded deliberately on your tenderness for your father. I was horrified at myself. It was my only chance of getting you to take the Communion.

JOHN: If you'd had any affection for me, you couldn't have done such an abominable thing. If you'd had any respect for me, you couldn't have done it.

SYLVIA: Let me speak, John.

JOHN: Be quiet! You've insisted on talking about it, and now, by God, you're going to listen to me. Do you know what I felt? Shame. When I took the bread and the wine, I thought they'd choke me. Because once I believed so devoutly it seemed to me that I was doing an awful thing. Deliberately, with full knowledge of what I was doing, I told a dirty lie. And I feel dirty to the depths of my soul.

SYLVIA: I thought perhaps it wouldn't be a lie. I had to do it, John. It was my only chance.

JOHN: Why did you do it?

SYLVIA: Don't look at me so sternly. I can't bear it. You frighten me. I can't collect my thoughts.

JOHN: Why did you do it? Shall I tell you? Because at the back of all your Christian humility there's the desire to dominate. It isn't so much that I didn't believe as that I didn't believe what you wanted me to believe. You wanted to grind my face in the dust.

SYLVIA: [*Passionately.*] John, if you only knew! I only thought of you. I only thought of you all the time.

JOHN: Don't be such a hypocrite.

SYLVIA: [*Brokenly.*] I expected a miracle.

JOHN: At this time of day?

SYLVIA: For God's sake have mercy on me! It was your mother who put the idea in my head. Your father received the Communion last night.

JOHN: You have no charity for human weakness. You were all so terrified that he shouldn't make an edifying end. As if it mattered if the poor dear's nerve failed him at the last.

SYLVIA: [*Eagerly.*] But it didn't. That's just it. You noticed your mother's face yourself. Notwithstanding all her grief she's happy. Do you know why?

JOHN: Why?

SYLVIA: [*As though suddenly inspired.*] Because when he'd received the Blessed Sacrament the fear of death left him. He was once more a brave and gallant gentleman. He had no dread any longer of the perilous journey before him. He was happy to die.

JOHN: [*More gently.*] Is that true? Dear father, I'm very glad.

SYLVIA: It was a miracle. It was a miracle.

JOHN: I still don't follow.

SYLVIA: I thought that when you knelt at the chancel steps, and received the Communion as you used to receive it when you were a boy, all the feelings of your boyhood would rush back on you. I had to make you take it.

JOHN: In my frame of mind? Surely I had no right to.

SYLVIA: I know. That's what makes my sin the greater. Perhaps I was mad. To God all things are possible. I felt certain you'd believe.

JOHN: [*Very gravely.*] Perhaps you have worked a miracle, but not the one you expected.

SYLVIA: What do you mean?

JOHN: When you said you wouldn't marry me I was—I was knocked endways—I felt like a man who's been shipwrecked. All my plans for the future had been bound up with you. I couldn't imagine it without you. I felt utterly forlorn.

SYLVIA: But don't you know what it cost me?

JOHN: At first I couldn't think you meant it. When you said you didn't love me, I couldn't believe it. It seemed too preposterous. I was awfully miserable, Sylvia.

SYLVIA: John, I didn't want you to be unhappy.

JOHN: And then, when I received the Communion something quite strange took place in me. I can't tell you what I felt. I felt as though mother had heard me saying something obscene. I forced myself to go through with it, because I really did think it might give poor father some peace of mind. But it was you who made me do it. The thought of you filled me with horror.

SYLVIA: [*With dismay.*] John!

JOHN: You've cured me, Sylvia. I ought to be grateful to you for that. My love for you has fallen from me as a cloak might fall from one's shoulders. I see the truth now. You were quite right. In these long years we've become different people and we have nothing to say to one another any more.

SYLVIA: [*Passionately.*] But I love you, John! How can you be so blind? Don't you see that I only did it because I loved you? Oh, John, you can't leave me now! I've waited for you all these years. I've longed for you to come back. Forgive me if I did wrong. I can't lose you now. I love you, John, you won't leave me?

JOHN: [*After a moment's pause.*] Of course I won't leave you. I thought you didn't want to marry me.

SYLVIA: [*Hardly knowing what she is saying.*] I'm not young any more. I've lost my freshness. I've got nobody but you now. Oh, John, don't forsake me! I couldn't bear it.

JOHN: [*As though he were talking to a child.*] My dear, don't distress yourself. I'm not thinking of forsaking you. We'll be married as soon as ever we can.

SYLVIA: Yes, we'll be married, won't we? I love you so much, John, I'll make you love me. I couldn't lose you now. I've waited too long.

JOHN: Come, darling, you mustn't be unhappy. It's all settled now. Dry your eyes. You don't want to look a fright, do you?

SYLVIA: [*Clinging to him.*] I'm so miserable.

JOHN: Nonsense, give me a nice kiss, and we'll forget all about our troubles. I'll try to make you a good husband, Sylvia. I'll do all I can to make you happy. Give me a kiss.

[*When he seeks to raise her face in order to kiss her, she tears herself violently from him.*]

SYLVIA: No, don't! Don't touch me! God give me strength! I'm so pitifully weak.

JOHN: Sylvia!

SYLVIA: Don't come near me! For God's sake! [*She puts her hands before her face, trying to control and to collect herself, and there is a moment's pause.*] It never occurred to me that you didn't care for me any more, and when you told me, for a moment I lost my head. Forgive me for that, dear, and forget it. I'm not going to marry you.

JOHN: Now, Sylvia, don't be idiotic. It would be so unseemly if I had to drag you to the altar by the hair of your head.

SYLVIA: You're very kind, John. I suppose it wouldn't be very good form to back out of it now. I'm poor, and I've wasted my best years waiting for you. You needn't worry about what is going to happen to me. I can earn my living as well as other women.

JOHN: Oh, Sylvia, you're torturing yourself and me. Can't you forget what I said in a moment of exasperation? You must know how deep my affection is for you.

SYLVIA: I don't want to forget. It is the will of God. I lied. I did an abominable and evil thing. I don't think you can imagine how terrible my sin has been. I risked my soul to save you, John, and God has inflicted on me a punishment infinitely less than I deserved. He has taken out of your heart the love you bore me.

JOHN: But you love me, Sylvia.

SYLVIA: Better than anyone in the world. I've loved you ever since I was a child of ten. That's only the weakness of my flesh. My soul exults in the great mercy that God has shown me.

JOHN: Oh, my dear, you're going to be so unhappy.

SYLVIA: No, don't be sorry for me. You've given me a great opportunity.

JOHN: I?

SYLVIA: I've been mortified because I was able to do so little in the war. I knew it was my duty to stay here and look after mother. But I wanted to go out to France and do my bit like all my friends.

JOHN: That was very natural.

SYLVIA: Now at last I have the chance to do something. No sacrifice is worthless in the eyes of God. A broken and a contrite heart, O God, thou wilt not despise. I sacrifice now all that was precious to me in the world, my love and my hope of happiness in this life, and I sacrifice it with a cheerful heart, and I pray that God may accept it. So shall I do my part to atone for the sins which have brought on this horrible war.

JOHN: It would have been better if I'd never come back. I've caused misery and suffering to all of you.

SYLVIA: John, you took away the ring you gave me when we became engaged. You threw it in the fire.

JOHN: I'm afraid that was very silly of me. I did it in a moment of bitterness.

SYLVIA: You went into Canterbury to buy a wedding ring. What have you done with it?

JOHN: I have it here. Why?

SYLVIA: Can I have it?

JOHN: Of course.

> [*He takes it out of his waistcoat pocket, and, wondering, gives it to her.*

SYLVIA: [*Slipping the ring on her finger.*] I will put the love of man out of my life. I will turn from what is poor and transitory to what is everlasting. I will be the bride of One whose love is never denied to them that seek it. The love of God is steadfast and enduring. I can put all my trust in that and I shall never find it wanting. . . . Good-bye, John, God bless you now and always.

JOHN: Good-bye, dear child.

> [*She goes out quickly. In a minute* KATE *comes in. She is carrying a square wooden box in which are papers, firewood a hearth-brush, and a large soiled glove.*

KATE: Please, sir, Mrs. Wharton says, will you go upstairs now?

JOHN: Yes.

> [*He goes out.* KATE *goes to the fireplace, kneels down, puts on the glove and begins to rake out the ashes. The* COOK *enters. She is a stout homely body of forty-five.*

COOK: The butcher's come, Kate. I don't exactly like to go up to Mrs. Wharton just now. I've got the cold beef for lunch, but they'll be wanting something for dinner.

KATE: Oh, well, they always like best end. You can't go far wrong if you have that.

COOK: I've got a fine lot of pease.

KATE: Well, they'll do nicely.

COOK: I was thinking I'd make a fruit tart. I think p'raps I'd better order two and a half pounds of best end.

> [*She goes out.* KATE *continues to lay the fire.*

THE END

FOR SERVICES RENDERED

A PLAY
in Three Acts

CHARACTERS

LEONARD ARDSLEY
CHARLOTTE ARDSLEY, his wife
SYDNEY, his son
EVA ⎫
LOIS ⎭ his unmarried daughters
ETHEL BARTLETT, his married daughter
HOWARD BARTLETT, her husband
COLLIE STRATTON, Commander, R.N.
WILFRED CEDAR
GWEN, his wife
DR. PRENTICE, Mrs. Ardsley's brother
GERTRUDE, the Ardsleys' parlourmaid

The action takes place in the Ardsleys' house at Rambleston, a small country town in Kent, near the cathedral city of Stanbury.

FOR SERVICES RENDERED

THE FIRST ACT

*The Scene is a terrace at the back of the Ardsleys' house. French
    windows lead out on it from the house, and beyond is the
    garden.*
LEONARD ARDSLEY *is the only solicitor in Rambleston and his
    house faces the village street. Part of it is used as his office.
    Tea is laid. It is five o'clock on a warm afternoon in September.*
MRS. ARDSLEY *is sitting in a chair, hemming a napkin. She is
    a thin, grey-haired woman of more than sixty, with a severe
    face but kind eyes. She is quietly dressed.*
The MAID *brings in the tea.*

MRS. ARDSLEY: Is it tea-time?

GERTRUDE: The church clock's striking now, ma'am.

MRS. ARDSLEY: [*Getting up and putting her sewing aside.*] Go
    down to the tennis court and tell them that tea is ready.

GERTRUDE: Very good, ma'am.

MRS. ARDSLEY: Have you told Mr. Sydney?

GERTRUDE: Yes, ma'am.
    [*She goes out into the garden.* MRS. ARDSLEY *brings
    two or three light chairs up to the table.* SYDNEY
    comes in from the house. He is a heavy man of hard
    on forty, with a big, fat face. He is blind and walks
    with a stick, but he knows his way about and moves
    with little hesitation.*

MRS. ARDSLEY: Where would you like to sit, dear?

SYDNEY: Anywhere.
    [*He lets himself down into a chair by the table and puts
    down his stick.*

MRS. ARDSLEY: What have you been doing all the afternoon?

SYDNEY: Nothing very much. Knitting a bit.

MRS. ARDSLEY: Ethel's here. Howard's coming to fetch her on his way home from Stanbury. He's gone to the cattle-market.

SYDNEY: I suppose he'll be as tight as a drum.

MRS. ARDSLEY: Sydney!

SYDNEY: [*With a little chuckle.*] What rot it all is. Does Ethel really think we don't know he drinks?

MRS. ARDSLEY: She's proud. She doesn't want to admit that she made a mistake.

SYDNEY: I shall never stop asking myself what on earth she saw in him.

MRS. ARDSLEY: Everything was so different then. He looked very nice in uniform. He was an officer.

SYDNEY: You and father ought to have put your foot down.

MRS. ARDSLEY: They were madly in love with one another. When all that slaughter was going on it seemed so snobbish to object to a man because he was just a small tenant farmer.

SYDNEY: Did you think the war was going on for ever?

MRS. ARDSLEY: No, but it looked as though the world would be a changed place when it stopped.

SYDNEY: It's funny when you think of it. Everything goes on in the same old way, except that we're all broke to the wide and a few hundred thousand fellows like me have had our chance of making a good job of life snatched away from us.

[MRS. ARDSLEY *gives a sigh and makes an unhappy gesture.* SYDNEY *utters a little sardonic chuckle.*

Cheer up, mother. You must console yourself by thinking that you've got a hero for a son. M.C. and mentioned in despatches. No one can say I didn't do my bit.

MRS. ARDSLEY: They're just coming.

> [GWEN CEDAR *and* ETHEL BARTLETT *come in from the garden.* ETHEL BARTLETT, MRS. ARDSLEY'S *second daughter, is a handsome woman of thirty-five, with regular features and fine eyes.* GWEN CEDAR *is fifty, a good deal painted, with dyed hair; she is too smartly dressed in a manner hardly becoming to her age. She has the mechanical brightness of a woman who is desperately hanging on to the remains of her youth.*

ETHEL: The others are coming as soon as they've finished the set. Hulloa, Sydney.

SYDNEY: Hulloa.

GWEN: [*Shaking hands with him.*] How are you to-day, Sydney? You're looking very well.

SYDNEY: Oh, I'm all right, thanks.

GWEN: Busy as a bee as usual, I suppose. You're simply amazing.

MRS. ARDSLEY: [*Trying to head her off.*] Let me give you some tea.

GWEN: I do admire you. I mean, you must have great strength of character.

SYDNEY: [*With a grin.*] A will of iron.

GWEN: I remember when I was ill last spring and they kept me in a darkened room for nearly a week, it was quite intolerable. But I kept on saying to myself, well, it's nothing compared to what poor Sydney has to put up with.

SYDNEY: And you were right.

MRS. ARDSLEY: One lump of sugar?

GWEN: Oh, no, I never take sugar. It's Lent all the year round for me. [*Brightly attacking* SYDNEY *again.*] It's a marvel to me how you pass the time.

SYDNEY: Charming women like you are very sweet to me, and my sisters are good enough to play chess with me. I improve my mind by reading.

GWEN: Oh, yes, Braille. I love reading. I always read at least one novel a day. Of course I've got a head like a sieve. D'you know, it's often happened to me to read a novel right through and never remember till the end that I'd read it before. It always makes me so angry. I mean, it's such a waste of time.

SYDNEY: How's the farm, Ethel?

ETHEL: We're making the most of the fine weather.

GWEN: It must be so interesting, living on a farm. Making butter and all that sort of thing.

ETHEL: One's at it from morning till night. It keeps one from thinking.

GWEN: But of course you have people to do all the rough work for you.

ETHEL: What makes you think that?

GWEN: You don't mean to say you do it yourself. How on earth d'you keep your hands?

ETHEL: [*With a glance at them, smiling.*] I don't.
> [*There is a sound of voices from the garden.*

MRS. ARDSLEY: Here are the others.

> [*Her two daughters come in with the two men they have been playing with. These are* WILFRED CEDAR *and* COLLIE STRATTON. WILFRED CEDAR *is a stout, elderly man, but well preserved, with a red face and grey, crisply curling hair. He is stout, jovial, breezy and sensual. He is out to enjoy all the good things of life.* COLLIE STRATTON *is between thirty-five and forty. He has been in the Royal Navy and has the rather school-boyish manner of those men who have never quite grown up. He has a pleasant, frank look.* EVA *is* MRS. ARDSLEY'S *eldest daughter. She is*

thin and of a somewhat haggard appearance. She is
very gentle, a trifle subdued, but she does not give you
the impression of being at peace with herself. Behind
the placidity is a strange restlessness. She is thirty-
nine. LOIS ARDSLEY is the youngest of the family.
She is twenty-six, but the peaceful, monotonous life
she has led has preserved her youth and she looks little
more than twenty. She is gay and natural. She is a
very pretty young woman, but what is even more
attractive in her than her blue eyes and straight nose
is the air she has of immense healthiness.

LOIS: Tea. Tea. Tea.

WILFRED: By George, they made us run about. Hulloa,
Sydney.

MRS. ARDSLEY: How were you playing?

WILFRED: Lois and me against Eva and Collie.

EVA: Of course Wilfred's in a different class from us.

COLLIE: That forehand drive of yours is devilish.

WILFRED: I've had a lot of practice, you know, playing in
tournaments on the Riviera and so on.

GWEN: Of course he was too old for singles, but a few
years ago he was one of the best doubles players in
Cannes.

WILFRED: [*Not too pleased.*] I don't know that I play any
worse than I played a few years ago.

GWEN: Well, you can't expect to get across the court as
you used to when you were young. I mean, that's silly.

WILFRED: Gwen always talks as if I was a hundred. What
I say is, a woman's as old as she looks and a man as
old as he feels.

SYDNEY: It has been said before.

MRS. ARDSLEY: [*To* WILFRED.] How do you like your tea?

LOIS: Oh, mother, I'm sure they want a drink.

WILFRED: Clever girl.

MRS. ARDSLEY: What would you like?

WILFRED: Well, a glass of beer sounds good to me. What about you, Collie?

COLLIE: Suits me.

EVA: I'll tell Gertrude.

MRS. ARDSLEY: [*As* EVA *is going.*] Tell your father that if he wants any tea he'd better come now.

EVA: Very well.

[*She goes into the house.*

WILFRED: Damned convenient for your husband having his office in the house.

LOIS: He's got a private door so that he can slip away without the clients seeing him.

GWEN: Evie's looking a little tired, I think.

MRS. ARDSLEY: She's been rather nervy lately. I've wanted her uncle to have a look at her, but she won't let him.

GWEN: So sad the man she was engaged to being killed in the war.

MRS. ARDSLEY: They were very much in love with one another.

ETHEL: She's never really got over it, poor dear.

GWEN: Pity she never found anyone else she liked.

MRS. ARDSLEY: In a place like this she could hardly hope to. By the end of the war there were very few young men left. And girls were growing up all the time.

GWEN: I heard there *was* someone.

MRS. ARDSLEY: Not very desirable. I believe he did ask her, but she refused him.

GWEN: I'm told he wasn't quite, quite. It's always a mistake to marry out of one's own class. It's never a success.

[GWEN *has dropped a brick.* ETHEL *has married beneath her.*

LOIS: Oh, what nonsense. As if that sort of thing mattered any more. It depends on the people, not on their class.

[GWEN *suddenly realises what she has said, gives* ETHEL *a hurried look and tries to make everything right.*

GWEN: Oh, of course. I didn't mean that. All sorts of people keep shops nowadays and go in for poultry farming and things like that. I don't mind what a man is as long as he's a gentleman.

COLLIE: It's a relief to hear you say that, as I run a garage.

GWEN: That's just what I mean. It doesn't matter your running a garage. After all you were in the Navy and you commanded a destroyer.

SYDNEY: To say nothing of having the D.S.O. and the Legion of Honour.

WILFRED: In point of fact what made you go into the motor business when you were axed, Collie?

COLLIE: I had to do something. I was a pretty good mechanic. I got a bonus, you know, and I thought I might just as well put it into that as anything else.

WILFRED: I suppose you do pretty well out of the motor-buses.

COLLIE: Lot of expenses, you know.

[GERTRUDE *comes out of the house with two tankards of beer on a tray.*

WILFRED: Look what's here.

[*He takes one of the tankards and takes a great pull at it.* EVA *comes back.*

EVA: Father's just coming. He wants to see you, Collie.

COLLIE: Oh, does he?

WILFRED: That doesn't look too good, old man. When a solicitor wants to see you it's generally that he has something disagreeable to say to you.

LOIS: Hurry up and finish your beer and we'll give them their revenge. It'll be getting dark soon.

GWEN: Oh, are you going to play again, Wilfred? Don't you think it's time we went home?

WILFRED: What's the hurry? You take the car. I'll have another set and I'll walk back.

GWEN: Oh, if you're not coming, I'll wait.

WILFRED: [*Trying to hide his irritation behind his joviality.*] Oh, come on, you can trust me out of your sight just this once. I promise to be a good boy.

> [*A little look passes between them. She stifles a sigh and smiles brightly.*

GWEN: Oh, all right. A brisk walk won't do your figure any harm.

> [*She turns towards* MRS. ARDSLEY *to say good-bye.*

MRS. ARDSLEY: I'll come as far as the door with you.

> [*The two of them go out.*

SYDNEY: Where's my stick, Evie? [*She gives it to him and he gets up.*] I think I'll totter down to the court and see how you all play.

ETHEL: I'll come with you, shall I?

EVA: I think I'd better get some fresh tea for father.

LOIS: Hurry up, then, or the light'll be going.

EVA: I shan't be a minute.

> [*She goes into the house.*

LOIS: What should we do in this house without Evie?

SYDNEY: What would Evie do without us? You can't sacrifice yourself unless there's someone about whom you can sacrifice yourself for.

WILFRED: You're a cynical bloke.

LOIS: [*With a smile.*] And ungrateful.

SYDNEY: Not at all. It's jam for Evie to have an invalid to look after. If she could make me see by saying a magic word, d'you think she'd say it? Not on your life. Nature destined her to be a saint and it's damned lucky for her that I'm around to give her the opportunity of earning a heavenly crown.

ETHEL: [*With a chuckle.*] Come on, give me your arm.

SYDNEY: [*Putting on a cockney accent.*] Spare a copper for a poor blind man, sir.

[*They go out.*

LOIS: I'll just go and hunt for that ball. I think I know more or less where it is.

WILFRED: I'd come with you if I weren't so lazy.

LOIS: No, stay there. You'll only wreck the flower beds with your big feet.

WILFRED: I like that. I flatter myself not many men of my size have smaller feet than I have.

LOIS: Modest fellow, aren't you? Give me a shout when Evie comes.

[*She disappears into the garden.*

WILFRED: Good-looking girl that. Nice too. And she's got a head on her shoulders.

COLLIE: Plays a good game of tennis.

WILFRED: Funny she shouldn't have been snapped up before now. If I was a young fellow and single I shouldn't hesitate.

COLLIE: She hasn't got much chance here, poor thing. Who the devil is there she can marry in a place like this?

WILFRED: I wonder you don't have a cut in yourself.

COLLIE: I'm fifteen years older than she is. And I haven't got a bean.

WILFRED: Girls nowadays who live in the country have to take what they can get.

COLLIE: Nothing doing as far as I'm concerned.

WILFRED: [*With a shrewd look at him.*] Oh!

COLLIE: Why d'you want to know?

WILFRED: Only that she's a nice girl and I'd like to see her settled.

COLLIE: I say, old man, I suppose you wouldn't do me a favour.

WILFRED: Of course I will, old boy. What is it?

COLLIE: Well, to tell you the truth, I'm in a bit of a hole.

WILFRED: Sorry to hear that. What's it all about?

COLLIE: Business has been rotten lately.

WILFRED: I know it has. And I don't know when things are going to improve. I can tell you I'm damned glad I got out when the going was good.

COLLIE: I expect you are.

WILFRED: Everyone told me I was a fool to retire. But I smelt a rat. I said, no, I've worked a good many years and I've made a packet. Now I'm going to live like a gentleman. I sold out at the top of the market. Just in time.

COLLIE: Lucky.

WILFRED: Lucky be damned. Clever, I call it.

COLLIE: Look here, old man. I hate asking you, but I'm terribly hard up just now. I should be awfully grateful if you could lend me a bit.

WILFRED: [*Very heartily.*] Why, my dear old boy, of course I will. I'm always glad to oblige a friend. How much d'you want?

COLLIE: That's awfully kind of you. Could you manage two hundred pounds?

WILFRED: Oh, I say, that's real money. I thought you were going to say a tenner. Two hundred pounds is quite another story.

COLLIE: It's not very much for you.

WILFRED: I'm not made of money, you know. My investments have gone down like everybody else's. Believe me, I haven't got more than I can spend.

COLLIE: I'm in a most awful jam.

WILFRED: Why don't you go to the bank?

COLLIE: I'm overdrawn already. They won't lend me a bob.

WILFRED: But haven't you got any security?

COLLIE: Not that they'll accept.

WILFRED: Then what d'you expect me to lend you the money on?

COLLIE: I'll give you my word of honour to return it as soon as ever I can.

WILFRED: My dear old boy, you're a damned good chap and a D.S.O. and all that sort of thing, but this is business.

COLLIE: You've known me for six months now. You must know I'm honest.

WILFRED: I took a furnished house down here for my wife's health, and when I heard you'd been in the navy of course I came to you for my petrol and tyres and repairs. I know it's hard for you fellows who've been axed. I've paid all my bills on the nail.

COLLIE: I've given you good service.

WILFRED: I know you have. I'm very sorry your garage hasn't proved a good proposition. If you'd been a business man you'd have known it was crazy to settle down in a little tin-pot place like this. But I really don't see that I'm called upon to make you a present of two hundred pounds.

COLLIE: I'm not asking it as a present.

WILFRED: It comes to the same thing. I've lent dozens of fellows money and they never pay it back. I think it's a bit thick to ask me to lend you a sum like that.

COLLIE: You don't think I like it. I tell you I'm absolutely up against it. It means life and death to me.

WILFRED: I'm awfully sorry, old boy, but there's nothing doing. . . . I wonder if Lois has found that ball yet.

> [*He gets up and goes into the garden.* COLLIE *sits on dejectedly. In a moment* EVA *comes in with the teapot.*

EVA: What's the matter? You're looking terribly depressed.

COLLIE: [*Trying to collect himself.*] I'm sorry.

EVA: Are they waiting for us?

COLLIE: [*With a slight sigh.*] I suppose so.

EVA: Tell me what the matter is.

COLLIE: [*Forcing a smile.*] It wouldn't interest you.

EVA: Why do you say that? Don't you know that anything that concerns you interests me.

COLLIE: That's very sweet of you.

EVA: I suppose I'm rather reserved. It's difficult for me to show my feelings. I should like you to look upon me as a friend.

COLLIE: I do.

EVA: Tell me what it is then. Perhaps I can help you.

COLLIE: I'm afraid not. I think you've got troubles enough of your own without sharing mine.

EVA: You mean looking after Sydney. I don't look upon that as a trouble. I'm glad to do what I can for the poor boy. When I think of what the war did to him, it's only right that I should sacrifice myself.

COLLIE: It's very good of you, all the same.

EVA: You see, Ethel was married and Lois was so young. Mother isn't very strong. Looking after Sydney helped me to bear the loss of poor Ted.

COLLIE: That was the man you were engaged to?

EVA: Yes. I was terribly unhappy when he was killed.

I'm afraid I was rather morbid about it. One can't afford to give in, can one? I mean, life is given to us, and it's our duty to make the best we can out of it.

COLLIE: [*Rather vaguely.*] Naturally one gets over everything in course of time.

EVA: I suppose one ought to consider oneself fortunate that one can. And I think a girl ought to marry, don't you? I mean, it's a woman's province to have a home of her own and children to look after.

COLLIE: Yes, I suppose it is.

[*There is a moment's pause.*

EVA: It's rather strange that you should never have married, Collie.

COLLIE: [*With a grin.*] I never had anything to marry on.

EVA: Oh, money isn't everything. A clever woman can manage on very little. [*Brightly.*] I must have a look round and see if I can't find someone to suit you.

COLLIE: I'm afraid I'm too old now.

EVA: Oh, what nonsense. You're just the same age as I am. Every woman loves a sailor. Between you and me and the gate-post I don't believe there's a girl here who wouldn't jump at the chance if you asked her.

COLLIE: [*A trifle embarrassed.*] I'm not likely to do that.

EVA: Are you waiting for her to ask you? That's wanting almost too much.

COLLIE: I suppose it is really.

EVA: After all, a nice girl can't do much more than show a man she's not indifferent to him and leave him to draw what conclusions he pleases.

COLLIE: I've got an awful headache. I wonder if you'd tell the others that I can't play tennis again to-day. Perhaps Ethel will make a four.

EVA: Oh, my dear, I am sorry. Of course you mustn't play. That's quite all right.

> [LEONARD ARDSLEY *comes out from the house. He is a red-faced, hearty man of sixty-five, with blue eyes and white hair. He looks more like the old-fashioned sporting squire than the country solicitor. He is on familiar terms with the local gentry and in the season enjoys a day's shooting.*

Oh, there you are, father. We've all had tea.

ARDSLEY: I had somebody with me. [*With a nod to him.*] How are you, Stratton? Run along, Evie, I'll help myself. I want to have a word with our young friend.

EVA: Oh, all right.

> [*She goes out into the garden.*

ARDSLEY: I've just seen Radley.

COLLIE: Yes.

ARDSLEY: I'm afraid I haven't got very good news for you.

COLLIE: He won't wait?

ARDSLEY: He can't wait.

COLLIE: Then what's to be done?

ARDSLEY: The only sensible thing is to file your petition.

COLLIE: It's ridiculous. It's only a matter of a hundred and eighty-seven pounds. I'm sure if I can hang on a little longer I can manage. When does Radley want to be paid?

ARDSLEY: The first of the month.

COLLIE: I've just got to get the money before then, that's all.

ARDSLEY: You've had a hard struggle and you've deserved to succeed. Believe me, no one will be sorrier than I if you're beaten. You know, you needn't worry about my fees. We'll forget about them.

COLLIE: That's very kind of you.

ARDSLEY: Not a bit of it. I think it's very tough on you

fellows who've been kicked out of the navy. A man with your record. You put all your eggs in the one basket, didn't you?

COLLIE: Everything. If I go bust I haven't a shilling. I'll be thankful if I can get a job driving a motor bus.

ARDSLEY: [*Cheerily.*] Oh, I hope it won't come to that. It would be rather a come-down for a man who's commanded a destroyer and has all the ribands you have.

[MRS. ARDSLEY *comes out of the house with* DR. PRENTICE. *He is a thin, elderly man with iron-grey hair, a stern face and searching eyes.*]

Hulloa, Charlie.

PRENTICE: How are you? Oh, Stratton.

ARDSLEY: Just in time for a cup of tea. [*To* COLLIE.] Don't you bother about us if you want to go and play tennis.

COLLIE: No, I'm not playing any more. I'll hop it. Good-bye, Mrs. Ardsley.

MRS. ARDSLEY: Are you going already?

COLLIE: I'm afraid I must.

MRS. ARDSLEY: Well, good-bye. Come again soon.

COLLIE: Good-bye.

[*He nods to the two men and goes out through the house.*]

MRS. ARDSLEY: [*To* PRENTICE.] Will you have some tea?

PRENTICE: No, thank you.

MRS. ARDSLEY: Collie looks rather worried. Is anything the matter?

PRENTICE: I'm told his garage isn't doing any too well.

ARDSLEY: It's the same old story. All these ex-officers. They go into business without knowing anything about it. And by the time they've learnt how many beans make five they've lost every bob they'd got.

MRS. ARDSLEY: It's very hard on them.

ARDSLEY: Of course it is. But what's to be done about it?

The nation can't afford itself the luxury of supporting an army of officers it has no use for.

PRENTICE: The unfortunate thing is that the lives they've led in the service has unfitted them for the rough and tumble of ordinary life.

ARDSLEY: Well, I must get back to my office. Is this just a friendly call, Charlie, or are you hunting a patient? Personally, I am in robust health, thank you very much.

PRENTICE: [*With grim humour.*] That's what you say. I expect your blood pressure's awful.

ARDSLEY: Get along with you. I've never had a day's illness in my life.

PRENTICE: Well, don't blame me if you have a stroke. I always have my suspicions about a man who looks as well as you do.

MRS. ARDSLEY: As a matter of fact, I wanted to have a little talk with Charlie about Eva. She's been very jumpy lately.

ARDSLEY: Oh, that's only your fancy, my dear. She's getting a little old maidish. The great thing is to give her occupation. Fortunately Sydney gives her plenty to do.

PRENTICE: Sydney keeping pretty fit?

MRS. ARDSLEY: As fit as can be expected.

ARDSLEY: Poor old Sydney. The only thing we can do is to make things as easy for him as we can. It's been a great blow to me. I was hoping he'd go into the business. He'd have been able to take a lot of the work off my hands now. I've paid for the war all right.

PRENTICE: [*With a twinkle in his eye.*] He has too, in a way.

ARDSLEY: Of course. But he's got used to it. Invalids do, you know. Well, it's lucky I've got my health and strength. Anyhow, I must go back and do a job of work.

[*He nods to the doctor and goes into the house.*

PRENTICE: Leonard's a wonderful fellow. He always looks at the bright side of things.

MRS. ARDSLEY: It's a strength.

PRENTICE: You've spoilt him.

MRS. ARDSLEY: I've loved him.

PRENTICE: I wonder why.

MRS. ARDSLEY: [*With a smile.*] I can't imagine. I suppose because he can never see further than the end of his nose and I've always had to take care that he didn't trip over the obvious and hurt himself.

PRENTICE: You've been a good wife and mother, Charlotte. There aren't many left like you now.

MRS. ARDSLEY: Times are difficult. I think one should make allowances for all these young things who are faced with problems that we never dreamed of.

PRENTICE: What did you want to say to me about Evie?

MRS. ARDSLEY: I want her to come and see you. She's been losing weight. I'm rather uneasy about her.

PRENTICE: I daresay she wants a holiday. I'll have a talk to her. But you know I'm more concerned about you. I don't like this pain you've been complaining of.

MRS. ARDSLEY: I don't think it's very important. It's just pain, you know. I suppose most women of my age have it now and then.

PRENTICE: I've been thinking about it. I want you to let me make a proper examination.

MRS. ARDSLEY: I'd hate it.

PRENTICE: I'm not a bad doctor, you know, even though I am your brother.

MRS. ARDSLEY: You can't do anything for me. When the pain gets bad I take some aspirin. It's no good making a fuss.

PRENTICE: If you won't let me examine you I shall go to Leonard.

MRS. ARDSLEY: No, don't do that. He'll have a fit.

PRENTICE: Come along, then.

MRS. ARDSLEY: Now?

PRENTICE: Yes, now.

MRS. ARDSLEY: I disliked you when you were a little boy and used to make me bowl to you, and every year that has passed since then has made me dislike you more.

PRENTICE: You're a wrinkled old hag, Charlotte, and women ought to be young and pretty, but upon my word there's something about you that I can't help liking.

MRS. ARDSLEY: [*Smiling.*] You fool.

[LOIS *and* WILFRED CEDAR *saunter in from the garden.*

LOIS: Hulloa, Uncle Charlie. Tennis is off. Evie says Collie's got a bad head.

MRS. ARDSLEY: He's gone home.

PRENTICE: I'm just taking your mother off to have a look at her.

LOIS: Oh, mother, you're not ill?

MRS. ARDSLEY: No, darling, of course not. Uncle Charlie's an old fuss-pot.

[*They go into the house.*

WILFRED: D'you want me to take myself off?

LOIS: No, sit down. Would you like a drink?

WILFRED: Not at the moment. Let's have a talk.

LOIS: The days are drawing in. Oh, how I hate the winter.

WILFRED: It must be pretty grim down here.

LOIS: The wind! When d'you go south?

WILFRED: Oh, not for another month.

LOIS: Shall you take a house here again next year?

WILFRED: I don't know. Would you like me to?

LOIS: Naturally. It's awful when there's no one at the Manor.

WILFRED: D'you know, you're a very pretty girl.

LOIS: It doesn't do me much good.

WILFRED: I wonder you don't go on the stage.

LOIS: One can't go on the stage just like that.

WILFRED: With your looks you could always get a job in the chorus.

LOIS: Can you see father's face if I suggested it?

WILFRED: You haven't got much chance of marrying in a place like this.

LOIS: Oh, I don't know. Someone may turn up.

WILFRED: I believe you'd be a success on the stage.

LOIS: One has to have training. At least a year. I'd have to live in London. It costs money.

WILFRED: I'll pay.

LOIS: You? What *do* you mean?

WILFRED: Well, I'm not exactly a poor man. I can't bear the thought of your going to seed in a rotten little hole like this.

LOIS: Don't be silly. How can I take money from you?

WILFRED: Why not? I mean, it's absurd at this time of day to be conventional.

LOIS: What do you think Gwen would say?

WILFRED: She needn't know.

LOIS: Anyhow, it's too late. I'm twenty-six. One has to start at eighteen. . . . It's extraordinary how the years slip by. I didn't realise I was grown up till I was twenty. I vaguely thought of becoming a typist or a hospital nurse. But I never got beyond thinking of it. I suppose I thought I'd marry.

WILFRED: What'll you do if you don't?

LOIS: Become an old maid. Be the solace of my parents' declining years.

WILFRED: I don't think much of that.

LOIS: I'm not complaining, you know. Life's so monotonous here. Time slips by without your noticing it.

WILFRED: Has no one ever asked you to marry him?

LOIS: Oh, yes. An assistant of Uncle Charlie's did. An odious little man. And there was a widower with three children and no money. I didn't think that much catch.

WILFRED: I don't blame you.

LOIS: What made you suggest that just now? Paying for my training?

WILFRED: Oh, I don't know. I was sorry for you.

LOIS: You don't give me the impression of a philanthropist.

WILFRED: Well, if you must know, I'm crazy about you.

LOIS: And you thought I'd show my gratitude in the usual way.

WILFRED: I never thought about it.

LOIS: Oh, come off it.

WILFRED: You're not angry with me? It's not my fault if I'm just dotty about you.

LOIS: After all, you are old enough to be my father.

WILFRED: I know. You needn't rub it in.

LOIS: I think it's just as well that you're going away in a month.

WILFRED: I'd do anything in the world for you, Lois.

LOIS: Thank you very much, but there's nothing you can do.

WILFRED: You don't know what you're talking about. You're just mouldering away here. I can give you a better time than you've ever dreamed of. Paris. You've

never been there, have you? By God, you'd go mad
over the clothes. You could buy as many as you liked.
Cannes and Monte. And what price Venice? Gwen
and I spent the summer before last at the Lido. It was
a riot, I can tell you.

LOIS: You're a monstrous old man. If I were a properly
brought up young woman I should ring for a flunkey
and have you shown the door.

WILFRED: I'm not a bad sort. I'm sure I could make you
happy. You know, you could turn me round your
little finger.

LOIS: [*Looking at her fingers.*] Blazing with jewels?

WILFRED: Rather.

LOIS: [*With a laugh.*] You fool.

WILFRED: God, how I love you. It's a relief to be able to
say it, at all events. I can't make out how you never
guessed it.

LOIS: It never occurred to me. Does Gwen know?

WILFRED: Oh, no, she never sees anything. She hasn't got
the brains of a louse.

LOIS: You're not going to make a nuisance of yourself,
are you?

WILFRED: No, I'm going to leave you to think about it.

LOIS: That's not necessary. There's nothing doing. I can
tell you that at once. Take care, there's someone
coming.

> [HOWARD BARTLETT *comes in from the house. He is
> a big, fine man of forty, somewhat on the stout side,
> but still with the dashing good looks that had attracted
> ETHEL during the war. He wears rather shabby plus-
> fours and a golf coat of rather too loud a pattern.
> He is altogether a little showy. He does not drop his
> aitches often, but his accent is slightly common. At
> the moment he is not quite sober. You would not say*

*he was drunk, but the liquor he has had during the
day has made him jovial.*

HOWARD: Well, here I am.

LOIS: Hulloa, Howard.

HOWARD: I've caught you, have I? What are you doing
with my sister-in-law, Cedar? Eh? You be careful of
that man, Lois. He's up to no good.

LOIS: [*With a laugh.*] Oh, shut up, Howard.

HOWARD: I know him. He's just the kind of fellow to lead
a poor girl astray.

LOIS: [*Coolly.*] Howard, you've had a couple.

HOWARD: I know I have, and I'm feeling all the better for it.
[*Harking back.*] Don't you listen to a word he says.
He's a wicked old man.

WILFRED: Go on. I like flattery.

HOWARD: You know, his intentions aren't honourable.
[*To* WILFRED.] Now, as one man to another, are your
intentions honourable?

WILFRED: If you put it like that . . .

HOWARD: One man to another, mind you.

WILFRED: I don't mind telling you they're not.

HOWARD: There, Lois, what did I tell you?

LOIS: At all events I know where I am now.

HOWARD: Don't say I didn't warn you. When you're
walking the streets of London, with a baby on your
arm and no home to go to, don't say, Howard never
warned me.

LOIS: Ethel's waiting for you, Howard. She wants to go
home.

HOWARD: No place like home and home's a woman's place.

LOIS: You'll find her somewhere in the garden.

HOWARD: A good woman. You always know where to find

her. She's not one of your gad-abouts. One of the best.
And a lady, mind you. [*To* WILFRED.] I don't mind
telling you I'm not a gentleman by birth.

WILFRED: Aren't you?

HOWARD: The King made me a gentleman. His Majesty.
I may be only a farmer now, but I've been an officer
and a gentleman. And don't you forget it.

LOIS: You're drivelling, Howard.

HOWARD: What I mean to say is, leave the girl alone, Cedar.
A poor motherless child. An innocent village maiden.
I appeal to your better nature.

WILFRED: D'you know what's the matter with you,
Bartlett?

HOWARD: I do not.

WILFRED: You're tight.

HOWARD: Me? I'm as sober as a judge. How many drinks
d'you think I've had to-day?

WILFRED: More than you can count.

HOWARD: On the fingers of one hand, maybe. [*With
triumph.*] But not on the fingers of two. It wants more
than that to make me tight.

WILFRED: You're getting older. You can't carry your
liquor like you used to.

HOWARD: Do you know, when I was an officer and a gentleman, I could drink a bottle of whisky at a sitting and
not turn a hair. [*He sees* MRS. ARDSLEY *and* DR. PRENTICE
coming through the drawing-room.] Here's the Doctor. We'll
ask him.

[*They come out.*

MRS. ARDSLEY: Oh, Howard, I didn't know you were here.

HOWARD: As large as life.

DR. PRENTICE: Been in to Stanbury?

HOWARD: Market-day to-day.

DR. PRENTICE: Do any business?

HOWARD: Business is rotten. Just wasting my time, I am. Farming's gone all to hell.

MRS. ARDSLEY: You look tired, Howard. Would you like me to have a cup of tea made for you?

HOWARD: Tired? I'm never tired. [*Pointing to* WILFRED.] Do you know what this chap says? He says I'm tight.

WILFRED: I was only joking.

HOWARD: [*Solemnly.*] I'm going to get a professional opinion. Uncle Charlie and Dr. Prentice, as one man to another, tell me, am I tight? Don't mind hurting my feelings. I'll bear it, whatever you say, like an officer and a gentleman. 'Shun.

DR. PRENTICE: I've seen men a lot tighter.

HOWARD: You examine me. I want to get to the bottom of this. Tell me to say British Constitution.

PRENTICE: Say British Constitution.

HOWARD: I've already said it. You can't catch me that way. Now what about the chalk line?

DR. PRENTICE: What about it?

HOWARD: Look here, do you want me to teach you your business? Draw a chalk line and make me walk along it. That'll prove it. Go on. Draw a chalk line. Draw it straight, mind you.

DR. PRENTICE: I don't happen to have any chalk.

HOWARD: You haven't got any chalk?

DR. PRENTICE: No.

HOWARD: Then I shall never know if I'm tight or not.

> [SYDNEY *comes from the garden, accompanied by* ETHEL. *A moment later* EVA *follows them.*

ETHEL: Howard. Had a good day?

SYDNEY: Hulloa.

HOWARD: Yes, I met a lot of good chaps, white men, fine upstanding fellows. Straight as a die. Pick of the British nation.

> [ETHEL *gives a little start as she realises that he is tipsy, but pretends to notice nothing.*

ETHEL: [*Brightly.*] How was business?

HOWARD: Rotten. Everybody's broke. Farming—what a game. What I ask you is, why the Government don't do something.

ETHEL: Well, they've promised to.

HOWARD: Are they going to keep their promises? You know they're not, I know they're not, and they know they're not.

ETHEL: Then the only thing is to grin and bear it as we've grinned and borne it all these years.

HOWARD: Are we the backbone of the country or not?

SYDNEY: I've never heard a Member of Parliament who didn't say so.

HOWARD: [*About to get angry.*] I know what I'm talking about.

ETHEL: [*Soothingly.*] Of course you do.

HOWARD: Then why does he contradict me?

SYDNEY: I wasn't contradicting you. I was agreeing with you.

HOWARD: [*Mollified.*] Were you, old boy? Well, that's damned nice of you. You're a sport. I've always liked you, Sydney.

SYDNEY: Good.

HOWARD: I was born on a farm. Born and bred. Except when I was an officer and a gentleman, I've been a farmer all me life. Shall I tell you what's wrong with farming?

SYDNEY: No.

HOWARD: No?

SYDNEY: No.

HOWARD: All right, I won't.

> [*He sinks back, comatose, into his chair. At that moment* GWEN CEDAR *comes in from the drawing-room. She has a fixed, bright smile on her face.*

MRS. ARDSLEY: [*A little surprised.*] Oh, Gwen.

GWEN: I'm like a bad penny. I was just passing your door and the maid told me Wilfred was still here, so I thought I'd step in for him.

MRS. ARDSLEY: Of course.

> [WILFRED'S *face is sullen with anger.*

WILFRED: What's the idea, Gwen?

GWEN: I didn't think you'd want to walk all that way.

WILFRED: You said you were going home.

GWEN: I remembered I had some things to do.

WILFRED: I prefer to walk.

GWEN: [*With a bright smile.*] Why?

WILFRED: Good God, surely I don't have to explain why I want a walk.

GWEN: It seems so silly when the car is there.

WILFRED: I need the exercise.

GWEN: You've had lots of exercise.

WILFRED: You're making a fool of yourself, Gwen.

GWEN: How rude you are, Wilfred.

WILFRED: It's maddening that you can never trust me out of your sight for ten minutes.

GWEN: [*Still very bright.*] You're so fascinating. I'm always afraid some bold bad woman will be running after you.

WILFRED: [*Surly.*] Come on, then. Let's go.

GWEN: [*Turning to shake hands with* MRS. ARDSLEY.] Tiresome creatures men are, aren't they?

WILFRED: Good-bye, Mrs. Ardsley. Thank you very much.

GWEN: It's been a lovely afternoon. So kind of you to ask us.

MRS. ARDSLEY: I hope you'll come again very soon.

> [WILFRED *gives a sullen nod to the others. He waits at the window for his wife and when she flutters out he follows her.*

SYDNEY: What's the trouble?

LOIS: What a fool of a woman.

SYDNEY: I bet he gives her hell in the car.

> [HOWARD *gives a little snore. He has fallen into a drunken sleep.* ETHEL *gives a start.*

ETHEL: Listen to Howard. He's tired out, poor dear. One of the cows has something the matter with her and he was up at five this morning.

MRS. ARDSLEY: Let him sleep for a little, Ethel. Sydney, hadn't you better come in? It's beginning to get quite chilly.

SYDNEY: All right.

> [MRS. ARDSLEY, DR. PRENTICE *and* SYDNEY *go into the house.*

DR. PRENTICE: [*As they go.*] How has the neuralgia been lately?

SYDNEY: Bearable, you know.

> [MRS. ARDSLEY'S *three daughters are left with the drunken, sleeping man.*

ETHEL: Poor Howard, he works so hard. I'm glad to see him get a few minutes' rest.

EVA: You work hard too and you get no rest.

ETHEL: I love it. I'm so interested in it, and Howard's a wonderful person to work with.

EVA: Would you marry him over again if you could put the clock back?

ETHEL: Why, of course. He's been a wonderful husband.

> [MRS. ARDSLEY *comes to the door of the drawing-room.*

MRS. ARDSLEY: Evie, Sydney would like a game of chess.

EVA: All right, mother. I'll come.

> [MRS. ARDSLEY *withdraws into the room.* EVA *gets up.*

LOIS: Don't you hate chess?

EVA: I loathe it.

ETHEL: Poor Evie.

EVA: It's one of the few games Sydney can play. I'm glad
to do anything I can to make life a little easier for him.

ETHEL: That horrible war.

LOIS: And the chances are that it'll go on like this till we're
all weary old women.

> [HOWARD *gives another snore.*

EVA: I'll go.

> [*She makes her way into the house.*

LOIS: At all events you've got your children.

ETHEL: I've got nothing to complain of.

> [LOIS *gets up and bending over* ETHEL *kisses her on the
> cheek. Then she saunters away into the darkening
> garden.* ETHEL *looks at her husband and the tears flow
> down her cheeks. She takes out her handkerchief and
> nervously pulls it about as she tries to control herself.*

END OF THE FIRST ACT

THE SECOND ACT

The Scene represents the dining-room of the ARDSLEYS' *house. It is furnished in an old-fashioned style, with a mahogany sideboard, mahogany chairs with leather seats and backs, and a solid mahogany dining-table. On each side of the fireplace are two easy chairs, one with arms for the master of the house and one without for the mistress. On the walls are large framed engravings of academy pictures.*

There is a bow window, looking on the High Street, and here EVA *and* SYDNEY *are seated, playing chess. Luncheon is just over and* GERTRUDE, *the maid, is clearing away.*

MRS. ARDSLEY *is sitting in her easy chair reading the paper.*

EVA: Uncle Charlie's car has just driven up.

SYDNEY: Do attend to the game, Evie.

EVA: It's your move.

MRS. ARDSLEY: You'd better go and open the door, Gertrude.

GERTRUDE: Very good, ma'am.

[She goes out.

EVA: He's been here rather often lately.

MRS. ARDSLEY: You know what he is. He will fuss.

SYDNEY: You're not ill, mother, are you?

MRS. ARDSLEY: No, only old.

SYDNEY: I doubt whether even Uncle Charlie can do much about that.

MRS. ARDSLEY: That's what I tell him.

*[GERTRUDE *shows in* DR. PRENTICE.*

GERTRUDE: Dr. Prentice.

[*He comes in, kisses* MRS. ARDSLEY *and waves to the others.*

DR. PRENTICE: How are you? Don't let me disturb your game.

SYDNEY: D'you want us to leave you?

DR. PRENTICE: No. This isn't a doctor's visit. I'm only stopping a minute.

SYDNEY: Queen's knight to queen's bishop third.

[EVA *moves the piece he indicates. The* DOCTOR *sits down and holds out his hands to the fire.*

DR. PRENTICE: Chilly to-day.

MRS. ARDSLEY: Have you arranged something?

DR. PRENTICE: Yes, three o'clock to-morrow afternoon.

MRS. ARDSLEY: That'll suit very well.

DR. PRENTICE: Where's Lois?

MRS. ARDSLEY: She's playing golf. She thought it would be a rush to get back, so she lunched at the club house.

SYDNEY: She's playing with Wilfred. She said she'd bring him back with her and Collie's coming in so that we can have a rubber or two of bridge.

MRS. ARDSLEY: Oh, that'll be nice for you, Sydney.

SYDNEY: Is there a fire in the drawing-room?

MRS. ARDSLEY: I'll have one lit. Gertrude.

[GERTRUDE *has been clearing the rest of the things away and now has finished.*

GERTRUDE: Very good, ma'am.

[*She puts the table-cloth away in the sideboard drawer and goes out.*

MRS. ARDSLEY: [*To* DR. PRENTICE.] Can't you stay and have a man's four?

DR. PRENTICE: I wish I could. I'm too busy.

EVA: King's knight to queen's third.

SYDNEY: That's an idiotic move, Evie.

EVA: There's no reason why I shouldn't make it if I want to.

SYDNEY: You must protect your bishop.

EVA: Play your own game and let me play mine.

MRS. ARDSLEY: Evie.

SYDNEY: You won't look ahead.

EVA: [*Violently.*] Good God, don't I spend my life looking ahead? And a damned cheerful prospect it is.

SYDNEY: My dear, what on earth's the matter with you?

EVA: [*Regaining her self-control.*] Oh, nothing. I'm sorry. I'll protect my bishop. Queen's bishop's pawn to bishop's fourth.

SYDNEY: I'm afraid that's not a very good move.

EVA: It'll do.

SYDNEY: There's not the least use playing chess unless you're prepared to give it some attention.

EVA: Oh, can't you stop nagging? It's enough to drive one insane.

SYDNEY: I didn't mean to nag. I won't say another word.

EVA: Oh, I'm sick of it.

[*She takes the board and throws all the pieces on the floor.*

MRS. ARDSLEY: Evie.

EVA: Damn it. Damn it. Damn it.

MRS. ARDSLEY: Evie, what's the matter with you? You mustn't lose your temper because you're losing a game. That's childish.

EVA: As if I cared whether I lost or won. I hate the filthy game.

DR. PRENTICE: [*Soothingly.*] I think it's very boring myself.

MRS. ARDSLEY: Sydney has so few amusements.

EVA: Why should I be sacrificed all the time?

SYDNEY: [*With an amused smile.*] My dear, we thought you liked it.

EVA: I'm sick of being a drudge.

MRS. ARDSLEY: I'm sorry, I never knew you looked at it like that. I thought you wanted to do everything you could for Sydney.

EVA: I'm very sorry he's blind. But it's not my fault. I'm not responsible for the war. He ought to go into a home.

MRS. ARDSLEY: Oh, how cruel. How callous.

EVA: He took his chance like the rest of them. He's lucky not to have been killed.

SYDNEY: That of course is a matter of opinion.

EVA: It's monstrous that he should try to prevent anyone else from having a good time.

MRS. ARDSLEY: I thought it was a privilege to be able to do what we could to make life easier for him when he gave so much for us. And I felt that it wasn't only for him we were doing it, but also for all those others who, for our sakes, and for what at least they thought was honour, have sacrificed so much of what makes life happy and good to live.

EVA: I've given enough. I gave the man I was going to marry. I adored him. I might have had a home of my own and children. I never had another chance. And now . . . now. Oh, I'm so unhappy.

> [*Bursting into tears, she rushes out of the room. There is a moment's awkward pause.*

MRS. ARDSLEY: What is the matter with her?

SYDNEY: She wants a man, that's all.

MRS. ARDSLEY: Oh, Sydney, don't. That's horrible.

SYDNEY: But not unnatural.

MRS. ARDSLEY: You mustn't take any notice of what she said to you.

SYDNEY: [*With an indulgent smile.*] Oh, my dear, I knew it

already. The day's long past since I was a wounded hero for whom nothing was good enough. Fifteen years is a long time.

MRS. ARDSLEY: If you could bear it there's no reason why others shouldn't.

SYDNEY: It was easier for me, you know. Being blind is an occupation in itself. It's astonishing how quickly the time passes. But of course it's hard on the others. At first it gives them a sort of exaltation to look after you, then it becomes a habit and they take you as a matter of course, but in the end, human nature being what it is, you become just a damned bore.

MRS. ARDSLEY: You'll never be a bore to me, Sydney.

SYDNEY: [*Affectionately.*] I know. You've got that queer, incomprehensible thing that's called the mother instinct.

MRS. ARDSLEY: I can't live for ever. It was a comfort to me to think that you'd always be safe with Evie.

SYDNEY: [*Almost gaily.*] Oh, don't bother about me, mother, I shall be all right. They say suffering ennobles. It hasn't ennobled me. It's made me sly and cunning. Evie says I'm selfish. I am. But I'm damned artful. I know how to get people to do things for me by working on their sympathy. Evie'll settle down. I shall be as safe as a house.

MRS. ARDSLEY: Her not marrying and all that. It seemed so natural that she should look after you. Ethel's got her husband and children. Lois is so much younger. She doesn't understand. She's hard.

SYDNEY: [*With a good-natured shrug of the shoulders.*] Oh, I don't know. She's got the healthy, normal selfishness of youth. There's no harm in that. She doesn't see why she should be bothered with me, and she damned well isn't going to. I don't blame her. I know exactly where I am with her.

MRS. ARDSLEY: I suppose I ought to go to Evie.

DR. PRENTICE: I'd leave her alone for a little longer.

> [GERTRUDE *comes in with a note*.

GERTRUDE: Mrs. Cedar asked me to give you this, ma'am.

MRS. ARDSLEY: Oh. [*She opens the letter and reads it*.] Is she in the drawing-room?

GERTRUDE: No, ma'am. She's waiting in her car.

MRS. ARDSLEY: Ask her to come in.

GERTRUDE: Very good, ma'am.

> [GERTRUDE *goes out*.

MRS. ARDSLEY: How very strange.

DR. PRENTICE: What is it?

MRS. ARDSLEY: It's from Gwen. She asks if she can see me alone for a few minutes.

SYDNEY: I'll get out then.

> [*He rises, takes his stick and stumps out of the room.*

DR. PRENTICE: I'll go, too.

MRS. ARDSLEY: I wonder what she wants.

DR. PRENTICE: Probably an address or something.

MRS. ARDSLEY: She could have telephoned.

DR. PRENTICE: Am I right in thinking she's a very silly woman?

MRS. ARDSLEY: Quite right.

> [DR. PRENTICE *has been watching* SYDNEY *go and as soon as the door is closed on him he changes his manner*.

DR. PRENTICE: I've had a long talk with Murray.

MRS. ARDSLEY: I hate this consultation that you've forced me into.

DR. PRENTICE: My dear, it's essential. I don't want to alarm you, but I must tell you I'm not satisfied with your condition.

MRS. ARDSLEY: Oh, well. It's at three o'clock to-morrow afternoon?

DR. PRENTICE: Yes. He's promised to ring me up after he's seen you.

MRS. ARDSLEY: [*Giving him her hand.*] You're very nice to me.

DR. PRENTICE: [*Kissing her cheek.*] I'm very fond of you.

> [*He goes out. In a minute* GERTRUDE *shows* GWEN CEDAR *into the room, and after announcing her, goes out.*

GERTRUDE: Mrs. Cedar.

MRS. ARDSLEY: How d'you do?

GWEN: I hope you don't think it very strange my sending in a note like that. I simply had to see you.

MRS. ARDSLEY: Do sit down. We shan't be disturbed.

GWEN: I thought I'd better talk it over with you. I mean, I thought it only fair to you.

MRS. ARDSLEY: Yes?

GWEN: I think I'd better come straight to the point.

MRS. ARDSLEY: [*With a little smile.*] It's always a good plan.

GWEN: You know that I'm Wilfred's second wife.

MRS. ARDSLEY: No, I didn't.

GWEN: He's my second husband. We fell very much in love with one another. And there were divorce proceedings. We've been married for twelve years. It's all so long ago, I didn't see any reason to say anything about it when we came down here.

MRS. ARDSLEY: It was nobody's business but your own.

GWEN: We've been awfully happy together. It's been a great success.

MRS. ARDSLEY: I imagine he's a very easy man to get on with.

GWEN: Of course he's always been very attractive to women.

K

MRS. ARDSLEY: That's a thing I'm no judge about.

GWEN: He's got a way with him that takes them. And he pays them all kinds of little attentions that flatter them. But of course it doesn't mean anything.

MRS. ARDSLEY: It seldom does.

GWEN: All women don't know that. It's the kind of thing that's quite likely to turn a girl's head. It would be silly to take him seriously. After all he's a married man and *I* would never divorce him whatever he did. Never.

MRS. ARDSLEY: My dear, you said you were coming straight to the point. Aren't you beating about the bush a good deal?

GWEN: Don't you know what I mean?

MRS. ARDSLEY: I haven't an idea.

GWEN: I'm very relieved to hear it.

MRS. ARDSLEY: Won't you explain?

GWEN: You won't be angry with me?

MRS. ARDSLEY: I shouldn't think so.

GWEN: He's been paying a lot of attention to your Lois.

MRS. ARDSLEY: [*With a chuckle.*] Oh, my dear, don't be so ridiculous.

GWEN: I know he's attracted by her.

MRS. ARDSLEY: How can you be so silly?

GWEN: They're together all the time.

MRS. ARDSLEY: Nonsense. They play tennis and golf together. They're playing golf now. There are very few men for your husband to play with during the week. It's been nice for both of them. You don't mean to say you're jealous of that?

GWEN: But you see, I know he's madly in love with her.

MRS. ARDSLEY: Oh, my dear, that's only fancy.

GWEN: How do you know that she isn't in love with him?

MRS. ARDSLEY: He's old enough to be her father.

GWEN: What does that matter?

MRS. ARDSLEY: A lot, I should say. I don't want to hurt your feelings, but you know, a girl of Lois's age looks upon you and me, your husband and mine, as older than God.

GWEN: It isn't as if there were a lot of men here. A girl can't pick and choose in a place like this.

MRS. ARDSLEY: Now I'm afraid I think you're not being very polite.

GWEN: I'm sorry. I don't mean to be rude. I'm so utterly miserable.

MRS. ARDSLEY: [*With kindness.*] You poor dear. I'm sure you're mistaken. And in any case you're going away soon and that'll end it.

GWEN: [*Quickly.*] Then you think there's something to end?

MRS. ARDSLEY: No, no. End your fear, I mean. I know very little about men like your husband. I daresay men of that age are often rather taken by bright young things. I think a sensible wife just shrugs her shoulders and laughs. Her safety is that the bright young things look upon her husband as an old fogey.

GWEN: Oh, I hope you're right. If you only knew the agony I've been through since I found out.

MRS. ARDSLEY: I'm sure I'm right. And if there is any truth in what you think, I'm convinced that a fortnight after you've left here he'll have forgotten all about her.

> [*She gets up to put an end to the conversation.* GWEN *rises too. She glances out of the window and sees a car stopping at the door.*

GWEN: Here they are.

MRS. ARDSLEY: [*Looking out of window.*] Who? Oh, your husband and Lois.

GWEN: He's coming in.

MRS. ARDSLEY: He promised Sydney to play bridge. You don't object to that, do you?

GWEN: I don't want him to see me. He'll think I'm spying on him. He'll be furious.

MRS. ARDSLEY: He won't come in here. He'll go into the drawing-room.

GWEN: You won't say anything to Lois, will you? I don't want to put her back up.

MRS. ARDSLEY: Of course I won't say anything. I'm sure she's absolutely unconscious of what you've been talking about. It would only make her shy and uncomfortable.

GWEN: I'll slip away the moment the coast is clear.

> [*The door is burst open and* LOIS *comes in. She is radiant with health and spirits.*

LOIS: Hulloa! Are you here, Gwen?

GWEN: Yes, your mother wanted to see me about the sale of work. I'm just going.

LOIS: Wilfred is here.

GWEN: Is he? Give him my love and tell him not to be late for dinner. You're going to play bridge, aren't you?

LOIS: Yes. Collie and Howard are coming. They'll have a man's four.

GWEN: Wilfred says your brother plays just as well as if he could see.

LOIS: Yes, it's rather marvellous. Of course we have special cards.

GWEN: [*Catching sight of a pearl necklace* LOIS *has on.*] Pretty chain that is you're wearing. I've never seen it before.

LOIS: [*Instinctively putting her hand to her neck and fingering the beads.*] I bought it the other day when I went into Stanbury.

GWEN: How extravagant of you. I didn't know anyone could afford to buy pearls now.

LOIS: It only cost a pound.

GWEN: Aren't they real?

LOIS: Of course not. How could they be?

GWEN: [*Going up to* LOIS *and feeling the pearls.*] I think I know something about pearls. I would have sworn they were real.

LOIS: I wish they were.

GWEN: It's the most wonderful imitation I've ever seen.

LOIS: They do make them marvellously now. I wonder anyone bothers to have real pearls at all.

> [GWEN *is taken aback. She still looks at the pearls doubtfully. Then she makes an effort over herself.*

GWEN: Good-bye, Mrs. Ardsley. I'll have everything ready in good time.

MRS. ARDSLEY: Good-bye, my dear. Lois will see you out.

> [GWEN *and* LOIS *go out.* MRS. ARDSLEY *is left reflective. She is a little puzzled.* LOIS *comes in again.*

MRS. ARDSLEY: Lois dear, I've been thinking you looked rather peaked. Don't you think it would be a good idea if you went to stay at Aunt Emily's for a week or two?

LOIS: I should hate it.

MRS. ARDSLEY: She does love having you there.

LOIS: It's so incredibly boring.

MRS. ARDSLEY: You'll have to go before the end of the year. Much better go now and get it over.

LOIS: I loathe the idea.

MRS. ARDSLEY: Think about it a little. I can't have you not looking your best, you know, or I shall never get you off my hands.

> [*She goes out. Her voice is heard through the still open door:* Oh, here's Collie. You'll find Sydney in the

drawing-room. *As* COLLIE *passes the door he sees* LOIS.

COLLIE: Hulloa, Lois.

LOIS: You're early.

> [*He pauses at the door.*

COLLIE: I had an appointment with your father, but he's had to go out. I've left a message with the clerk to say I'm here when I'm wanted.

LOIS: Oh, good.

COLLIE: I'll go along to the drawing-room.

LOIS: Right-ho.

> [*He passes on.* LOIS *goes to the looking-glass and looks again at the little string round her neck. She feels the pearls.* WILFRED'S *voice is heard:* LOIS.

LOIS: Hulloa.

WILFRED: [*Still outside.*] Where are you?

LOIS: In the dining-room.

> [*He comes to the door.*

WILFRED: As Collie's here why shouldn't we start?

LOIS: Howard's coming.

WILFRED: I know. But there's no reason why you shouldn't play a rubber or two before he does.

LOIS: Come in a minute, will you?

WILFRED: Why?

LOIS: Shut the door.

WILFRED: [*Closing the door behind him.*] It's shut.

LOIS: These pearls you gave me, they are false, aren't they?

WILFRED: Of course.

LOIS: How much did they cost?

WILFRED: I told you. A pound.

LOIS: Gwen's just been here.

WILFRED: Why?

LOIS: Oh, I don't know. She came to see mother about the sale of work.

WILFRED: Oh, is that all? She's been very funny lately.

LOIS: She says they're real.

WILFRED: What does she know about it?

LOIS: She says she knows a great deal. She has pearls of her own.

WILFRED: And a pretty packet they cost me.

LOIS: Is she right?

WILFRED: [*Smiling.*] I wouldn't swear she wasn't.

LOIS: Why did you say they were false?

WILFRED: I didn't think you'd take them if you thought they were real.

LOIS: Naturally.

[*She puts her fingers to the clasp.*

WILFRED: What are you going to do?

LOIS: I'm going to give them back to you.

WILFRED: You can't do that now. You'll give the whole show away.

LOIS: There's nothing to give away.

WILFRED: Oh, isn't there? You don't know Gwen. She's got the tongue of a serpent.

LOIS: I can't accept a valuable pearl necklace from you.

WILFRED: At all events you must go on wearing it till we go away.

LOIS: How much did you pay for it?

WILFRED: My dear, it's not very good manners to ask what a present costs.

LOIS: Several hundred pounds?

WILFRED: I shouldn't wonder.

LOIS: D'you know, I've never had a valuable thing in my life. I shall be scared stiff of losing it.

WILFRED: Don't give it a thought. I'm not a very poor man, and if you do I shall survive it.

LOIS: But I might never have known. I might have worn it for years under the impression it was worth nothing.

WILFRED: That's what I hoped.

LOIS: [*With a smile.*] You know, that's rather sweet of you. I would never have thought you capable of that.

WILFRED: Why?

LOIS: Well, I've always looked upon you as rather a show-off. I should have thought you the sort of man who, when he gave a present that cost a lot of money, made pretty sure that you knew it.

WILFRED: That's not very flattering.

LOIS: You couldn't expect me to be so awfully grateful. I mean, a string of false pearls. Howard might have bought me that when he'd won a fiver on a horse.

WILFRED: I liked to think of you wearing pearls I'd given you. It gave me rather a thrill to think of them round your pretty neck.

LOIS: It seems a lot to pay for it.

WILFRED: You see, I'm so terribly in love with you. Give me a kiss, Lois.

> [*He puts his arm round her waist. He tries to kiss her lips, but she turns her face away, and he kisses her cheek.*] You do like me a little, don't you?

LOIS: [*Coolly.*] Yes.

WILFRED: D'you think you could ever love me?

LOIS: It wouldn't be much use, would it?

WILFRED: I'd do anything in the world for you. You know Gwen and I don't get on. We'd be much happier apart.

I know I could make you happy. After all, you don't want to stay in this deadly little place all your life.

LOIS: What are you asking me to do now? Run away with you?

WILFRED: Why not?

LOIS: And be chucked the moment you were sick of me? Thank you.

WILFRED: I'll settle twenty thousand pounds on you to-morrow, and if you don't like to run away with me you needn't.

LOIS: Don't be such a donkey.

WILFRED: Gwen would divorce me if I made it worth her while and then we'd be married.

LOIS: I've always understood that when the gay seducer had worked his wicked will on the village maiden he screamed like a hyena at the thought of making an honest woman of her.

WILFRED: Oh, Lois, don't laugh at me. I love you with all my heart. Oh, I know I'm as old as the hills. I wish to God I was twenty years younger. I want you so awfully. I want you for keeps.

[LOIS *looks at him for a moment seriously.*

LOIS: Let's go and play bridge.

[ETHEL *comes in.*

ETHEL: Sydney's getting impatient. [*To* WILFRED, *humor-ously.*] And Howard says, if you don't come along at once you'll have to marry the girl.

LOIS: I didn't know you were here.

ETHEL: We've only just come.

LOIS: Oh, well, if Howard's here you don't want me.

WILFRED: All right, we'll start a rubber. But come and cut in later, won't you?

LOIS: I must go and powder my nose.

[WILFRED *goes out.*

ETHEL: I hear Evie's been making a scene.

LOIS: Has she? What about?

ETHEL: Oh, I don't know. Nerves. She ought to get married.

LOIS: Whom can she marry, poor dear?

ETHEL: Collie. They're just about the same age. I think it would be very suitable.

LOIS: Wilfred says he's going smash.

ETHEL: They could manage. Nobody's got any money nowadays, but one gets along somehow. Even a marriage that isn't quite satisfactory is better than not being married at all.

LOIS: Is that your experience?

ETHEL: I wasn't talking of myself. I haven't got anything to grumble at.

LOIS: Wilfred wants me to run away with him.

ETHEL: Wilfred? What do you mean? Why?

LOIS: He says he's in love with me.

ETHEL: The dirty old man. I don't understand. What does he suggest?

LOIS: Well, I suppose his idea is to keep me till he gets his divorce and then I suppose his idea is to marry me.

ETHEL: The beast.

LOIS: I'm getting on, you know. I'm twenty-six.

ETHEL: [*Aghast.*] Lois.

LOIS: What have I got to look forward to exactly? Getting jumpy like Eva or making the best of a bad job like you.

ETHEL: I have my children. Howard has his faults like everybody else. But he's fond of me. He looks up to me.

LOIS: My dear, you've got a wonderful character. I haven't. D'you think I haven't seen what a strain it is on you sometimes?

ETHEL: Of course it's a hard life. I ought to have known it would be when I married a tenant farmer.

LOIS: But you didn't expect he'd drink.

ETHEL: I don't suppose he drinks any more than most men of his class.

LOIS: Have you ever really quite got used to him?

ETHEL: [*Defiantly.*] I don't know what you mean?

LOIS: Well, he's common, isn't he?

ETHEL: [*Smiling.*] Are you quite sure that you and I are any great shakes?

LOIS: At all events we do talk the King's English. We have decent table manners and we wash.

ETHEL: I don't believe you'd wash much if you had to get up at six and milk the cows. All that's convention. One oughtn't to let oneself be upset by things like that.

LOIS: But aren't you?

ETHEL: Sometimes. I blame myself.

LOIS: What have you got in common with him, really?

ETHEL: A recollection. That first year or two when I loved him so madly. He was gallant and young. He was manly. I loved him because he was of the soil and his strength had its roots in it. Nothing mattered then. Nothing that he did offended me.

LOIS: My dear, you're so romantic. I'm not. Romance doesn't last. When it's dead what is left but dust and ashes?

ETHEL: And the consciousness that you've done your best.

LOIS: Oh, that.

ETHEL: It's something. I've made my bed and I'm ready to lie on it. Have you ever heard me complain?

LOIS: Never.

ETHEL: I've carried my head high. I've tried to make Howard a good wife. I've tried to be a good mother to my children. Sometimes I'm inclined to be a little proud of myself.

LOIS: I suppose it's never occurred to you that it would have been better for Howard really if he'd married someone in his own class?

ETHEL: Oh yes, often. That's why I feel I must always have patience with him. I ought to have known. I oughtn't to have been carried away.

LOIS: My dear, you're so noble it makes me positively sick.

ETHEL: I'm not noble at all. I merely have a good deal of common sense . . . Lois, you're not really thinking of going away with that man?

LOIS: No, not really. It's only that it's rather exciting to have the chance.

ETHEL: Oh, I'm so glad.

[LEONARD ARDSLEY *comes in.*

ARDSLEY: What are you two girls doing in here? Discussing frocks and frills, I'll be bound.

ETHEL: [*Kissing him.*] How are you, father?

ARDSLEY: Chatter, chatter, chatter all day long. I know you. It's a marvel to me that you never get tired of talking about clothes. Collie's here, isn't he?

LOIS: Yes, he's playing bridge.

ARDSLEY: Well, run along both of you and send him in here. I want to see him.

LOIS: All right.

ARDSLEY: Kiddies well?

ETHEL: Oh yes. They always are.

ARDSLEY: Fine thing for them living on a farm like that. Grand thing a country life.

ETHEL: They've gone back to school now.

ARDSLEY: Of course. I remember. Best thing in the world for them. Happiest time in their lives. [*The two girls go out.* ARDSLEY *catches sight of a ladies' paper and takes it up.*] I knew it.

> [*He gives a complacent smile at his own perspicacity. The door opens and* COLLIE *comes in.* ARDSLEY *at the sight of him assumes his professional air.*] How d'you do?

COLLIE: You weren't in when I turned up at the office just now.

ARDSLEY: No. I've got someone waiting that I thought you'd better not meet, and I wanted to see you before I saw him. So I came through my private door.

COLLIE: I'm just as glad. I'm not used to solicitors' offices and I'm always rather intimidated.

ARDSLEY: I'm afraid I've got something very serious to say to you.

COLLIE: Oh, Lord.

ARDSLEY: In the three years you've been here we've seen a good deal of you. We all liked you.

COLLIE: It's been a snip for me having this house to come to. Except for all of you I should have had a pretty thin time.

ARDSLEY: I'm sure you'll realise that it's not very pleasant for me to find myself in my present position.

COLLIE: I suppose that means the game's up. I've made a damned good fight for it. Have I got to file my petition?

ARDSLEY: The bank wrote to you last month telling you that you were overdrawn and that they wouldn't cash any further cheques you drew until your account was put in order.

COLLIE: Yes.

ARDSLEY: And after that you gave several post-dated cheques in payment of various accounts.

COLLIE: I was being pestered for money all over the shop. I couldn't help myself.

ARDSLEY: You were hopelessly insolvent. How did you expect to meet them?

COLLIE: I thought something would turn up.

ARDSLEY: Don't you know that's a criminal offence?

COLLIE: Oh, what rot. It's the sort of thing anyone might do when he was up against it.

ARDSLEY: Not without going to gaol.

COLLIE: Good God, you don't mean to say they're going to prosecute?

ARDSLEY: You can't expect the injured parties to take it lying down.

COLLIE: But it's absurd. They know I didn't mean any harm.

ARDSLEY: It's almost incredible that you should be so unbusinesslike.

COLLIE: What should I know about business? I'm a sailor. I was in the navy for twenty years.

ARDSLEY: I'm afraid you've been very unwise.

COLLIE: Then what's going to happen?

ARDSLEY: The bank manager is in my office now. You must be prepared for the worst, Collie. A warrant will be applied for.

COLLIE: Does that mean I shall be arrested?

ARDSLEY: Of course you'll be released on bail. I'll arrange that. If you elect to be tried by a jury the justices will refer the case to quarter sessions. It's early days yet to decide, we'll see what counsel has to say. My own opinion at the moment is that the best thing you can do is to plead guilty and throw yourself on the mercy of the court.

COLLIE: But I'm not guilty.

ARDSLEY: Don't be such a fool. You're just as guilty as the thief who sneaks ten bob from your till when no one is looking.

COLLIE: What will they do to me?

ARDSLEY: In consideration of your previous good character and your record in the navy, I have little doubt that the judge will be lenient. I should be very disappointed if you got more than from three to six months in the second division.

COLLIE: [*With a flash of anger at the casual way he takes it.*] You don't care, do you?

ARDSLEY: My dear boy, don't think I'm happy about it. In my profession one often finds oneself in very disagreeable situations, but I don't remember ever having found myself in a more painful one than this.

COLLIE: Fortunately most people get over seeing the other fellow come a cropper.

ARDSLEY: It's not only the pleasant social relations we've always had with you, but that you should have got the D.S.O. and been in command of a destroyer—it all makes your fall so much more distressing. I'm afraid it makes it also much more disgraceful.

COLLIE: They'll take my D.S.O. away from me?

ARDSLEY: I suppose so.

COLLIE: I suppose it doesn't occur to you that when a fellow has served the country for twenty years in a job that's unfitted him for anything else, it's rather distressing and rather disgraceful that he should be shoved out into the world with no means of earning his living and nothing between him and starvation but a bonus of a thousand pounds or so?

ARDSLEY: I can't go into that. Though of course it's a good point to take up at the trial. I'll make a note of that. Of course the answer is that the country was up against it and had to economise and if a certain number of individuals had to suffer it can't be helped.

COLLIE: When I was torpedoed during the war and they fished me out, "God, what a bit of luck!" I said. I never knew.

ARDSLEY: Do me the justice to admit that I begged you six months ago to file your petition. You wouldn't take my advice.

COLLIE: I'd had it drummed into me for so many years that nothing is impossible in the British Navy. It was hard to give in while I still had some fight in me.

ARDSLEY: You mustn't despair.

COLLIE: There's not much of a future for an ex-naval officer, forty years of age, after six months in gaol.

ARDSLEY: I've been a hunting man. It's a very good plan not to take your fences before you come to them. Now look here, I must be off. There's whisky and soda on the sideboard. You help yourself to a drink. I'm sure you want it.

COLLIE: Thank you.

ARDSLEY: [*Giving him his hand.*] Good-bye, my boy. I'll let you know about things as soon as I hear.

COLLIE: Good-bye.

> [ARDSLEY *goes out.* COLLIE, *sinking into a chair, buries his face in his hands; but hearing the door open he looks up and pulls himself together.* EVA *comes in.*

EVA: Oh, I beg your pardon. I was looking for my bag. I didn't know anyone was here.

COLLIE: I was just going.

EVA: Please don't. I won't disturb you.

COLLIE: What are you talking about? Surely you can come into your own dining-room.

EVA: I wasn't speaking the truth. I knew you were here

and my bag's upstairs. I heard father go. I wanted to
see you. I'm so frightfully anxious.

COLLIE: What about?

EVA: Everyone knows you're in difficulties. Father let fall
a hint at luncheon. I knew he was seeing you this
afternoon.

COLLIE: It's kind of you to bother, Evie. I've had rather a
rough passage, but at all events I know where I am
now.

EVA: Can nothing be done?

COLLIE: Not very much, I'm afraid.

EVA: Won't you let me help you?

COLLIE: [*With a smile.*] My dear, how can you?

EVA: It's only a matter of money, isn't it?

COLLIE: "Only" is good.

EVA: I've got a thousand pounds that my god-mother left
me. It's invested and I've always dressed myself on the
interest. I could let you have that.

COLLIE: I couldn't possible take money from you. It's out
of the question.

EVA: Why? If I want to give it you.

COLLIE: It's awfully generous of you, but . . .

EVA: [*Interrupting.*] You must know how frightfully fond I
am of you.

COLLIE: It's very nice of you, Evie. Besides, your father
would never hear of it.

EVA: It's my own money. I'm not a child.

COLLIE: Can't be done, my dear.

EVA: Why shouldn't I buy an interest in your garage? I
mean, then it would be just an investment.

COLLIE: Can you see your father's face when you suggested
it? It looked all right when I bought it. Things were

booming then. But the slump has killed it. It isn't worth a bob.

EVA: But surely if you can get more capital you can afford to wait till times get better?

COLLIE: Your father doesn't think much of me as it is. He'd think me a pretty mean skunk if he thought I'd induced you to put your money into an insolvent business.

EVA: You keep on talking of father. It's nothing to do with him. It's you and I that are concerned.

COLLIE: I know you're a damned good sort and you're always going out of your way to do things for people, but there are limits. Perhaps you'll want to get married one of these days and then you'll find your thousand pounds devilish useful.

EVA: I shall never have a better use for it than to give it to someone who means so much to me as you do.

COLLIE: I'm awfully sorry, God knows I want the money, but I really can't take it from anyone like you.

EVA: I thought you liked me.

COLLIE: I like you very much. You're a jolly good friend.

EVA: I thought perhaps some day we might be more than friends. [*There is a moment's silence. She is very nervous, but forces herself to go on.*] After all, if we were engaged, it would be very natural that I should come to the rescue when you were in a hole.

COLLIE: But we're not engaged.

EVA: Why shouldn't we pretend to be? Just for a little while, I mean. Then I could lend you the money and father would help you to get straight.

COLLIE: Oh, my dear, that's absurd. That's the sort of thing they do in novels. You mustn't be so romantic.

EVA: You could always break it off when you got straight.

COLLIE: That's not a very pretty role you're asking me to play.

EVA: [*In a husky voice.*] Perhaps when you got used to the idea you wouldn't want to break it off.

COLLIE: My dear, what on earth ever put such an idea in your head?

EVA: You're alone and I'm alone. There's no one in the world that cares twopence for either of us.

COLLIE: Oh, what nonsense. Your family's devoted to you. They depend on you so enormously. Why, the whole house centres round you.

EVA: I want to get away. I'm so unhappy here.

COLLIE: I can't believe that. You're just nervous and run down. I daresay you want a bit of change.

EVA: You won't understand. How can you be so cruel?

COLLIE: I'm not cruel. I'm awfully grateful to you.

EVA: I can't say any more than I have. It's so humiliating.

COLLIE: I'm dreadfully sorry. I don't want to hurt your feelings.

EVA: After all, I'm not so old as all that. Plenty of men have wanted to marry me.

COLLIE: I don't doubt that for a minute. I'm quite convinced that one of these days you'll find someone that you really like and I'm sure you'll make him a perfectly grand wife. [*She begins to cry and he looks at her with troubled eyes.*] I'm sorry.

> [*She does not answer and quietly he leaves the room. She sobs. But she hears the door open and starts to her feet, turning her face away so that her tears should not be seen. The newcomer is* HOWARD. *He is quite sober.*]

HOWARD: Where's Collie?

EVA: How should I know?

HOWARD: We want him for bridge.

EVA: Well, you can see he isn't here, can't you?

HOWARD: He was here.

EVA: [*Stamping her foot.*] Well, he isn't here now.

HOWARD: Temper, temper. What price the angel of mercy now?

EVA: You're very funny, aren't you? Terribly amusing.

HOWARD: I know what you've been doing. You've been asking him to marry you.

EVA: [*Furiously.*] You drunken brute. Damn you. Blast you.

> [*She flings out of the room.* HOWARD *purses his lips and grins. Then he goes over to the sideboard and helps himself to a whisky and soda. While he is sipping it* LOIS *comes in.*]

LOIS: Hulloa, I thought you were playing bridge.

HOWARD: No. Your father wanted to see Collie, and Sydney and Wilfred are having a game of piquet.

LOIS: So you seized the opportunity to have a drink on the quiet.

HOWARD: My dear girl, I had to have something to pull myself together. Evie's been swearing at me. Such language, my dear. Called me a drunken brute. I mean, it shakes a chap's morale when a properly brought-up young lady forgets herself like that.

LOIS: Are you obliged to drink?

HOWARD: Well, in a manner of speaking I am. My poor old father died of drink and his poor old father died of drink. So it's in the family. See?

LOIS: It is rotten for Ethel.

HOWARD: She has a lot to put up with, poor girl. You

don't have to tell me. I know it. Fact is, she's too good
for me.

Lois: Much.

Howard: That's what I say. She's a lady. I mean, you only
have to look at her to know that. And mind you, she
never lets up. I can be a gentleman when I want to, but I
don't want to all the time. I mean to say, I like to have a
good old laugh now and again. She never does. Truth
is, between you and me, she has no sense of humour.

Lois: I daresay after being married to you for fifteen years
it's worn rather thin.

Howard: I like a girl as has a bit of fun in her. Let's have a
good time while we're alive, I say; we can do all the
sitting quiet we want when we're dead and buried.

Lois: There's something in that.

Howard: Mind you, I'm not complaining of Ethel. Too
much of a gentleman to do that. She's class. I know
that. And I'm only a common farmer. Only, you know
what I mean, you don't always want to be looking up to
your wife, do you?

Lois: No one asked you to marry Ethel.

Howard: Pity you wasn't old enough then. I'd have
married you instead.

Lois: Complimentary, aren't you?

Howard: You're not half the lady what Ethel is. And
you're a bit of a devil, I shouldn't wonder. You and
me'd get on like a house on fire.

Lois: You're drunk.

Howard: No, I'm not. I'm cold stone sober.

Lois: Then I like you better drunk.

Howard: Give me a kiss, honey.

Lois: D'you want your face slapped?

HOWARD: I don't mind.

LOIS: The nerve of it.

HOWARD: Come on. Be a sport.

LOIS: Go to hell.

HOWARD: I would with you.

> [*With a sudden movement he catches hold of her and gives
> her a kiss full on the lips. She tears herself away from
> him.*

LOIS: How dare you?

HOWARD: Oh, come off it. You didn't mind. You liked it.

LOIS: It almost made me sick. You stink of cows.

HOWARD: A lot of girls like that. Makes them go all
funny.

LOIS: You filthy beast.

HOWARD: Want another?

LOIS: If it weren't for Ethel I'd go straight to father.

HOWARD: Don't make me laugh. D'you think I don't
know about girls? And if you don't know about men
it's high time you did. A good-looking girl like you.
You ought to be ashamed of yourself. I mean, think
what you're missing.

LOIS: You've got a pretty good opinion of yourself, haven't
you?

HOWARD: And not without cause. Of course I don't say
it's like the war. God, I wish it had gone on for ever.
Those were the days. If you liked the look of a girl you
just walked her up the garden path. Of course the
uniform had a lot to do with it and being a blasted hero.

LOIS: Brute.

HOWARD: [*Confidentially.*] Look here, why don't you come
up to the farm for a few days? We could have a grand old
time.

LOIS: I don't know what you take me for, Howard.

HOWARD: Don't talk that sort of rot to me. You're human, same as I am, aren't you? What's the good of mouldering away without having a bit of fun in your life? You come up to the farm. Now the kids have gone to boarding-school their room's empty.

LOIS: If you're not drunk you're crazy.

HOWARD: No, I'm not. You'll come, my girl.

LOIS: [*Contemptuously.*] And what makes you think that?

HOWARD: I'll tell you. Because I want you and you know I want you and there isn't a thing that takes a girl like that. By God, I want you.

> [*He looks at her and the violence of his desire seems heavy in the room.* LOIS *instinctively puts her hand to her breast. Her breathing is oppressed. There is a silence.* MRS. ARDSLEY *comes in.*]

LOIS: [*Recovering herself.*] Oh, mother.

HOWARD: I've just been telling this young woman she ought to come up to the farm for a few days. She looks to me as if she wanted a change.

MRS. ARDSLEY: I'm glad you agree with me. Only a little while ago I was suggesting that she should go and stay with Aunt Emily for two or three weeks.

LOIS: I've been thinking it over, mother. I daresay you're quite right. When d'you think I'd better go?

MRS. ARDSLEY: The sooner the better. To-morrow.

LOIS: All right. I'll send the old girl a wire and tell her I'm coming.

MRS. ARDSLEY: You needn't do that. I've just written to her to say that you'll arrive in time for dinner.

LOIS: Have you? You domineering old lady.

MRS. ARDSLEY: You're a very good girl, Lois. I didn't think you'd disregard my wishes.

LOIS: I don't think I'm a very good girl. But you're a darling old mother.

> [*She kisses her tenderly.* MRS. ARDSLEY, *smiling, pats her hand.*

END OF THE SECOND ACT

THE THIRD ACT

The drawing-room at the ARDSLEYS' *house. It is a large low room, with french windows leading on to the terrace that was the scene of the first act. It is furnished in an old-fashioned, commonplace and comfortable way. Nothing much has been added since it was all new when the* ARDSLEYS *married. The walls are overcrowded with framed engravings and water colours, copies of Florentine bas-reliefs, weapons on wooden shields and plates in old English china. The occasional tables are laden with knick-knacks. The arm-chairs and sofas are covered with loose-covers of faded cretonne.*

It is a rainy, windy day and there is a fire burning on the hearth. The light is failing. It is about half-past four.

WILFRED *is standing at the fire warming his hands.* LOIS *comes in. She is wearing a coat and skirt.*

LOIS: [*Coming towards him with outstretched hand.*] How d'you do? Mother's out. She'll be back to tea. She's gone to Stanbury.

WILFRED: I know. I asked the maid if I could see you. Is it true you're going away to-day?

LOIS: Yes, I'm spending a fortnight with an aunt near Canterbury.

WILFRED: But in a fortnight I shall be gone.

LOIS: Will you?

WILFRED: Were you going without saying good-bye to me?

LOIS: I thought mother would say it for me.

WILFRED: [*In a husky, agitated tone.*] Don't go, Lois.

LOIS: [*Indifferently.*] Why not?

WILFRED: Why are you going?

LOIS: Mother thought I wanted a change. I generally spend a fortnight with Aunt Emily once or twice a year. She's my god-mother and she says she's going to leave me something in her will.

WILFRED: I was going up to London to-morrow to settle that money on you.

LOIS: Don't be so silly. As if I wanted that. If I ran away with you I wouldn't take it. I'd rather have my independence.

WILFRED: You might have given me the last fortnight. It means nothing to you. And so much to me.

LOIS: How did you know I was going?

WILFRED: Gwen told me.

LOIS: How did she know?

WILFRED: Your mother rang up.

LOIS: Oh!

WILFRED: Are you quite sure it was about the sale of work that Gwen came to see your mother yesterday?

LOIS: She wouldn't have dared. You don't know mother. She'd never let anyone say a word against any of us. You've only seen her when she's being nice. She can be as stiff as a poker if one tries to take a liberty with her.

WILFRED: Gwen spotted the pearls all right.

LOIS: [*Beginning to unclasp them.*] Oh, I forgot. I can give them back to you now.

WILFRED: Won't you keep them? Please. It can't hurt you and it'll give me so much pleasure.

LOIS: I don't see how. The chances are that we shall never see one another again. As far as you're concerned it's just throwing money away.

WILFRED: I want to be able to think that you're wearing something I gave you. I've held them in my hands. I want to think that they have the warmth of your body and they touch the softness of your neck.

LOIS: [*Tempted.*] I've never had anything so valuable. I suppose I'm half a strumpet.

WILFRED: They only cost a pound, Lois.

LOIS: Oh, you liar. Does Gwen know you gave them to me?

WILFRED: She hasn't said so. She knows there's no one else who could.

LOIS: Has she been making a scene?

WILFRED: Oh, no, she's been holding herself in. She's afraid.

LOIS: Why? Are you so terrifying?

WILFRED: I don't think you'd find me so.

LOIS: Are you awfully in love with me?

WILFRED: Awfully.

LOIS: Strange, isn't it? I wonder why.

WILFRED: I'm broken-hearted, Lois. I know you don't love me. There's no reason why you should. But you might. If I were very kind to you. And patient. I'd do anything in the world to make you happy.

LOIS: It's curious, it does give one rather a funny feeling to know someone's in love with you.

WILFRED: When Gwen told me you were going, the whole world went black. She tried to say it casually, but she knew she was thrusting a dagger in my heart and she watched my face to see me writhe.

LOIS: Poor Gwen. I suppose people can be rather foul when they're jealous.

WILFRED: Oh, damn Gwen. I can only think of myself. You're everything in the world to me, and every one else can go to hell. It's my last chance, Lois.

> [*She slowly shakes her head. He looks at her for a moment with despair.*]

WILFRED: Is there nothing I can say to persuade you?

LOIS: Nothing.

WILFRED: I'm done. I'm finished.

LOIS: I don't think so. You'll get over it. When are you going to the Riviera?

WILFRED: It's only a joke to you. [*Violently.*] Oh, I hate being old.

[*EVA comes in.*

EVA: Why haven't the curtains been drawn? Oh, Wilfred.

WILFRED: [*Trying to seem naturally casual.*] How are you to-day?

EVA: I'll turn on the lights.

[*She switches on the electricity while* LOIS *draws the curtains.*

LOIS: It is a foul day.

WILFRED: I'll be getting along.

EVA: Oh, aren't you going to stay to tea? Sydney's just coming. He'd love to play piquet with you.

WILFRED: I'm sorry, I must be off. I only came to say good-bye to Lois.

EVA: We shall be seeing you again soon, I suppose?

WILFRED: I expect so.

[*They shake hands.* LOIS *gives him her hand.*

LOIS: Good-bye. Give my love to Gwen.

WILFRED: Good-bye.

[*He goes out quickly.*

EVA: What's the matter with him? He seems all funny to-day.

LOIS: I didn't notice that he was any different.

EVA: Are you all packed up and everything?

LOIS: Yes.

EVA: Are you taking the five-fifty?

Lois: Yes.

Eva: That gives you nice time to have tea. Ethel's coming in.

Lois: I know. She wants me to take some partridges to Aunt Emily.

[Sydney *comes in.*

Sydney: Tea ready?

Eva: It's not five yet.

Sydney: Thank God for the fire. I hate that gas stove in my room. Mother's not back yet, I suppose?

Eva: No. She said she'd be in to tea.

Lois: Howard says he's expecting a very hard winter.

Sydney: Cheerful.

Lois: Oh, I hate the winter.

Eva: If it weren't for the winter we shouldn't enjoy the spring.

Sydney: Are you obliged to say things like that, Evie?

Eva: It happens to be true.

Sydney: It happens to be true that two and two are four, but one needn't make a song and dance about it.

Lois: I'll put on a record, shall I?

Eva: Oh, for goodness' sake don't, it drives me mad.

Lois: Oh, all right.

[*They both give her a little look of surprise.*

Eva: I'm rather jumpy to-day. I suppose it's the east wind.

Sydney: Give me my tatting, Lois, will you?

Lois: I will.

[*She gives it to him and while he talks he proceeds mechanically with his work.*

Sydney: I wonder if Collie will turn up?

EVA: I rang up to ask him to come in to tea. He hasn't been at the garage all day.

[ETHEL *and* HOWARD *come in.*

ETHEL: How's everybody?

SYDNEY: Hulloa.

HOWARD: We've brought the partridges. They'd better be hung for a couple of days. They were only shot yesterday.

SYDNEY: Got many birds this year, Howard?

HOWARD: A few. What's that you're doing?

SYDNEY: Tatting.

EVA: Put on the gramophone if you want to.

HOWARD: I'll put it on.

[*He goes over, gives the machine a wind and starts a record.*

ETHEL: I'm afraid it won't be very amusing for you at Aunt Emily's.

LOIS: I shall read a lot.

SYDNEY: Let's hope she'll die soon and leave you a packet.

LOIS: She's got very little to leave.

[*Suddenly* MR. ARDSLEY *bursts into the room.*

ETHEL: Oh, father.

ARDSLEY: Turn off the gramophone.

EVA: What's the matter?

[HOWARD *who is still at the gramophone stops the record.*

ARDSLEY: Something dreadful's happened. I thought I'd better come in and tell you at once.

EVA: [*With a cry.*] Collie.

ARDSLEY: How d'you know?

SYDNEY: What is it, father?

ARDSLEY: They've just telephoned to me from the police station. There's been an accident. Collie's been shot.

HOWARD: Shot? Whom by?

ARDSLEY: I'm afraid he shot himself.

HOWARD: Good God.

EVA: He isn't dead?

ARDSLEY: Yes.

> [EVA *gives a loud, long shriek. It is a sound that is only just human.*

ETHEL. EVIE.

> [EVA *goes up to her father with arms raised high in the air and clenched hands.*

EVA: You killed him, you fiend.

ARDSLEY: I? What *are* you talking about?

EVA: You fiend. You beast.

ETHEL: [*Putting a restraining hand on her.*] Evie.

EVA: [*Shaking her off angrily.*] Leave me alone. [*To* ARDSLEY.] You could have saved him. You devil. I hate you. I hate you.

ARDSLEY: Are you mad, Eva?

EVA: You hounded him to his death. You never gave him a chance.

ARDSLEY: Good heavens, we all gave him chance after chance.

EVA: It's a lie. He begged for money. He begged for time. And not one of you would help him. Not one of you remembered that he'd risked his life for you a hundred times. You brutes.

ARDSLEY: Oh, what rubbish.

EVA: I hope you're shamed before the whole world. Let everyone know that a brave and gallant gentleman went to his death because there's wasn't a soul in this bloody place who would lend him two hundred pounds.

ARDSLEY: Pretty language, Eva. In point of fact two hundred pounds wouldn't have helped him. It would have saved him from going to gaol, but that's all.

EVA: Gaol?

ARDSLEY: Yes, a warrant for his arrest was issued this morning.

EVA: [*With anguish.*] Poor Collie. I can't bear it. Cruel. Cruel.

[*She begins to sob desperately.*

ARDSLEY: Now, my dear, don't take it so much to heart. Go and lie down in your room. Ethel will come and bathe your forehead with eau-de-Cologne. Of course the whole thing is very unfortunate. No one regrets it more than I do. The poor fellow was in a hopeless mess and perhaps he took the best way out of a situation that could only have thrown discredit on the uniform he'd worn.

[*While he says this* EVA *raises her head and looks at him with eyes of horror.*

EVA: But he was alive and he's dead. He's gone from us for ever. He's been robbed of all the years that were before him. Haven't you any pity for him? He used to come here almost every day.

ARDSLEY: He was a very nice fellow and a gentleman. Unfortunately he wasn't a very good business man.

EVA: As if I cared if he was a good business man.

ARDSLEY: There's no reason why you should. But his creditors did.

EVA: He was everything in the world to me.

ARDSLEY: My dear, what an exaggerated way to speak. You ought to have more sense at your age.

EVA: He loved me and I loved him.

ARDSLEY: Don't talk such nonsense.

EVA: We were engaged to be married.

ARDSLEY: [*With astonishment.*] What's that? Since when?

EVA: Since ages.

ARDSLEY: Well, my dear, you're well out of that. He was in no position to marry.

EVA: [*With anguish.*] It was my only chance.

ARDSLEY: You have a good home. You'd much better stay here.

EVA: And make myself useful?

ARDSLEY: There's no harm in that.

EVA: I've got just as much right to life and happiness as anyone else.

ARDSLEY: Of course you have.

EVA: You've done everything you could to prevent me from marrying.

ARDSLEY: Rubbish.

EVA: Why should I be sacrificed all the time? Why should I be at everybody's beck and call? Why should I have to do everything? I'm sick of being put upon. I'm sick of you, I'm sick of Sydney, I'm sick of Lois. I'm sick of you all.

> [*During the speech her agitation has become quite uncontrolled. There is a table covered with ornaments by her, and now with a violent gesture she throws it over so that everything is scattered on the floor.*

ETHEL: Evie.

EVA: Damn you. Damn you. Damn you.

> [*Shrieking she throws herself down and hysterically beats upon the floor with her fists.*

ARDSLEY: Stop it. Stop it.

HOWARD: Better get her out of here.

> [*He picks her up and carries her out of the room.* ARDSLEY *opens the door. He and* ETHEL *follow her out.* LOIS *and* SYDNEY *are left alone.* LOIS, *pale and trembling, has watched the scene with terror.*

M

LOIS: What's the matter with her?

SYDNEY: Hysterics. Upset you?

LOIS: I'm frightened.

SYDNEY: I'll telephone for Uncle Charlie. I think she wants
a doctor.

> [*He makes his way out of the room.* LOIS *stands stock-
> still. She cannot control the nervous trembling that
> seizes her.* HOWARD *comes in.*

HOWARD: I've put her on the dining-room sofa.

LOIS: Are Ethel and father with her?

HOWARD: Yes. [*He looks at her and sees the condition she is in.
He puts his arm round her shoulders.*] Poor old girl, gave
you quite a turn, didn't it?

LOIS: [*Unconscious of his touch.*] I'm frightened.

HOWARD: It's not serious, you know. Do her good to let
off steam like that. You mustn't take it to heart.

> [*He bends down and kisses her on the cheek.*

LOIS: Why do you do that?

HOWARD: I don't like to see you miserable.

> [*She turns round a little and gives him a thoughtful look.
> He smiles rather charmingly.*

HOWARD: I'm quite sober.

LOIS: You'd better take your arm away. Ethel can come
in any minute.

HOWARD: I'm terribly fond of you, Lois. Don't you
like me?

LOIS: [*Miserably.*] Not much.

HOWARD: Shall I come over and see you when you're
staying at Aunt Emily's?

LOIS: Why should you?

HOWARD: [*In a low passionate whisper.*] Lois.

> [*She looks at him curiously and with a cold hostility.*

LOIS: Isn't human nature funny? I know with my mind that you're a rotter. And I despise you. Isn't it lucky you can't see into my heart?

HOWARD: Why, what should I see there?

LOIS: Desire.

HOWARD: What for? I don't know what you mean.

LOIS: I didn't think you would or I shouldn't have told you. How shameful and ugly. I see that all right. It's funny, it doesn't seem to make any difference.

HOWARD: Oh, I see what you mean now. That's quite O.K. Give it time, girlie. I'll wait.

LOIS: [*Coolly, indifferently.*] You swine.

[SYDNEY *comes in.*

SYDNEY: Uncle Charlie's on his way round now.

LOIS: Mother will be back in a minute.

SYDNEY: How are you going to get to the station?

HOWARD: I'll drive you if you like.

LOIS: Oh, it's all arranged.

[ARDSLEY *comes in.*

ARDSLEY: Prentice has come. They're putting Evie to bed.

LOIS: I'll go and see if I can do anything.

[*She goes out.*

ARDSLEY: [*To* SYDNEY.] Sydney, did you know anything about her being engaged to Collie?

SYDNEY: I don't believe she was.

ARDSLEY: D'you mean to say you think it was pure invention?

SYDNEY: I shouldn't wonder. But I think she'll stick to it. After all no one can now prove she wasn't.

ARDSLEY: It's a terrible thing about poor Collie. No one can be more distressed than I.

SYDNEY: It seems a bit hard that after going through the war and getting a D.S.O., he should have come to this end.

ARDSLEY: He may have been a very good naval officer. He was a very poor business man. That's all there is to it.

SYDNEY: We might put that on his tombstone. It would make a damned good epitaph.

ARDSLEY: If that's a joke, Sydney, I must say I think it in very bad taste.

SYDNEY: [*With bitter calm.*] You see, I feel I have a certain right to speak. I know how dead keen we all were when the war started. Every sacrifice was worth it. We didn't say much about it because we were rather shy, but honour did mean something to us and patriotism wasn't just a word. And then, when it was all over, we did think that those of us who'd died hadn't died in vain, and those of us who were broken and shattered and knew they wouldn't be any more good in the world were buoyed up by the thought that if they'd given everything they'd given it in a great cause.

ARDSLEY: And they had.

SYDNEY: Do you still think that? I don't. I know that we were the dupes of the incompetent fools who ruled the nations. I know that we were sacrificed to their vanity, their greed and their stupidity. And the worst of it is that as far as I can tell they haven't learnt a thing. They're just as vain, they're just as greedy, they're just as stupid as they ever were. They muddle on, muddle on, and one of these days they'll muddle us all into another war. When that happens I'll tell you what I'm going to do. I'm going out into the streets and cry: Look at me; don't be a lot of damned fools; it's all bunk what they're saying to you, about honour and patriotism and glory, bunk, bunk, bunk.

HOWARD: Who cares if it is bunk? I had the time of my life in the war. No responsibility and plenty of money. More than I'd ever had before or ever since. All the girls you wanted and all the whisky. Excitement. A roughish time in the trenches, but a grand lark afterwards. I tell you it was a bitter day for me when they signed the armistice. What have I got now? Just the same old thing day after day, working my guts out to keep body and soul together. The very day war is declared I join up and the sooner the better, if you ask me. That's the life for me. By God!

ARDSLEY: [*To his son.*] You've had a lot to put up with, Sydney. I know that. But don't think you're the only one. It's been a great blow to me that you haven't been able to follow me in my business as I followed my father. Three generations, that would have been. But it wasn't to be. No one wants another war less than I do, but if it comes I'm convinced that you'll do your duty, so far as in you lies, as you did it before. It was a great grief to me that when the call came I was too old to answer. But I did what I could. I was enrolled as a special constable. And if I'm wanted again I shall be ready again.

SYDNEY: [*Between his teeth.*] God give me patience.

HOWARD: You have a whisky and soda, old boy, and you'll feel better.

SYDNEY: Will a whisky and soda make me forget poor Evie half crazy, Collie doing away with himself rather than go to gaol, and my lost sight?

ARDSLEY: But, my dear boy, that's just our immediate circle. Of course we suffered, perhaps we've had more than our fair share, but we're not everyone.

SYDNEY: Don't you know that all over England there are families like ours, all over Germany and all over

France? We were quite content to go our peaceful way, jogging along obscurely, and happy enough. All we asked was to be left alone. Oh, it's no good talking.

ARDSLEY: The fact is, Sydney, you think too much.

SYDNEY: [*Smiling.*] I daresay you're right, father. You see, I have little else to do. I'm thinking of collecting stamps.

ARDSLEY: That's a very good idea, my boy. If you go about it cleverly there's no reason why it shouldn't be a very sound investment.

> [MRS. ARDSLEY *comes in. She is still wearing her hat and coat.*

SYDNEY: Hulloa, mother.

> [*As she sits down, a trifle wearily, her eye catches the litter on the floor of all the things* EVA *threw over when she upset the table.*

MRS. ARDSLEY: Been having a picnic?

ARDSLEY: Evie upset the table.

MRS. ARDSLEY: In play or anger?

HOWARD: I'd better pick the things up.

MRS. ARDSLEY: It does look rather untidy.

> [*He picks up one piece after the other and sets the table straight.*

ARDSLEY: Poor Collie's killed himself.

MRS. ARDSLEY: Yes, I've heard. I'm sorry.

ARDSLEY: Evie's in rather a state about it.

MRS. ARDSLEY: Poor thing, I'll go to her.

ARDSLEY: Charlie Prentice is with her.

SYDNEY: Why don't you wait till you've had a cup of tea, mother? You sound tired.

MRS. ARDSLEY: I am rather. [DR. PRENTICE *comes in and*

she gives him a smile.] Oh, Charlie. I was just coming upstairs.

PRENTICE: I wouldn't. I've given Evie a hypodermic. I'd rather she were left alone.

ARDSLEY: Take a pew, Charlie. I'm going back to my office. One or two things I want to finish up. I'll be along for tea in a quarter of an hour.

MRS. ARDSLEY: Very well.

[*He goes out.*

HOWARD: [*Having finished.*] There. That's all right, I think.

MRS. ARDSLEY: Thank you.

HOWARD: I say, I think I'll just go along to Collie's garage. There are one or two bits and pieces that I've got my eye on. I'd just as soon make sure that nobody sneaks them.

SYDNEY: Oh, yeah.

HOWARD: Tell Ethel I'll come back for her. I shan't be long.

[*He goes out.*

SYDNEY: What did the specialist say, mother?

MRS. ARDSLEY: What specialist, Sydney?

SYDNEY: Come off it, darling. You don't generally favour your family with a very detailed account of your movements. When you took such pains to tell us exactly why you were going into Stanbury this afternoon, I guess that you were going to see a specialist.

MRS. ARDSLEY: I never believe a word doctors say to me.

PRENTICE: Don't mind me.

MRS. ARDSLEY: Tell me about Evie.

PRENTICE: I hardly know yet. It may be it would be better if she went into a home for a few weeks.

MRS. ARDSLEY: She isn't mad?

PRENTICE: She's very unbalanced. . . . I was just coming round when Sydney telephoned. Murray rang me up after he'd seen you.

MRS. ARDSLEY: Why didn't he mind his own business?

PRENTICE: It was his business.

SYDNEY: Would you like me to leave you?

[MRS. ARDSLEY *gives him a little, thoughtful look.*

MRS. ARDSLEY: No, stay if you like. But go on with your tatting and pretend you don't hear.

SYDNEY: All right.

[*He takes his work and goes on as though absorbed in it.*

MRS. ARDSLEY: Don't interrupt.

PRENTICE: I'm afraid Murray could only confirm my diagnosis, Charlotte.

MRS. ARDSLEY: [*Cheerfully.*] I had an idea he would, you know. You stick together, you doctors.

PRENTICE: He agrees with me that an immediate operation is necessary.

MRS. ARDSLEY: I believe he does.

PRENTICE: When I spoke to him on the telephone he said you were—hesitating a little.

MRS. ARDSLEY: Not at all. I didn't hesitate for a minute.

PRENTICE: I'm delighted to hear it. I know your courage. I was confident in your good sense.

MRS. ARDSLEY: I'm glad.

PRENTICE: I'll make all the arrangements and we'll have it done as soon as possible.

MRS. ARDSLEY: I'm not going to be operated on, Charlie.

PRENTICE: My dear, I must be frank with you. It's the only chance we have of saving your life.

MRS. ARDSLEY: That's not true, Charlie. It's the only chance you have of prolonging my life. For a few months or a year perhaps. And then it'll start all over again. Do you think it's worth it? I don't.

PRENTICE: You have your husband and your children to think of.

MRS. ARDSLEY: I know. It would be a frightful expense. If I got over the operation I should always be an invalid. I should have to have a nurse. I should be much more bother than I was worth.

PRENTICE: That's unkind, Charlotte. And it's untrue.

MRS. ARDSLEY: You've known me a great many years, Charlie. Haven't you noticed that when once I make up my mind I don't change it?

PRENTICE: Don't be a damned fool, Charlotte.

MRS. ARDSLEY: I have nothing to complain of, I haven't had an unhappy life. I'm prepared to call it a day.

PRENTICE: I don't know if Murray made himself quite clear.

MRS. ARDSLEY: I asked him to.

PRENTICE: Listen to me. I mean every word I say. If you won't consent to an operation I'm afraid you have only a few months to live.

MRS. ARDSLEY: [*Coolly.*] How odd! Those were his very words.

PRENTICE: Well?

MRS. ARDSLEY: I've often wondered in the past how I should take it when I was told that I was going to die. I've wondered if I'd scream or faint. You know, I didn't do either. It gave me a funny sort of thrill. I felt as if I'd drunk a glass of port on an empty stomach. I had some shopping to do at Stanbury afterwards. I'm afraid I was rather extravagant. I felt so gay and light-hearted.

PRENTICE: That's more than I do.

MRS. ARDSLEY: It shows how right Leonard is when he

says it's silly to take your jumps before you come to them.

PRENTICE: Oh, damn Leonard.

MRS. ARDSLEY: I'm free. Nothing matters very much any more. It's a very comfortable feeling.

PRENTICE: And the rest?

MRS. ARDSLEY: Oh, the rest, my dear, is between me and the pale, distant shadow that is all you clever people have left me of God.

PRENTICE: [*After a moment's reflection.*] If you take that view of it, if you know the facts and are prepared to take the consequences, I have no more to say. Perhaps you're right. I admire your courage. I should like to think that I should have enough to follow your example.

MRS. ARDSLEY: There is one thing I'm going to ask you to do for me.

PRENTICE: My dear, anything in the world.

MRS. ARDSLEY: I don't want to suffer more than I need. We've always had a great deal of affection for one another, Charlie.

PRENTICE: I suppose we have.

MRS. ARDSLEY: You doctors are a brutal lot and there's no end to the amount of pain you can bear in other people.

PRENTICE: I will do everything medical practice permits me to save you from suffering.

MRS. ARDSLEY: But I'm going to ask you to do something more.

[*A long, intent look passes between them.*

PRENTICE: I'll do even that.

MRS. ARDSLEY: [*With a change of manner, cheerfully.*] Then that's all right. And now let's forget that I have anything the matter with me.

[SYDNEY *gets up and coming over to his mother bends down and kisses her on the forehead.*

MRS. ARDSLEY: As you're up you might ring the bell, Sydney. I'm simply dying for a cup of tea.

[*As he rings* ETHEL *comes in.*

ETHEL: I didn't know you were back, mother.

MRS. ARDSLEY: Yes, I got in a few minutes ago. [ETHEL *kisses her.*] I was going up to see Evie, but Uncle Charlie thought I'd better wait.

ETHEL: She's quite comfortable.

MRS. ARDSLEY: Asleep?

ETHEL: No, but resting.

MRS. ARDSLEY: Where's Lois?

ETHEL: She's in her room. She's just coming.

[*The* MAID *comes in with a tray, which she puts on a little table.*

MRS. ARDSLEY: [*To her.*] Oh, Gertrude, if anyone calls I'm not at home.

GERTRUDE: Very good, ma'am.

MRS. ARDSLEY: I don't feel inclined to cope with visitors this afternoon.

PRENTICE: I'll take myself off.

MRS. ARDSLEY: Don't be so stupid. You're going to stay and have a cup of tea.

PRENTICE: I have other patients, you know.

MRS. ARDSLEY: They can wait.

[LOIS *comes in.*

MRS. ARDSLEY: You ought to be starting soon, Lois, oughtn't you?

LOIS: I've got time yet. It won't take me five minutes to get to the station.

ETHEL: You won't forget the partridges?

LOIS: No.

MRS. ARDSLEY: Give Aunt Emily my love.

PRENTICE: You might remember me to her, Lois.

LOIS: I will.

MRS. ARDSLEY: Her chrysanthemums ought to be coming on just now.

> [GERTRUDE *has gone out of the room after bringing in the tray and now comes back.*

GERTRUDE: Mrs. Cedar has called, ma'am.

MRS. ARDSLEY: I told you to say I wasn't at home.

GERTRUDE: I said you wasn't, ma'am, but she says it's very important.

MRS. ARDSLEY: Tiresome woman. Tell her I've just come back from Stanbury and I'm very tired. Say, will she forgive me, but I don't feel up to seeing anybody to-day.

GERTRUDE: Very good, ma'am.

> [*She is about to go, when the door is burst open and* GWEN *comes in. She is wrought up.*

GWEN: I'm sorry to force myself on you. It's a matter of life and death. I must see you.

MRS. ARDSLEY: I'm not very well, Gwen. Don't you think you can wait till to-morrow?

GWEN: No, no, no, to-morrow it'll be too late. Oh, God, what shall I do?

MRS. ARDSLEY: Well, since you're here, perhaps the best thing would be to sit down and have a cup of tea.

GWEN: [*In a strangled voice.*] Lois and Wilfred are going to elope.

MRS. ARDSLEY: Oh, my dear, don't be so silly. You're making a perfect nuisance of yourself.

GWEN: It's true, I tell you, it's true.

MRS. ARDSLEY: Lois is going to spend a fortnight with my sister-in-law. I didn't think there was anything in what you said to me, but I didn't want any unpleasantness, so I arranged that she should be away till after you'd gone.

GWEN: She's not going to your sister-in-law's. Wilfred's meeting her at Stanbury. They're going to London.

LOIS: What are you talking about, Gwen?

GWEN: I heard every word you said on the 'phone.

LOIS: [*Trying to hide that she is startled.*] When?

GWEN: Just now. Ten minutes ago. You didn't know I'd had an extension put up into my room. I'm not such a perfect fool as you thought me. Can you deny that you spoke to Wilfred?

LOIS: No.

GWEN: You said, Wilfred, it's a go. And he said, what d'you mean? And you said, I'm trusting myself to your tender mercies. You're for it, my boy. I'm going to elope with you.

ETHEL: She was joking with him.

GWEN: A funny joke. He said, my God, you don't mean it. And she said, I'll get out of the train at Stanbury. Meet me in the car and we'll talk it over on the way to London.

MRS. ARDSLEY: Is it true, Lois?

LOIS: Yes.

SYDNEY: You damned fool, Lois.

GWEN: Oh, Lois, I've never done you any harm. I've been a good friend to you—you can't take my husband from me.

LOIS: I'm not taking him from you. You lost him years ago.

GWEN: You're young, you'll have plenty of chances before you're through. I'm old and he's all I've got. If he leaves me I swear to you that I'll kill myself.

MRS. ARDSLEY: But why have you come here? Why didn't you go to your husband?

GWEN: He won't listen to me. Oh, what a fool I've been. I ought to have known when I saw the pearls.

MRS. ARDSLEY: What pearls?

GWEN: She's wearing them now. She pretends they're false, but they're real, and he gave them to her.

MRS. ARDSLEY: Take them off, Lois, and give them to Gwen.

> [*Without a word* LOIS *undoes the clasp and throws the string on the table.*

GWEN: Do you think I'd touch them? He hates me. Oh, it's so awful to love someone with all your heart and to know that the very sight of you maddens him beyond endurance. I went down on my knees to him. I begged him not to leave me. He said he was sick to death of me. He pushed me over. I heard the door slam. He's gone. He's gone to join her.

> [*She falls to her knees and bursts into a passion of tears.*

MRS. ARDSLEY: Gwen, Gwen, don't give way like that.

> [GWEN, *still on her knees, drags herself up to* MRS. ARDSLEY.

GWEN: Don't let her go to him. You know what it feels like to be old. You know how defenceless one is. She'll regret it. You don't know what he's like. He'll throw her aside when he's tired of her as he's thrown all the others aside. He's hard and cruel and selfish. He's made me so miserable.

MRS. ARDSLEY: If that's true, if he's all you say I should have thought you were well rid of him.

GWEN: I'm too old to start afresh. I'm too old to be left alone. Alone. [*She struggles up to her feet.*] He's mine. I went through the divorce court to get him. I won't let him go. [*Turning on* LOIS.] I swear to you before God that you shall never marry him. He forced his first wife to divorce him because she hadn't money, but I've got money of my own. I'll never divorce him.

LOIS: Nothing would induce me to marry him.

GWEN: Take him if you want to. He'll come back to me. He's old. He tries to keep up. It's all sham. I know the effort it is. He's tired to death and he won't give in. What good can he be to you? How can you be so stupid? You ought to be ashamed.

MRS. ARDSLEY: Gwen. Gwen.

GWEN: Money. Oh, curse the money. He's a rich man and you haven't got a bob between you. You're all in it. All of you. You all want to get something out of it. You brutes. You beasts.

> [DR. PRENTICE *gets up and takes her by the arm.*

PRENTICE: Come, Mrs. Cedar, we've had enough of this. You go too far. You must get out of this.

GWEN: I won't go.

PRENTICE: If you don't, I shall put you out.

> [*He urges her towards the door.*

GWEN: I'll make such a scandal that you'll never be able to hold up your heads again.

PRENTICE: That's enough now. Get out.

GWEN: Leave me alone, damn you.

PRENTICE: I'm going to take you home. Come on.

> [*They both go out. There is a moment's awkward silence when the door is closed on them.*

LOIS: I'm sorry to have exposed you to this disgusting scene, mother.

SYDNEY: You may well be.

ETHEL: You're not really going off with that man, Lois?

LOIS: I am.

ETHEL: You can't be in love with him.

LOIS: Of course not. If I were, d'you think I'd be such a fool as to go?

ETHEL: [*Aghast*.] Lois.

LOIS: If I loved him I'd be afraid.

ETHEL: You don't know what you're doing. It would be awful and unnatural if you loved him, but there would be an excuse for you.

LOIS: Has love done very much for you, Ethel?

ETHEL: Me? I don't know what you mean. I married Howard. I took him for better, for worse.

LOIS: You've been a good wife and a good mother. A virtuous woman. And a lot of good it's done you. I've seen you grow old and tired and hopeless. I'm frightened, Ethel, frightened.

ETHEL: I wasn't obliged to marry. Mother and father were against it.

LOIS: You could have stayed on at home like Evie. So can I. I'm frightened, Ethel. I'm frightened. I don't want to become like Evie.

ETHEL: Mother, can't you do something? It's so awful. It's such madness.

MRS. ARDSLEY: I'm listening to what Lois has to say.

ETHEL: [*With a catch in her breath*.] You're not running away from anybody here?

LOIS: [*Smiling*.] Oh, my dear, that isn't at all in my character.

ETHEL: [*Ashamed and awkward*.] I thought that perhaps someone had been trying to make love to you.

Lois: Oh, Ethel, don't be so silly. Who is there to make love to me in this God-forsaken place?

Ethel: I didn't know. Perhaps it was only my fancy. It's just the money?

Lois: Yes, and what money brings. Freedom and opportunity.

Ethel: Those are mere words.

Lois: I'm sick of waiting for something to turn up. Time is flying and soon it'll be too late.

Mrs. Ardsley: When did you decide, Lois?

Lois: Half an hour ago.

Mrs. Ardsley: Have you considered all the consequences?

Lois: Oh, mother dear, if I did that I should stay here twiddling my thumbs till my dying day.

Mrs. Ardsley: It's not a very nice thing that you're doing.

Lois: I know.

Mrs. Ardsley: It's cruel to Gwen.

Lois: [*With a shrug.*] I or another.

Mrs. Ardsley: It'll be a dreadful blow to your father.

Lois: I'm sorry.

Mrs. Ardsley: And the scandal won't be very nice for us.

Lois: I can't help it.

Ethel: It would be bad enough if you were going to be married. Gwen says she won't divorce.

Lois: I don't want to marry him.

Ethel: What's to happen to you if he chucks you?

Lois: Darling, you're years older than I am and a married woman. How can you be so innocent? Has it never occurred to you what power it gives a woman when a man is madly in love with her and she doesn't care a row of pins for him?

[GERTRUDE *comes in with the teapot and the hot water on a tray.*

MRS. ARDSLEY: [*To* ETHEL.] Go and tell your father tea is ready, Ethel.

[*With a disheartened gesture* ETHEL *goes out.*

LOIS: I'll go and put on my hat. [GERTRUDE *goes out.*] I'm sorry to disappoint you, mother. I don't want to cause you pain.

MRS. ARDSLEY: Have you quite made up your mind, Lois?

LOIS: Quite.

MRS. ARDSLEY: That is what I thought. Then perhaps you *had* better go and put on your hat.

LOIS: What about father? I don't want him to make a scene.

MRS. ARDSLEY: I'll tell him after you've gone.

LOIS: Thank you.

[*She goes out.* MRS. ARDSLEY *and* SYDNEY *are left alone.*

SYDNEY: Are you going to let her go, mother?

MRS. ARDSLEY: How can I stop her?

SYDNEY: You can tell her what the surgeon told you this afternoon.

MRS. ARDSLEY: Oh, my dear, with one foot in the grave it's rather late to start blackmail.

SYDNEY: She wouldn't go, you know.

MRS. ARDSLEY: I don't think she would. I can't do that, Sydney. I shouldn't like to think of her waiting for my death. I should feel like apologising for every day I lingered on.

SYDNEY: She might change her mind.

MRS. ARDSLEY: She's young, she has her life before her, she

must do what she thinks best with it. I don't belong to life any longer. I don't think I have the right to influence her.

SYDNEY: Aren't you afraid she'll come an awful cropper?

MRS. ARDSLEY: She's hard and selfish. I don't think she's stupid. She can take care of herself.

SYDNEY: She might be a stranger, to hear you speak.

MRS. ARDSLEY: Does it sound unkind? You see, I feel as if nothing mattered very much any more. I've had my day. I've done what I could. Now those who come after me must shift for themselves.

SYDNEY: You're not frightened at all?

MRS. ARDSLEY: Not a bit. I'm strangely happy. I'm rather relieved to think it's over. I'm not at home in this world of to-day. I'm pre-war. Everything's so changed now. I don't understand the new ways. To me life is like a party that was very nice to start with, but has become rather rowdy as time went on, and I'm not at all sorry to go home.

[ETHEL *comes back.*

ETHEL: I've told father. He's just coming.

MRS. ARDSLEY: I'm afraid we've let the tea stand rather a long time.

SYDNEY: Father likes nothing better than a good strong cup.

[LOIS *comes in. She has her hat on.*

LOIS: [*Startled and anxious.*] Mother, Evie is coming down the stairs.

MRS. ARDSLEY: Isn't she asleep?

SYDNEY: Uncle Charlie said he'd given her something.

[*The door is opened and* EVA *comes in. Her eyes are bright from the drug the doctor has given her. She has a queer, fixed smile on her face. She has changed into her best frock.*

MRS. ARDSLEY: I thought you were lying down, Evie. They told me you didn't feel quite up to the mark.

EVA: I had to come down to tea. Collie's coming.

LOIS: [*Shocked.*] Collie!

EVA: He'd have been so disappointed if I hadn't come.

MRS. ARDSLEY: You've put on your best dress.

EVA: It is rather an occasion, isn't it? You see, I'm engaged to be married.

ETHEL: Evie, what do you mean?

EVA: I'm telling you beforehand so that you should be prepared. Collie's coming here this afternoon to talk to father about it. Don't say anything about it till he comes.

> [*There is a moment's awkward pause. They none of them know what to say or do.*

MRS. ARDSLEY: Let me give you your tea, darling.

EVA: I don't want any tea. I'm too excited. [*She catches sight of the string of pearls that* LOIS *had put on the table.*] What are these pearls doing here?

LOIS: You can have them if you like.

MRS. ARDSLEY: Lois.

LOIS: They're mine.

EVA: Can I really? It'll be an engagement present. Oh, Lois, that is sweet of you. [*She goes up to her and kisses her, then, standing in front of the glass, puts them on.*] Collie always says I have such a pretty neck.

> [MR. ARDSLEY *and* HOWARD *come in.*

ARDSLEY: Now what about this cup of tea?

HOWARD: Hulloa, Evie. All right again?

EVA: Oh, yes. There's nothing the matter with me.

ARDSLEY: All ready to start, Lois?

LOIS: Yes.

ARDSLEY: Don't cut it too fine.

HOWARD: I may look you up one of these days, Lois. I've got to go over to Canterbury to see a man on business. I don't suppose I shall be able to get back for the night, Ethel.

ETHEL: No?

HOWARD: I'll come over and fetch you in the car, Lois, and we'll do a picture together.

LOIS: [*Mocking him.*] That would be grand.

ARDSLEY: Well, I must say it's very nice to have a cup of tea by one's own fireside and surrounded by one's family. If you come to think of it we none of us have anything very much to worry about. Of course we none of us have more money than we know what to do with, but we have our health and we have our happiness. I don't think we've got very much to complain of. Things haven't been going too well lately, but I think the world is turning the corner and we can all look forward to better times in future. This old England of ours isn't done yet and I for one believe in it and all it stands for.

[EVA *begins to sing in a thin cracked voice.*

EVA: God save our gracious King!
                 Long live our noble King!
                 God save our King!

[*The others look at her, petrified, in horror-struck surprise. When she stops* LOIS *gives a little cry and hurries from the room.*

THE END

SHEPPEY

A PLAY
in Three Acts

CHARACTERS

Sheppey

Ernest Turner

Bradley

Mr. Bolton

Albert

Cooper

Dr. Jervis

Two Customers

A Reporter

A Hairdresser

Mrs. Miller

Florrie

Bessie Legros

Miss Grange

Miss James

SHEPPEY

ACT ONE

The Scene is Bradley's *Hairdressing and Barber's Saloon in
Jermyn Street.*

*At the back is the front shop in which the cashier sits, and the door
from the street leads into it. From this a doorway, closed by a
curtain, gives entrance to the saloon. This is lined with mirrors,
with basins, and in front of each basin is a barber's chair. In
the middle of the room is a table on which are papers and
magazines, two or three chairs for customers to sit on if they
have to wait, and a round coat and hat rack and umbrella stand.
A door in one of the side walls leads to the room where the
assistants sit when they are not occupied.*

When the curtain rises Two Customers *are being served. One of
them has just had his hair cut by* Albert, *and* Miss Grange,
*the manicurist, is finishing his nails. The other customer is in
process of being shaved by* Sheppey. Sheppey *is a stoutish,
middle-aged man, with a red face and twinkling eyes. He has a
fine head of black wavy hair. He has a jovial, well-fed look.
He is a bit of a character and knows it.* Miss Grange *is very
refined.*

Albert: Anything on the 'air, sir?

Customer: As long as it's not greasy.

Albert: Number three, sir?

Customer: All right.

> [Albert *sprinkles some hair wash on the customer's head.
> During the next few speeches he brushes and combs the
> hair.*

ALBERT: Anything you're wanting to-day, sir?

CUSTOMER: No.

ALBERT: 'Air's very dry, sir.

CUSTOMER: That's how I like it.

ALBERT: Getting a bit thin on top, sir.

CUSTOMER: I think it's rather becoming.

ALBERT: Matter of taste, sir. I can thoroughly recommend
our number three. We sell a rare lot of it.

CUSTOMER: You're not going to sell any to me.

ALBERT: Very good, sir. All I meant to say is, it can't 'elp
but do the 'air good. Mr. Bradley makes it 'imself.
It's made of the very best materials. I can guarantee that.

CUSTOMER: Shut up!

MISS GRANGE: You don't want a high polish on them, do
you?

CUSTOMER: Just ordinary.

MISS GRANGE: I'll put a high polish on them if you like.

CUSTOMER: I don't want to see my face in them, you know.

MISS GRANGE: I never like to see a gentleman's nails too
highly polished.

CUSTOMER: I daresay you're right.

MISS GRANGE: I mean to say, I always think it makes one
look like a foreigner.

CUSTOMER: Oh, do you think it does?

MISS GRANGE: I'm positive of it. And one doesn't want to
look like one of them Argentines, does he?

CUSTOMER: They look terribly rich, you know.

MISS GRANGE: I can put as much polish on your nails as
you like, you know.

CUSTOMER: Oh no, don't trouble.

MISS GRANGE: Oh, it's no trouble. I mean, you've only got
to say the word.

CUSTOMER: As long as they're neat and clean that'll do me.

MISS GRANGE: That's what I always say, neat but not gaudy.

SHEPPEY: [*To the customer he is shaving.*] Razor all right, sir?

SECOND CUSTOMER: Yes.

SHEPPEY: Very mild to-day, sir.

SECOND CUSTOMER: Yes.

SHEPPEY: I shouldn't be surprised if we 'ad a bit of rain to-night, sir.

SECOND CUSTOMER: Yes?

SHEPPEY: I 'ear the French 'orse won the three-thirty, sir.

SECOND CUSTOMER: Yes.

SHEPPEY: 'Ave anything on, sir?

SECOND CUSTOMER: Yes.

SHEPPEY: Bit of luck for you, sir.

SECOND CUSTOMER: Yes.

SHEPPEY: I backed Varsity Boy meself, sir. Shilling each way.

SECOND CUSTOMER: Yes?

SHEPPEY: 'E 'ad a pretty good chance.

SECOND CUSTOMER: Yes.

SHEPPEY: You 'ave to be pretty smart to spot a winner every time.

SECOND CUSTOMER: Yes.

SHEPPEY: It's a mug's game, backing 'orses.

SECOND CUSTOMER: Yes.

SHEPPEY: That's what I say. But one must 'ave a bit of excitement. Sport of Kings, they call it.

SECOND CUSTOMER: Yes.

SHEPPEY: Pity so many owners giving up.

SECOND CUSTOMER: Yes.

SHEPPEY: 'Ard times for all of us.

SECOND CUSTOMER: Yes.

> [MR. BOLTON *comes in. He is a smart-looking, middle-aged man.* BRADLEY, *the proprietor, precedes him through the curtains.*

BRADLEY: This way, sir.

BOLTON: I'm not too late, am I?

BRADLEY: No, sir, we don't shut till seven. I told my other young lady she might go, but Miss Grange is here. [*Calling.*] Number Three.

BOLTON: I'll wait for Sheppey.

BRADLEY: Just as you like, sir.

SHEPPEY: I shan't be above two minutes, sir.

> [No. 3 *comes through the door.*

BRADLEY: All right, Victor. Mr. Bolton's going to wait for Sheppey.

> [No. 3 *nods and goes back again.*
>
> [*Taking* MR. BOLTON's *hat and stick.*] Evening paper, sir?

BOLTON: Afternoon, Miss Grange.

MISS GRANGE: Afternoon, sir. You're quite a stranger. I'm just finished.

BOLTON: I don't know that I want a manicure to-day.

MISS GRANGE: It's nearly a fortnight since you had them done last, Mr. Bolton.

BOLTON: I'm only going to have a shave.

MISS GRANGE: That'll give me plenty of time. I can finish by the time Sheppey does.

SHEPPEY: Don't you put me on my mettle, Miss Grange. I can shave a customer in four and a 'alf minutes if I want to.

BOLTON: You needn't try to make any records on me, Sheppey.

MISS GRANGE: I don't say I can make an absolutely first-

rate job of it in the time it takes you to give a gentleman
a shave, but I *can* make his nails look decent.

BRADLEY: That's right, Mr. Bolton. I've 'ad to do with a
good many young ladies in my time. I can't off 'and
remember one as was quicker than Miss Grange.

MISS GRANGE: Well, practice makes perfect, they say. I
like a gentleman's hands to look as if they were a gentleman's hands, and I don't mind who knows it. [*To the
customer she is serving.*] There, sir, I think that's all
right.

CUSTOMER: Grand.

> [*He gets up.* ALBERT *removes his gown, and takes up a
> brush and gives him a rapid brush down.*]

ALBERT: Allow me, sir.

CUSTOMER: Oh, that's all right.

MISS GRANGE: [*Archly.*] We must send you out of the shop
nice and tidy, you know.

CUSTOMER: How much do I owe?

ALBERT: Pay at the desk, sir.

> *The* CUSTOMER *takes a shilling out of his pocket and gives
> it to* MISS GRANGE.

CUSTOMER: Here you are.

MISS GRANGE: Thank you, sir.

BRADLEY: [*Helping him on with his coat.*] Allow me, sir.

ALBERT: [*Producing a bottle of hair wash.*] This is our number
three, sir.

CUSTOMER: Very pretty.

BRADLEY: We sell a rare lot of it, sir.

CUSTOMER: So the gentleman who was cutting my hair said.
The information left me speechless.

BRADLEY: There isn't a preparation on the market to come
up to it. And it's not because I make it myself that I say
that.

ALBERT: You'd be surprised what it would do for your 'air, sir.

CUSTOMER: I hate surprises. [*He nods.*] Afternoon.

> [*The* CUSTOMER *is ushered out by* ALBERT.

SHEPPEY: A little off the ears, sir?

SECOND CUSTOMER: No.

SHEPPEY: Very good, sir. Shall you be wanting any 'air wash to-day, sir?

SECOND CUSTOMER: No.

SHEPPEY: Razor blades?

SECOND CUSTOMER: No.

SHEPPEY: There's a new safety razor just been put on the market. Beautiful bit of work. I suppose you wouldn't like just to 'ave a look at it.

SECOND CUSTOMER: No.

SHEPPEY: Very good, sir. Shall I just give the 'air a brush, sir?

SECOND CUSTOMER: No.

SHEPPEY: Very good, sir. Then I think that'll be all, sir.

> [*The* CUSTOMER *gets up and* SHEPPEY *takes his gown off him.* *The* CUSTOMER *tips him.*

Thank you, sir. [*To* MR. BOLTON.] Now I'm ready for you, sir.

BRADLEY: I'll just give you a brush, sir.

> MR. BOLTON *sits down in* SHEPPEY'S *chair and* MISS GRANGE *brings up her little stool.* SHEPPEY *fetches a clean gown. Meanwhile* BRADLEY *brushes down the second customer and gives him his hat.*

MISS GRANGE: Now let me have a look at those nails of yours, Mr. Bolton. Oh, Mr. Bolton. I do believe you've been unfaithful to me.

BOLTON: What makes you think that, Miss Grange?

MISS GRANGE: Well, I can see with half an eye that someone

has been messing about with your hands. Oh, Mr. Bolton, that is too bad of you.

BOLTON: I broke a nail playing golf down in the country. I had to do something about it.

MISS GRANGE: Well, I am disappointed. I never thought you'd do a thing like that. I shall have no end of a job getting your nails nice again. The fact is you can't trust anyone in this world.

BOLTON: I apologise, Miss Grange.

MISS GRANGE: Oh, I didn't mean you, sir. You're a gentleman and that nobody can deny. I meant that girl that done your nails. Well, I ask you.

[SHEPPEY *comes back with a gown and puts it on* MR. BOLTON.

BOLTON: Sheppey, I regret to inform you that Miss Grange is upset.

MISS GRANGE: I am and I'm not going to deny it.

SHEPPEY: Why, what's the trouble?

MISS GRANGE: Mr. Bolton's been unfaithful to me.

SHEPPEY: You know what men are, Miss Grange. You can't trust them out of your sight.

MISS GRANGE: And no one knows that better than me, Sheppey.

[SHEPPEY *begins to lather* MR. BOLTON'S *face.* ALBERT *comes in again.*

BOLTON: You didn't seem to be doing very well with your last customer, Sheppey.

SHEPPEY: Not what you'd call a brilliant conversationalist, was he? I knew there was nothing doing the moment he sat down. I only asked 'im if he was wanting anything to-day so as he shouldn't feel slighted.

BOLTON: [*To* ALBERT.] You didn't have much luck with your number three either, Albert.

o

ALBERT: You're right there, sir. He was one of them tight ones and no mistake.

MISS GRANGE: I'll say this for you, Albert. You had a good try.

SHEPPEY: I was listening to you. You didn't try the right way.

ALBERT: When a gent says he likes being bald—well, I ask you.

MISS GRANGE: He was aggravating, I must say. He had an answer to everything.

SHEPPEY: When a customer tries to be funny 'e's easy.

MISS GRANGE: Well, Sheppey, I don't believe even you could have got him to buy anything.

BOLTON: Is Sheppey a good salesman?

MISS GRANGE: You ask Mr. Bradley.

BRADLEY: Best I've ever had.

BOLTON: How d'you do it, Sheppey?

SHEPPEY: Oh, it's just knack, sir. Of course you want a lot of tact.

BOLTON: You needn't mind telling me, you know. You'll never catch me if you try till doomsday. All these preparations of yours. A lot of damned nonsense. I wouldn't take one of them as a gift.

> [SHEPPEY, *unseen by* BOLTON, *gives* BRADLEY *and* ALBERT *a wink*. BRADLEY *presently goes out*.

SHEPPEY: I know I couldn't sell you anything not in a hundred years. You 'ave to be a judge of character in my business and I know it would be just waste of time to try.

BOLTON: Thank you for those kind words.

SHEPPEY: You see, we make our money out of the vanity of the 'uman race. And I don't mind telling you that men are every bit as vain as women.

MISS GRANGE: Vainer, if you ask me.

SHEPPEY: Now I don't think I'm wrong in stating that you 'aven't got a spark of vanity in your composition.

BOLTON: I daresay you're right.

SHEPPEY: I know I'm right. I mean, if you was vain you wouldn't want to look any older than you need, would you?

BOLTON: I'm only just over forty, you know.

SHEPPEY: Is that a fact, sir? Of course, being so grey over the temples makes you look more.

MISS GRANGE: Oh, I like the grey over the temples, Sheppey. I always think it makes a gentleman look so distingay.

SHEPPEY: I don't say it don't look distingay. I only say it adds a good five years to one's age. If Mr. Bolton 'adn't got that grey 'e wouldn't look a day over thirty-five.

MISS GRANGE: He wouldn't look that, Sheppey.

BOLTON: I'm not going to dye my hair to please you, Sheppey.

SHEPPEY: I don't blame you. I'd never recommend a gentleman to dye his hair. It seems unnatural somehow.

MISS GRANGE: I always think it makes a face look so hard.

SHEPPEY: What I mean to say is, I don't suppose you mind if you look thirty-five or forty-eight. Why should you?

BOLTON: I don't know that I want to look as though I had one foot in the grave, you know.

SHEPPEY: You know what I'm thinking of, Miss Grange?

MISS GRANGE: That German stuff.

SHEPPEY: Mind you, sir, I'm not trying to sell it to you.

BOLTON: That's a good job because you won't succeed.

SHEPPEY: I'm all for British goods. I don't 'old with

foreigners or their doings. When the traveller come in with it I was all against it meself, but 'e persuaded Mr. Bradley to give it a trial. And you'd be surprised at the amount we've sold of it.

MISS GRANGE: Especially when you think what it costs.

SHEPPEY: What with the duty and one thing and another we can't sell it for less than twenty-five shillings a bottle.

BOLTON: What is it, a dye?

SHEPPEY: No, that's what it isn't. It just makes the 'air grow its natural colour. The result is so gradual that nobody notices. I can tell you this, if you give it a trial, at the end of three weeks you wouldn't 'ave a grey 'air on your 'ead.

BOLTON: You don't really expect me to believe that?

SHEPPEY: What reason 'ave I got for saying it? I know you're not going to try it, sir. Why should you? I know you're not the sort of gentleman as minds what 'e looks like.

BOLTON: You're not pulling my leg, are you?

SHEPPEY: How d'you mean, sir?

BOLTON: I thought you might be up to some hanky-panky.

SHEPPEY: Trying to sell you that stuff? That's not the way I'd go about it. Look here, sir, I don't mind telling you a secret. If you want to sell something to a customer you've got to keep your eye on 'im all the time. You've got to watch 'im like as if you was a boxer in the ring. Now, 'ave I been looking at you?

BOLTON: I haven't noticed it.

SHEPPEY: Well, then. A funny thing 'appened the other day. I expect you know the Marquess of Twickenham, sir.

BOLTON: No, I don't.

SHEPPEY: 'E's one of our customers and so's 'is brother,

Lord John. He absolutely insisted on trying this preparation. He was getting terribly grey and it upset 'im like. Well, one morning a gentleman come in and sat down in my chair. Good-morning, Lord John, I said to 'im. He began to laugh. I'm not Lord John, 'e said, I'm the Marquess of Twickenham. Would you believe it, I'd taken 'im for 'is younger brother. 'E 'adn't got a grey 'air in 'is 'ead.

MISS GRANGE: I couldn't help laughing at the sight of Sheppey's face.

SHEPPEY: Well, his lordship told me there was fifteen years between them.

MISS GRANGE: Almost a miracle, I call it.

BOLTON: What's the stuff called?

SHEPPEY: Get a bottle, Albert, and let Mr. Bolton 'ave a look at it.

BOLTON: Don't bother. It doesn't matter at all.

SHEPPEY: [*With a wink at* ALBERT.) Just as a matter of curiosity. 'Ave anything on the race to-day, sir?

BOLTON: No, I didn't.

SHEPPEY: I wish I 'adn't.

[ALBERT *goes into the front shop.*

BOLTON: Mug's game, betting.

MISS GRANGE: Sheppey doesn't think so. You'd be surprised the winners he picks.

SHEPPEY: Of course I never 'ave more than a shilling each way. With a wife and daughter to provide for I can't afford to take risks. I must say I like to 'ave a bit on.

BOLTON: You must be pretty smart if you don't lose more than you win.

SHEPPEY: Well, I'll tell you, I'm lucky. I always 'ave been.

MISS GRANGE: They say it's better to be born lucky than rich, don't they?

BOLTON: Did you have a ticket for the Irish Sweep?

SHEPPEY: Yes, I wouldn't miss that for anything. I've always 'ad one, ever since they started.

BOLTON: You've never won anything, I suppose?

SHEPPEY: Not yet, but I'm in 'opes.

BOLTON: The draw was yesterday, wasn't it?

SHEPPEY: Yes. They're drawing the consolation prizes to-day. I might win one of them.

MISS GRANGE: It would be a nice thing if you opened your paper to-morrow morning and saw your name there.

SHEPPEY: I shouldn't be surprised.

[ALBERT *comes in.*

ALBERT: Captain Fortescue's on the 'phone, Sheppey. He wants to know if you're free to-morrow morning at eleven-thirty.

SHEPPEY: Yes. I'm free. Book him, will you?

ALBERT: All right.

[*He goes out.*

MISS GRANGE: He was in this morning, Sheppey. He *was* in a way when he found you wasn't here.

SHEPPEY: Well, it wasn't my fault, was it?

MISS GRANGE: Cursing and swearing all over the place, he was.

SHEPPEY: I know. Only a captain and thinks 'imself a colonel.

[ALBERT *comes in again.*

ALBERT: He says, he ain't going to put up with any of your damned impudence again, and if you're not ready and waiting at eleven-thirty sharp he won't be responsible for the consequences.

SHEPPEY: I suppose they've made 'im commander-in-chief all of a sudden.

BOLTON: How is it that you weren't here this morning? I

thought you'd never missed a day for fourteen years.

SHEPPEY: No more I 'ave. Except for me fortnight's 'oliday in the summer. I was at Lambeth Police Court all the morning.

BOLTON: Drunk or disorderly?

SHEPPEY: Not me. 'Alf a pint of bitter to my dinner, and 'alf a pint when I go off work in the evening, that's all the liquor that ever passes my lips.

MISS GRANGE: He was witness in a case.

SHEPPEY: I caught a chap stealing the doctor's overcoat out of 'is car. It was standing outside the next 'ouse to mine and I come out of my front door just in the nick of time.

BOLTON: You can't leave a thing in your car now. It's rotten. You gave him in charge?

SHEPPEY: Yes. I almost wished I 'adn't afterwards. Out of work. Told the magistrate 'e 'adn't 'ad a bite for two days. You couldn't 'ardly 'elp feeling sorry for him really.

MISS GRANGE: You're too soft-hearted, Sheppey. All this unemployment. I believe if you really want a job you can always find one.

SHEPPEY: You wouldn't say that if you'd 'eard all I did this morning. My case didn't come on till near the end and I sat there and listened. It made me quite uncomfortable.

BOLTON: Why?

SHEPPEY: Well, you know, I'd 'ad a good breakfast before I left 'ome, and I was enjoying meself. It was a bit of a treat for me not 'aving to come to the shop for once in a way. A lot of cases there was.

BOLTON: Anything interesting?

SHEPPEY: Well, I don't know if you'd call 'em interesting. There was one woman who'd been caught stealing a bit of steak off a barrer. She 'ad eighteen bob a week to keep 'erself and three children. A respectable-looking woman she was too.

BOLTON: Of course there's a good deal of distress about nowadays, but there's nothing to do about it.

MISS GRANGE: That's what I say, there always have been rich and poor in the world and there always will be.

SHEPPEY: It seems funny in a country like this there should be a lot of people starving.

MISS GRANGE: If you have three good meals a day and a roof over your head, be thankful, I say, and don't worry about anybody else.

SHEPPEY: Well, I don't, not as a rule. Only you see, 'aving it brought 'ome to me all of a sudden, like it was this morning, it did give me a bit of a turn. There they was standing in the dock. They didn't look any different to anybody else. They looked just like you and me, if you understand what I mean. I couldn't 'elp saying to meself, not one of them'd be 'ere if they earned what I do.

BOLTON: You earn good money because you're steady and industrious.

SHEPPEY: I know that. But p'raps if they'd 'ad my chances they'd 'ave been just as good as me.

MISS GRANGE: You *are* morbid to-day, Sheppey. You can't be well.

BOLTON: Well, it's just on seven. You'll feel better after you've had your glass of beer.

SHEPPEY: Perhaps I shall. I generally 'ave a steak and veg. for my dinner, but some'ow to-day I didn't fancy it.

MISS GRANGE: I hope you haven't caught something sitting with all those dirty, unhealthy people.

SHEPPEY: You don't 'ave much 'eart to keep yourself clean when you don't know where your next meal is coming from and I don't expect it's so easy to keep 'ealthy when you don't get 'ardly enough nourishment to keep body and soul together.

MISS GRANGE: Oh, don't harp so. Why, you might be a Socialist to hear you talk. I always thought you were a good Conservative.

SHEPPEY: I'm a Conservative all right. I'll tell you what, Miss Grange, you let me take you to a police court one morning when we're slack and you see for yourself.

MISS GRANGE: Not me. I'm not going to upset myself. What the eye doesn't see the heart doesn't grieve over, I say. We've all got troubles enough of our own without bothering about other people's.

BOLTON: That's the only sensible way to look at it, you know, Sheppey. Everyone knows there's a lot of poverty in this world, but it can't be helped. It's just one of those things that you have to accept, like influenza or a run of bad luck at cards. And the fact remains that no one need starve to death in this country. There are institutions where he can always get a meal and there are shelters where he can always get a bed.

MISS GRANGE: My belief is that a lot of those people who sleep out on the Embankment sleep there because they really like it.

BOLTON: What did your fellow get?

SHEPPEY: Remanded for a week, sir.

BOLTON: Well, I wouldn't mind betting they'll find out that's not the only thing he's done. A man doesn't steal because he's hungry, he steals because he's a thief.

MISS GRANGE: And if he's hungry I should have thought he was better off in prison than outside.

BOLTON: It's no good fashing oneself about things one can't help. Better brains than yours have tried to find a way out, and if they haven't it's not likely you will.

MISS GRANGE: Everyone for himself and the devil take the hindmost, I say.

SHEPPEY: I'm a very ignorant man, I know that. All the same it does make me a bit uncomfortable to think it was me as gave the poor devil in charge.

BOLTON: You did quite right. Society must be protected, and it's a citizen's duty to uphold the law. A pretty state of things it would be if a fellow was justified in helping himself to whatever he fancied.

> [ALBERT *comes through the curtains.*

ALBERT: You're wanted on the 'phone, Sheppey.

SHEPPEY: Say I'm busy and ask 'em to leave a message.

ALBERT: It's your wife and she says it's urgent.

SHEPPEY: I don't care who it is. My wife knows very well I won't 'ave 'er ringing me up when I'm working.

BOLTON: Never mind about me, Sheppey. You go to the telephone. I don't mind waiting.

SHEPPEY: I wouldn't think of it. You know what women are, sir, give 'em an inch and they'll take an ell.

MISS GRANGE: Perhaps it's important, Sheppey. She's never rung you up before all the time I've been here.

SHEPPEY: I should think not indeed. When I'm at 'ome I'm at 'er beck and call, within reason, you know, but when I'm at the shop I'm me own master, as far as she's concerned.

> [ALBERT *comes in again.*

ALBERT: She says she can't leave a message and you've got to go to the 'phone yourself.

SHEPPEY: You tell 'er if it was the King of England ringing up from Buckingham Palace to give me the Order of the Garter I wouldn't go not while I was in the middle of shaving a customer.

> [ALBERT *goes out.*

BOLTON: How long have you been married, Sheppey?

SHEPPEY: Twenty-three years, sir, and if I may quote the words of our national bard it don't seem a day too much.

BOLTON: [*Smiling.*] Well, if this is the first time your wife has ever rung you up in working hours I don't think it would hurt you to see what she wants.

SHEPPEY: When you've been at the job as long as I 'ave, sir, you'll know there's one thing you must never do in married life, and that's create a precedent.

MISS GRANGE: The way you talk, Sheppey. A nicer woman than Mrs. Miller I never did know.

BOLTON: Who's Mrs. Miller?

SHEPPEY: That's my old lady. My name's Miller really.

BOLTON: Is it? I never knew that.

SHEPPEY: They call me Sheppey because I was born there. Isle of Sheppey. Kent, you know. They kid me because they say I've got Sheppey on the brain.

MISS GRANGE: To hear him talk you'd think there was no place like it.

SHEPPEY: No more there is. I always go there for me 'olidays and when I retire I'm going to settle down there.

MISS GRANGE: I went there one bank holiday. I didn't think so much of it.

SHEPPEY: The garden of England, that's what it is. I know the very 'ouse I'm going to buy when my ship comes home. Two acres of land. View of the sea. Just the place for me and my old woman.

[BRADLEY *comes in followed by* ALBERT *and the young lady who acts as cashier*, MISS JAMES *by name.*

BRADLEY: Put that razor down, Sheppey.

SHEPPEY: Why, what's the trouble?

BRADLEY: You've won a prize in the Sweep.

SHEPPEY: Is that all? That's no reason to leave a job unfinished.

> [*He is about to go on with his shaving when* Mr. Bolton
> *holds his arm.*

Bolton: No, you don't. I don't want my throat cut.

Sheppey: A little thing like that's not going to affect my
'and. Is that what you're frightened of? Why, I could
shave a gentleman if they was dropping bombs over
St. James's Palace and Jermyn Street was burning like
a load of straw.

Bolton: I don't mind telling you I'm not a gentleman who'd
be wanting a shave just at that moment.

Bradley: I'll finish Mr. Bolton myself. Give me your
razor.

Bolton: [*Passing his hand over his chin.*] No, that's all right.
That'll do.

> [Bradley *sponges and wipes his face.*

Albert: There's a wire for you from Dublin, and they've
rung up your house from the *Daily Echo.* They wanted
your business address.

Bradley: You haven't lost the ticket, Sheppey?

Sheppey: Not me. I've got it on me now. [*He takes out his
pocket book and produces the ticket.*]

Miss Grange: How much is it, Mr. Bradley?

Albert: Mrs. Miller didn't say. She was all excited. Crying
and laughing she was. The consolation prizes are a
hundred pounds.

Bolton: Well, even that's worth having.

Sheppey: I can do with it.

Miss Grange: You don't seem a bit excited, Sheppey.

Sheppey: Well, to tell you the truth I've been sort of
expecting it. I was born lucky.

Miss Grange: If it was me I'd be doing Catherine-wheels
all over the shop.

Sheppey: I don't believe Mr. Bradley would like that, Miss

Grange. Besides, it might put ideas in Albert's 'ead.
'Im not being a married man and all that.

MISS GRANGE: Oh, don't be so coarse, Sheppey. You know
I don't like that sort of joke.

[MR. BOLTON, *now ready, gets up from his chair*.

BOLTON: You'd better ring up the *Echo* and ask how much
it is.

BRADLEY: A hundred pounds.

BOLTON: What about the ten residuary prizes? How do you
know it's not one of them?

SHEPPEY: I never thought of that.

BRADLEY: Couldn't be.

ALBERT: There'll be a special edition. Perhaps it's out
by now.

BRADLEY: You nip along round the corner, Albert, and see
if it is.

ALBERT: All right, sir.

[*He goes out*.

BOLTON: [*Giving* SHEPPEY *a tip*.] Here you are, Sheppey,
and my best congratulations.

SHEPPEY: Thank you very much, sir.

BOLTON: Whatever it is don't blue it.

SHEPPEY: Not me, sir. I've made up my mind exactly what
I'm going to do with it.

MISS GRANGE: How can you when you don't know how
much it is yet? I mean, supposing it *is* one of the
residuary prizes? [*Pocketing* BOLTON's *tip*.] Thank
you, sir.

SHEPPEY: Anything up to thirty thousand pounds I've got
all fixed up.

BOLTON: I'll tell you what I'll do, Sheppey: to celebrate the
occasion I'll have a bottle of that German stuff you were
talking about.

SHEPPEY: Very good, sir. Shall I send it or will you take it with you?

BOLTON: Mind you, I don't believe in it, but to oblige you I'll try it.

SHEPPEY: Well, sir, I'm sure you'll be surprised.

BOLTON: I may just as well take it with me.

SHEPPEY: A bottle of Grayline for Mr. Bolton, please Mr. Bradley.

BRADLEY: I'll just do it up for you, sir. Cash, please.

BOLTON: Good-night.

THE OTHERS: Good-night, sir.

> [MISS JAMES *steps out and* BOLTON *follows.* BRADLEY *has held open the curtain for him and goes out after him.*

MISS GRANGE: You are a caution, Sheppey.

SHEPPEY: I know I am. I don't believe there's another man in the business could 'ave sold Mr. Bolton a bottle of 'air-dye. They can say what they like, that's all it is. If it's anything at all, that's to say.

MISS GRANGE: Oh, I wasn't thinking of that.

SHEPPEY: You wasn't? But it was a masterpiece the way I kidded him. 'E put me on my mettle, saying I'd never sell 'im anything not if I tried till doomsday. 'E's no fool either. Not like some of these young fellows as'll believe anything you tell them. You know, I was listening meself to what I was saying and I said to meself, you're a wonder, Sheppey, there's no doubt about it, you're a little wonder.

MISS GRANGE: Oh, you make me sick, Sheppey, patting yourself on the back because you sell a mug a bottle of hair restorer, when you've just won a prize in the Irish Sweep.

SHEPPEY: [*Taking off his long white working coat.*] Well, I'll tell you, Miss Grange, seeing's believing. I don't ever believe anything till I see it in the papers.

MISS GRANGE: There's Albert.

[ALBERT *comes in.*

ALBERT: The papers 'aven't come yet.

MISS GRANGE: Oh, bother.

BRADLEY: [*Coming in.*] I've told Miss James to try and get the *Echo*. It's just on seven. Draw the blind down, Albert.

ALBERT: Right you are, sir.

BRADLEY: I expect you'll be glad to be getting along home, Sheppey.

MISS GRANGE: Mrs. Miller and your daughter will be in a state.

[*The bell rings as the door opens.*

BRADLEY: Hulloa, who's that?

MISS GRANGE: My word, people think they can come at any old time.

BRADLEY: Oh, that's all right. Albert 'll say we're closed.

[ALBERT *re-enters.*

ALBERT: [*In a whisper.*] It's a fellow from the *Echo*. Wants to see Sheppey.

MISS GRANGE: [*Overwhelmed.*] No?

BRADLEY: Tell him to come along.

MISS GRANGE: Gracious! And me all anyhow.

[*She takes out her powder and begins to make up.*

SHEPPEY: Where do you come in?

MISS GRANGE: I don't want to disgrace the shop.

ALBERT: [*Through the curtains.*] Step this way, sir.

[*A young pasty-faced man with a camera enters.*

REPORTER: Mr. Miller?

SHEPPEY: That's my name. Sheppey for short.

REPORTER: [*Shaking hands with him.*] Best congratulations.

SHEPPEY: Don't mention it.

REPORTER: Paper sent me along to get a brief interview.

SHEPPEY: You've just come in time. Another five minutes and you'd have found us all gone.

REPORTER: Feeling pretty good, I suppose?

SHEPPEY: Not so bad.

REPORTER: Ever won anything before?

SHEPPEY: Never.

REPORTER: I suppose you've had tickets?

SHEPPEY: Never missed since they started.

REPORTER: Well, you don't mind if I say it's the first time you ever had one. I mean, it makes a better story.

SHEPPEY: No, I don't object to that.

BRADLEY: We were just trying to get on to your paper when you came in.

REPORTER: Oh, what about?

MISS GRANGE: It's one of the hundred-pound prizes, I suppose?

REPORTER: D'you mean to say you didn't know? It's one of the residuary prizes. Eight thousand five hundred pounds.

SHEPPEY: Is that what it is? That's real money that is.
> [MISS JAMES, *who has followed the reporter in, suddenly bursts into tears.*

BRADLEY: Hulloa, what's the matter with you, Miss James?

MISS JAMES: [*Sobbing.*] I do apologise. I can't help it. Eight thousand five hundred pounds. It makes me feel quite sick.

MISS GRANGE: If you're going to be sick you'd better go to the lavatory, I think.

MISS JAMES: Oh, it's all right. Excitement always takes me like that.

SHEPPEY: It's 'er stomach, poor girl.

REPORTER: What'll you do with the money? I suppose you've hardly had time to decide yet.

SHEPPEY: What makes you think a silly thing like that? I decided that when I bought the ticket. I'm going to pay off the rest of the money on my 'ouse. And there's a little place on the Isle of Sheppey I've got my eye on, two acres of land and just the sort of dinky little 'ouse I've always thought would suit me.

MISS GRANGE: Fancy you a landed proprietor, Sheppey. We shall have to call you squire.

SHEPPEY: Then there's my daughter wants to get married. I'll give her a slap-up wedding. Champagne and caviare. And I'll keep a girl to 'elp my wife. No more rough work for that old lady.

ALBERT: I'd buy a baby Austin if I was in your place.

SHEPPEY: And who says I won't buy a baby Austin? It would save me a lot of expense getting down to my property in the country.

REPORTER: You won't go on working, then?

SHEPPEY: Me? I wouldn't know what to do with myself if I stopped working. I'm what you might call an artist. Isn't that right, Governor?

BRADLEY: I wouldn't swear you weren't, not in a court of law.

SHEPPEY: No, young fellow, I'm not one to waste the gifts the Almighty has given me.

REPORTER: What about a photograph of you at work? I think the paper'd like that. Pity it's so late and no customers.

MISS GRANGE: Mr. Bradley can pretend he's a customer.

BRADLEY: That's right. Give me a gown, Albert.

ALBERT: Here you are, Governor.

P

BRADLEY: You put on your coat, Sheppey.

SHEPPEY: Half a tick. Shave or hair-cut?

REPORTER: Shave, I think. Looks more natural.

BRADLEY: I'll just put a bit of lather on my face.

MISS GRANGE: I'll get my stool and pretend I'm doing your nails.

SHEPPEY: 'Ere, who's being photographed, Miss Grange, you or me?

MISS GRANGE: Don't be a dog in the manger, Sheppey. I only want it to make a good picture.

SHEPPEY: You might be one of them Society beauties shoving yourself in like that. Albert 'll be wanting to come in next.

REPORTER: She's all right. I like that.

> [*They all get into attitudes. The* REPORTER *looks through his camera.*

BRADLEY: Don't stand like that, Sheppey. They won't see anything but my legs.

SHEPPEY: They want to see my face, don't they?

REPORTER: Get on the other side of him.

SHEPPEY: You won't be able to see me.

REPORTER: Yes, I shall. That's a good position. Let me see the razor.

BRADLEY: Not too near my face, Sheppey.

REPORTER: Hold it right out.

> [SHEPPEY *stretches out his arm.*

REPORTER: That's right. Fine.

BRADLEY: [*Noticing that* ALBERT *has edged in.*] What are you doing there, Albert? You get the hell out of there, see?

SHEPPEY: You don't want to break the camera, do you?

ALBERT: [*Sulkily.*] All right. One'd think you'd never been photoed before. Fuss you make of it.

REPORTER: Now look at me. Pleasant, now. This isn't a funeral. He's just won a prize in the Irish Sweep. Smile. That's right. Hold it. Thank you.

> [*They put on frozen smiles and when he says thank you return to their natural state.* BRADLEY *wipes the soap off his face and gets out of the chair.* MISS GRANGE *gathers up her stool and her box of utensils.*

MISS GRANGE: Will it be in the paper to-morrow?

REPORTER: It should be.

MISS GRANGE: I shall be excited.

SHEPPEY: It'll be in the papers to-night, won't it? I mean about the draw, the names and all that?

REPORTER: Yes. Haven't you seen a paper yet? I've got one on me. For the address, you know.

SHEPPEY: Mind letting me 'ave a squint? You know, I've never seen my name in print before. Fact is, I can't quite believe it's all true till I see it in black and white.

REPORTER: [*Taking the newspaper out of his pocket.*] Here you are. Front page.

> [SHEPPEY *takes the paper and looks at it.*

SHEPPEY: That's right. Eight thousand five hundred pounds. Isle of Sheppey. That's my synonym. Joseph Miller, The Rosary, Moore Street, Camberwell, S.E. 17. Well, well, well, who'd 'ave thought it. [*Without thinking he takes off his wig and discloses a very bald head. He meditatively scratches it.*]

REPORTER: [*Taken aback.*] Is that a wig you're wearing?

SHEPPEY: [*Coming down to earth.*] Me? Yes. I 'ave to in working hours. Customers are that funny. If you try and sell them a 'air tonic and you're bald like I am, they say it don't seem to 'ave done you much good.

REPORTER: It gave me quite a turn to see you take it off all of a sudden.

SHEPPEY: 'Ere, you're not going to say anything about it in the paper?

REPORTER: [*With a smile.*] That's asking something.

SHEPPEY: You wouldn't do that. I mean, you and me are in the same trade, so to speak. I mean, we 'ave to kid the public a bit, don't we? And you know what the public is, it wants to be kidded.

REPORTER: [*Good-naturedly.*] All right. I'll forget about it. Thank you very much. Good evening.

BRADLEY: Good evening, sir. Give us a look in when you want a hair-cut. Sheppey 'll attend to you himself.

SHEPPEY: I will with pleasure.

REPORTER: But I tell you what, you'll never sell me a hair-restorer.

SHEPPEY: I wouldn't be too sure, sir.

REPORTER: Good night.

ALL: Good night, sir.

> [*He goes out.* ALBERT *accompanies him to the door and soon after comes back.*

MISS GRANGE: Well, that's what I call luck.

SHEPPEY: Yes, I'll admit that.

MISS JAMES: And you so calm about it all. That's what I can't get over.

SHEPPEY: Well, I'm used to it, as you might say. I been lucky all my life.

BRADLEY: I wish I knew how it was done.

SHEPPEY: I'll tell you. You must believe in it. When I was a young fellow I was a rare one for the girls. And d'you know how I used to get 'em? Bounce. It's the same with luck, you've got to bounce it.

MISS GRANGE: [*With a toss of her head.*] I like that. No one will get me with bounce. The fellow who gets me has

got to have a good situation and a bit put by in the
savings bank.

MISS JAMES: Men are not what they were. There's no
denying that.

SHEPPEY: That's your poor stomach again, Miss James.

BRADLEY: Well, I'll be getting off. *Tempus fugit*, as they
say.

SHEPPEY: 'Alf a mo, governor. You must all drink my
'ealth first. I tell you what, I'll pop over to the Bunch
of Keys and get a bottle of champagne.

MISS GRANGE: Oh, Sheppey, if there's anything I like it's
a glass of fizz.

SHEPPEY: I shan't be a minute.

[*He hurries out.*

MISS GRANGE: It's funny when you think about it; I'm
almost as excited as if I'd won something myself.

BRADLEY: That shows you have a nice nature, Miss Grange.

MISS GRANGE: One has to have a nice nature in this business
or you couldn't listen to the silly things gentlemen say
to one all day long.

ALBERT: I never pay any attention. It just goes in at one
ear and out at the other with me.

MISS GRANGE: It's easy for you. Gentlemen expect a manicurist to be bright and snappy. And you've got to
laugh at their silly jokes or else they say you've got no
sense of humour.

BRADLEY: That's all part of the job.

MISS GRANGE: I know it is. I'm not complaining. And of
course you get a dinner and a theatre out of it now and
again.

ALBERT: To say nothing of a kiss and cuddle in the taxi
on the way home.

MISS JAMES: You are vulgar, Albert.

MISS GRANGE: Well, if a girl won't give a gentleman a kiss in return for dinner and a theatre more fool her, I say. I mean she must know when to stop, of course. But if you're a lady you can always keep a gentleman in his place.

ALBERT: I suppose they take you to the stalls, don't they?

MISS GRANGE: Well, it all depends. If they're bachelors, yes. But if they're married it's generally dress circles. They don't think it's so conspicuous.

BRADLEY: Of course we have a lot of tip-top swells coming to this establishment and naturally they have to be careful.

MISS GRANGE: Oh, I'm not blaming them. If they mention it, I always say I quaite understand. *Noblesse oblige*, if you know what I mean.

> [*The whole staff is gathered in the shop when* SHEPPEY *comes in with a bottle of champagne in his hand. He is accompanied by a pretty, painted woman, no longer very young, and flashily dressed in rather shabby clothes. This is* BESSIE LEGROS.

SHEPPEY: Here I am and here's the champagne. I got the best. Fourteen and nine.

ALBERT: Whew! It ought to be good at the price.

BRADLEY: Who's the lady, Sheppey?

SHEPPEY: A friend of mine. Well, not exactly a friend, but I know 'er, see? I always go in to the Bunch of Keys to 'ave my beer when I shut up of a evening and she's generally 'aving one at the same time.

BRADLEY: [*With a nod to* BESSIE.] Pleased to meet you.

BESSIE: The pleasure's mine.

SHEPPEY: So we got talking like. And so when I saw 'er just now, I said to 'er, no beer for you to-day, miss. You come along with me and 'ave a glass of fizz.

BESSIE: I didn't say yes and I didn't say no. You know the song, don't you?

BRADLEY: But you came along, I see.

BESSIE: I didn't want to, not really. I said to Mr. Miller, Oh, they won't want me, I shall only be in the way. But he said, Get along with you, it's months since you tasted fizz, I lay. And he was right there.

BRADLEY: Well, you're welcome as far as I'm concerned, and it's Sheppey that's standing the champagne.

ALBERT: Better let me open it, Sheppey. I'm more used to it than you are.

SHEPPEY: 'Ark at 'im. All right, only be careful. Now then, you girls, what about glasses?

MISS JAMES: We can manage.

MISS GRANGE: There's a glass in the lavatory, Victor.

> [VICTOR *goes out and comes in again in a moment with a glass.* MISS JAMES *goes round the shop and collects whatever there is that can be used to drink out of.*

BESSIE: [*To* BRADLEY.] You have got a beautiful place here.

BRADLEY: You have to have these days. Lots of competition, you know.

BESSIE: It's the same in everything. There ought to be a law against it, I think.

BRADLEY: You'd be surprised the amount of stuff we have to carry. You come and have a look at my show-cases.

> [*They walk into the front shop.*

MISS GRANGE: Come over here a minute, Sheppey. I want to say something to you.

SHEPPEY: [*Going over to her.*] What is it?

MISS GRANGE: She's a tart.

SHEPPEY: I know that.

MISS GRANGE: You didn't ought to have brought her in here, Sheppey.

SHEPPEY: Why?

MISS GRANGE: You ought to have more respect for me and Miss James.

SHEPPEY: Now look 'ere, my dear, you may be in the ladies' 'air-dressing yourself one day. If you think a ladies' salon can get along without tarts you're crazy.

MISS GRANGE: I don't say I've got any objection to them in business; it's meeting them socially I object to.

SHEPPEY: Oh, be a sport, Miss Grange. After all one doesn't win eight thousand five 'undred pounds in a sweep every day of one's life. To oblige me.

MISS GRANGE: Well, as long as you know, I don't mind so much. And they do say, to the pure all things are pure.

> [*By this time* ALBERT *has opened the bottle, and* BRADLEY *and* BESSIE *stroll in again.*]

ALBERT: Come on, all of you. First come first served.

> [*They gather round and take the tumblers he fills.*]

BRADLEY: Well, Sheppey, here's your very good health. If I couldn't win a prize myself there's no one I'd rather see win it than you.

ALBERT: And so say all of us.

ALL: [*Chanting.*] And so say all of us. For he's a jolly good fellow. For he's a jolly good fellow.

SHEPPEY: I'm very much obliged to you, ladies and gentlemen. This spontaneous effusion of good will has touched me to the bottom of me 'eart. Ladies and gentlemen, I drink your very good 'ealth.

MISS GRANGE: I must say, I like a glass of champagne.

BESSIE: It's class. That's what it is.

MISS GRANGE: Mind you, I wouldn't want it every day.

BESSIE: Oh, no, I mean if you drunk it every day it wouldn't be a treat, would it?

ALBERT: A1, Sheppey. Reminds me of the fizz we 'ad at my sister's wedding.

SHEPPEY: It ought to be good for the money. They 'ad some at twelve and six, but I said, No, on a day like this I want the best.

BRADLEY: Now, Sheppey, just because you've won a nice bit of money, don't you go wasting it on a lot of foolishness.

SHEPPEY: Not me. I've got me 'ead screwed on me shoulders all right.

BRADLEY: I'm very glad to hear you say it. Now I must be getting along home or my wife'll think I'm up to some hanky-panky. You'll shut up all right, Sheppey, won't you?

SHEPPEY: You can trust me.

ALBERT: I'll be going too. I'm taking my young lady to the pictures.

    [*He and* VICTOR *go out to take off their white coats*.

MISS GRANGE: Are you coming, Miss James?

MISS JAMES: I'm quite ready.

BRADLEY: Good night, all. See you to-morrow.

ALL: Good night, sir.

                    [BRADLEY *goes out*.

MISS GRANGE: Are you going anywhere to-night, dear?

MISS JAMES: No, I'm going to run up that *crêpe de Chine* I bought yesterday.

           [MISS GRANGE *and* MISS JAMES *go out*.

BESSIE: I'll be getting along too.

SHEPPEY: Don't you hurry. Here, there's a drop more in the bottle. Pity to waste it.

BESSIE: I won't say no.

> [ALBERT *and* VICTOR *come through.*

ALBERT: Good night.

SHEPPEY: Good night.

BESSIE: Hope you have a nice time with your young lady.

ALBERT: Trust me.

> [ALBERT *and* VICTOR *go out as* MISS JAMES *and* MISS
> GRANGE *come in with their hats on.*

SHEPPEY: You ain't been long.

MISS GRANGE: I haven't got too much time. It's partnership evening at my bridge club and I don't want to keep them waiting.

SHEPPEY: Well, good night.

MISS GRANGE: Night, Sheppey. [*She gives* BESSIE *a stiff bow.*] Good naight.

BESSIE: Good night, miss.

> [*The two girls go out.*

SHEPPEY: I'll just put the catch on the door.

> [*He goes out. When* BESSIE *is left alone she crumples
> up wearily on her chair. Her face is screwed up into
> a grimace and a sob is wrung from her. She clenches
> her hands in the effort to control herself, but the tears
> come and she takes her handkerchief out of her bag.*
> SHEPPEY *returns.*

SHEPPEY: 'Ulloa, what are you crying for?

BESSIE: I'm not crying. It's only tears running out of me eyes.

SHEPPEY: What's the trouble?

BESSIE: Nothing. Only it's cosy here. And you all being so friendly. I shall be all right in a minute.

SHEPPEY: Here, drink your champagne.

BESSIE: No, I daren't. Not on an empty stomach. I expect that's what upset me.

SHEPPEY: Didn't you have no tea?

BESSIE: No, nor dinner either. I'm banting.

SHEPPEY: Well, that's a silly thing to do.

BESSIE: Not if you've got no money. I only had tenpence. I spent threepence on my bus up west and I must keep threepence for me bus home if I don't click to-night. And I was going to spend the other fourpence on a beer when you come in.

SHEPPEY: Well, I saved you that anyway.

BESSIE: I felt I just couldn't walk up and down and round and round for hours if I didn't have my beer.

SHEPPEY: You must be pretty peckish, aren't you?

BESSIE: Oh, I don't mind that. I'm getting used to it by now. It's me room I'm worrying about. I'm three weeks behind with me rent and if I don't get a job to-night she'll turn me out.

SHEPPEY: Oh, I say.

BESSIE: Oh, well, the night's young yet. Never say die, that's my motto. It's fine and dry, that's something. It's when it's wet I don't like it.

SHEPPEY: It ain't exactly my idea of a life of pleasure, I must say.

BESSIE: Pleasure? Believe me or not, it's no pleasure to me.

SHEPPEY: What'll you do if you're turned out of your room?

BESSIE: I don't know. Salvation Army Shelter. But you have to sing hymns there. If it don't rain you're better off on the Embankment, they tell me, and the river's nice and close if you happen to feel like jumping in.

SHEPPEY: Ain't you got any family?

BESSIE: Not in London. And then they think I'm doing well. I wouldn't humiliate myself by going to them.

SHEPPEY: I don't want to hurt your feelings, and of course

I never mentioned it when we 'ad our little chats at
the Bunch of Keys, but you've always seemed a very
respectable woman to me, it surprised me that you was,
well, as you might say, on the streets.

BESSIE: And well you might be. It's a rare come-down for
me, I can tell you. If you'd told me eighteen months
ago I'd come to this, I'd have said, Why, you're
dreaming.

SHEPPEY: I knew I was right. The very first time we 'ad a
talk, afterwards I said to meself, That's a superior class
of woman. I mean, you're not silly. You can talk
sensibly. The dogs and football and politics.

BESSIE: I'm no fool. I know that.

SHEPPEY: Seems funny you should be doing this, if you
understand what I mean.

BESSIE: It's the slump done it. I was all right before that
come. I had a nice little flat in Kennington. And I had
three or four gentlemen used to visit me regular.
Respectable tradesmen, you know, with wives and
families, one was a J.P., nice class of men. I used to
make my seven or eight pounds a week. And they liked
me because they knew they could trust me. If you're
a married man and in a good position, you have to be
careful, don't you?

SHEPPEY: Yes, I suppose so. Speaking for meself, from
the day I married me wife I've never looked this way or
that way.

BESSIE: I don't blame you. But you don't find many like
that. My experience is, most men want a little bit of
fun now and again and somehow they don't want to
have it with their wives.

SHEPPEY: Well, what 'appened then?

BESSIE: I had a bit of bad luck. I got double pneumonia
and I had to go away for a bit. And when I come back

one of my gentlemen had been sold up and another said
he couldn't afford luxuries any more. I dare say I wasn't
as good-looking as I had been. Well, to cut a long story
short, things just went from bad to worse, and the end
of it was I had to put me pride in me pocket and come
up west.

SHEPPEY: I say, what's your name? You never told me.

BESSIE: Bessie Legros.

SHEPPEY: Oh, French.

BESSIE: Not really. But gentlemen think it is and when they
ask me me name and I tell them Bessie Legros, they get
all excited. Paris and all that. That's why I took the
name. When I had my little flat in Kennington I used
to call myself Mrs. Gloucester, because my first situation
when I come to London was in Gloucester Place. Very
nice lady, she was, not like some I could name, and I
thought I owed her something.

SHEPPEY: Sort of compliment you paid her, as you might
say.

BESSIE: [*Getting up.*] Well, I must be getting on the job if I
want to earn my rent. No rest for the weary. My God,
what a life.

SHEPPEY: It's slavery, that's what it is.

BESSIE: So's domestic service for the matter of that. And
in my business, well, it is a bit of a gamble, you know.

SHEPPEY: That 'elps, of course.

BESSIE: You may click and you may not. And that keeps
you going.

SHEPPEY: Look 'ere. I don't 'alf like the idea of you walking
about on an empty stomach. It can't be good for you.
'Ere's five bob. You can get a good meal on that and
there'll be something over in case you want it. [*He takes
two half-crowns out of his pocket and gives them to her.*]

BESSIE: I scarcely like to take it.

SHEPPEY: Why not?

BESSIE: Well, from a friend. I mean, it's not like as if it was from a gentleman. I'll pay it back as soon as ever I can. I promise you. I always have paid my way and except the rent I've never owed sixpence to nobody.

SHEPPEY: D'you know what I recommend? A nice bit of steak with a baked potato.

BESSIE: I'll have that, Mr. Miller, and thank you for the idea.

SHEPPEY: I'll come out with you. I expect my old woman's terribly excited. Crying and laughing, they said she was. Good old Ada. [*He gets up. He puts his hand to his forehead.*] Oh, my 'ead. I do feel funny.

BESSIE: Aren't you well, Mr. Miller? Sit down, do.

SHEPPEY: All muzzy.

> [*He sinks down on the chair and immediately falls over on the ground.*

BESSIE: My God! [*She sinks down on her knees beside him and shakes him.*] Mr. Miller. Mr. Miller. Sheppey. Pull yourself together. Don't be silly. Oh, my God, I believe he's fainted. Sheppey. Come on now. Wake up. Oh dear! Oh dear!

SHEPPEY: [*Coming to.*] I'm choking.

BESSIE: Half a mo'. I'll loosen your collar. My word, it is tight. The things men wear.

SHEPPEY: Where am I?

BESSIE: My God, you did give me a turn. I thought you was dead and I'd be had up for murder. How are you feeling?

SHEPPEY: Like a bit of fish that's gone wonky.

BESSIE: Well, lie still a minute.

SHEPPEY: I must have fainted. Thing I never done in my life before.

BESSIE: Looked more like a fit to me.

SHEPPEY: Never been fits in my family.

BESSIE: I expect it was the champagne.

SHEPPEY: Fourteen and nine a bottle. Couldn't 've been that. You saw me pay for it yourself.

BESSIE: You not being used to it and all.

SHEPPEY: I'm feeling better now. I'll just 'ave a set down for a minute.

BESSIE: I'll help you.

[*He gets up on his feet and sits down again in the chair.*

SHEPPEY: I'll be all right in two shakes now. Don't you bother about me. I can look after meself.

BESSIE: How are you going to get home?

SHEPPEY: Bus from Piccadilly Circus.

BESSIE: You're not fit to go by bus. You ought to take a taxi.

SHEPPEY: My old woman 'll think me off me nut if she sees me driving up in a taxi.

BESSIE: Well, a taxi you'll take, my boy. I don't think you're fit to go alone either. Like me to come with you?

SHEPPEY: I shall be all right. I don't want you to neglect your work for my sake.

BESSIE: Oh, that's all right. Trade's slack at this sort of time anyhow. I shall get back before things get busy.

SHEPPEY: Well, I don't mind telling you I do feel a bit queer.

BESSIE: The sooner you get home the better. Where's your hat?

SHEPPEY: Through that door, and me coat's with it. [*She goes out and comes in again immediately with his hat and coat.*] That's very good of you, I'm sure.

BESSIE: I'll just help you on. [*She helps him on with his coat.*] What about shutting up?

SHEPPEY: Only got to slam the gate behind us. There's the lights.

BESSIE: I'll put them out. [*They go to the door,* SHEPPEY *leaning on her arm.*] Feeling all right?

SHEPPEY: Feeling fine. All light inside. And 'appy.

BESSIE: That's a good thing. There ain't too much happiness in the world, I always say.

SHEPPEY: I'd like everybody to be happy.

BESSIE: Well, they can't be. There ain't enough happiness to go round.

SHEPPEY: [*Pointing.*] There are the switches.

BESSIE: Which do I turn? All of them?

SHEPPEY: That's right.

> [*As he says this she switches off the lights and they disappear through the curtains into the front shop.*

END OF ACT ONE

ACT TWO

The Scene represents the living room of SHEPPEY'S *house at Camberwell. It is furnished with a suite in fumed oak bought many years ago on the hire-purchase system. There is a shabby old cottage piano with yellow keys and a large grandfather's chair covered with faded twill. On an over-mantel above the fireplace are china ornaments. In the place of honour in the middle of the mantelshelf is an old silver-gilt snuff-box. The curtains are of plush. The walls are decorated with hand-painted plates, photogravures in gilt frames and enlarged photographs of family groups. It is stuffy and over-crowded.*

It is latish on Saturday afternoon. Just over a week has passed since the events shown in the preceding act.

MRS. MILLER *is sitting on a chair, darning socks, and her daughter* FLORRIE *is at the dining-table, studying a French grammar and writing an exercise.*

MRS. MILLER *is a stout, middle-aged woman, with a good-natured, homely face. She has kind eyes and a pleasant smile. She is neat enough in her person, but she has been married too long to bother much how she looks.* FLORRIE *is rather smart. She wears a frock bought at the sales, artificial silk stockings and very high-heeled shoes. Her short hair is permanently waved. She is pretty, alert and self-assured. She has been a typist in the city, and is confident that there is little worth knowing that she doesn't know.*

MRS. MILLER: I shall 'ave to be thinking about getting supper on the way soon.

FLORRIE: Oh, mum, how can I be expected to work if you keep on talking?

MRS. MILLER: Sorry. It's a bit of a change 'aving you 'ome on a Saturday afternoon.

FLORRIE: Ernie had to umpire. The first eleven are playing Cricklewood.

MRS. MILLER: Teaching in the Council School all the week, it seems a shame 'e shouldn't 'ave 'is Saturday afternoons.

FLORRIE: Oh, dry up, mother.

MRS. MILLER: Sorry. You'll strain your eyes reading too much.

FLORRIE: I'm not reading. I'm writing. Don't say anything to Ernie.

MRS. MILLER: How can I? I don't know what you're writing any more than the man in the moon.

FLORRIE: Exercises. I'm learning French. Only it's a secret.

MRS. MILLER: Whatever are you learning French for, Florrie? I don't believe any good can come of that.

FLORRIE: Now Dad's got this money, me and Ernie have made up our minds to spend our honeymoon in Paris.

MRS. MILLER: Oh, 'ave you? Well, it remains to be seen what your Dad and me 'ave got to say to that. Paris, indeed. A nice place for a young married couple to go to.

FLORRIE: [*With a grin.*] You mean it's a nice place for a young unmarried couple to go to.

MRS. MILLER: Don't be common, Florrie. You know I can't abide anything common.

FLORRIE: You're so old-fashioned, mum. Why, it's an education to go to Paris. You know how keen Ernie is on culture.

MRS. MILLER: I know he's an educated man. I mean, he wouldn't 'ave got a job as master in one of the County Council schools if he wasn't.

FLORRIE: You see, I want to surprise him. You look such
a fool if you can't say a word. I can see his face when
I start jabbering away at parlez-vous français, garçong,
apportez moi une café-au-lait, a quelle heure parti le
traing, oui, oui.

MRS. MILLER: Wonders will never cease.

FLORRIE: I've got a gift for languages. I know that. D'you
remember the gipsy last summer on the pier? That's
one of the things she said, that I had a gift for languages.

MRS. MILLER: I wasn't thinking of that. What amuses me
is, you was always going to the pictures and flattening
your nose against the shop windows, thinking of nothing
but dress, and now you read Ernie's books and you're
studying French and I don't know what all.

FLORRIE: Well, it's natural, isn't it? I don't want Ernie to
think I'm just an ignoramus.

MRS. MILLER: A what?

FLORRIE: An ignoramus. He says he knows I've got a good
brain, but I haven't had the chance to develop it that
he has; he says he's quite ready to make allowances.

MRS. MILLER: That's very kind of 'im, to be sure. I think
a young fellow's very lucky if 'e can find a girl as can
make her own clothes and cook his dinner for him and
not spend more money than 'e gives 'er. I know it was
in my time.

FLORRIE: Oh, well, things are different now. Now a girl's
got to be educated same as a fellow. Education's everything. I mean, it's only by having education that we
can make the world what it ought to be.

MRS. MILLER: Who's going to do that? You and Ernie?

FLORRIE: You see, I know Ernie looks upon it as a bit of
a come-down marrying me. Of course he hasn't said
so, but I know he feels it, Dad being only a hairdresser and
not even having a saloon of his own. Being an employee.

Mrs. Miller: Your Dad earns better money than many as are their own masters and 'e 'asn't got the responsibility.

Florrie: It's not the money, it's the position. Ernie's father was a clerk in the City. Quite a gentleman by all accounts and naturally that means a lot to Ernie. Mum, you won't ever let on that before you married Dad you were in service, will you?

Mrs. Miller: I'm not ashamed of it. If Ernie thinks I learnt to make them meat pies he likes so much without being a professional cook he's a bigger fool than I take 'im for.

Florrie: He never notices what he's eating. I mean, he knows it's good, but his mind is busy with his thoughts. What you don't understand is that Ernie's got a wonderful brain.

Mrs. Miller: [*With a fond smile.*] Perhaps not. But what I do understand is that you're more in love with 'im than I ever thought to see you with anybody.

Florrie: [*Charmingly.*] I know, mum, I can't help it, I'm just silly about him.

Mrs. Miller: I don't blame you, my girl. It only comes once in a lifetime, love like that. I daresay 'e's all right. You love 'im all you can. You've been a good daughter to me and a good daughter to your Dad. I 'ope you'll be as 'appy together as your Dad and me 'ave been and I can't say more than that.

Florrie: Dear old mum.

> [*There is a knock at the front door.*

Mrs. Miller: There's Ernie, I expect.

Florrie: [*Getting up and going to the window.*] No, it isn't. I'd know his knock in a thousand. It's more masterful than that. [*Looking out.*] It's a gentleman. He's come in a car.

MRS. MILLER: Go and see who it is.

FLORRIE: All right.

> [*She goes out.* MRS. MILLER *goes to the window and looks out.* FLORRIE *comes in again.*

FLORRIE: It's Mr. Bradley, mum. He's asking for Dad. Seems quite surprised he's out.

MRS. MILLER: Ask 'im to come in.

> [FLORRIE *goes to the door and opens it and speaks.*

FLORRIE: Will you come in, sir?

> [BRADLEY *enters.*

BRADLEY: My name's Bradley. I just came to see how your husband was getting on, Mrs. Miller.

MRS. MILLER: Won't you sit down, sir?

BRADLEY: I don't mind if I do.

MRS. MILLER: He's out just at the minute.

BRADLEY: Seems to be out a lot.

MRS. MILLER: I 'ad the doctor to 'im and the doctor said 'e ought to stay in bed. I tried to make 'im, but would 'e listen to me? Seems as though 'e couldn't sit still. Out all day long.

BRADLEY: Where does he go?

MRS. MILLER: Well, that's just what I don't know. 'E 'ardly seems to know 'imself.

BRADLEY: If he's well enough to go gadding about all over the place, I should have thought he was well enough to do a job of work.

MRS. MILLER: The doctor wouldn't 'ear of 'im working. 'E's not 'imself. Friday, not yesterday, Friday a week ago, the day we 'eard about the Sweep 'e come 'ome in a taxi. 'E said 'e'd fainted in the shop.

BRADLEY: I know. He told me when he came on the Saturday morning.

MRS. MILLER: I didn't want 'im to go to work that morning.

But 'e would go. Said 'e 'ad an appointment with the Commander-in-Chief.

BRADLEY: [*With a smile.*] That's right. Captain Fortescue. Sheppey calls him that because of the side he puts on.

MRS. MILLER: Well, on the Saturday afternoon, after dinner, I could see 'e wasn't well and suddenly 'e came all over queer. 'E just fell like a stone. My word, I was frightened. Fortunately Florrie was 'ere.

BRADLEY: Your daughter, I suppose?

FLORRIE: That's right.

BRADLEY: Pleased to meet you.

MRS. MILLER: She phoned for the doctor. The doctor said it looked more like a stroke to 'im than a faint.

BRADLEY: Lucky he's not paralysed if that's the case.

MRS. MILLER: The doctor says the shock and the excitement of winning all that money and Sheppey 'aving such a 'igh blood pressure and all, 'e's convinced it wasn't just an ordinary faint in the shop, but that was a sort of stroke too.

BRADLEY: I don't wonder you're anxious. If he's had two strokes. They always say three's fatal.

MRS. MILLER: The doctor says not to worry. 'E's only got to get 'is blood pressure down and 'e'll be good for another twenty years.

BRADLEY: Doctors don't know everything.

MRS. MILLER: 'E's going back to work on Monday morning.

BRADLEY: Oh, is he? That's just what I wanted to see him about.

MRS. MILLER: It would break 'is 'eart if 'e couldn't go on working. He takes such a pride in his profession.

BRADLEY: [*With a shrewd look at her.*] He wrote me a letter last night.

MRS. MILLER: Did 'e? 'E never told me.

BRADLEY: He must have left it himself. It hadn't got a stamp on.

FLORRIE: What did he say?

BRADLEY: I don't know that I'm quite at liberty to divulge the contents. Perhaps I ought to have a talk to him about it first.

MRS. MILLER: 'E's bound to be in soon. 'E knows we're 'aving supper early because Florrie and the gentleman she's engaged to are going to the pictures.

BRADLEY: [*To* FLORRIE.] Oh, yes. Sheppey told me you were engaged to be married. And when is the happy event going to take place, may I ask?

FLORRIE: [*Becoming very refined.*] July. My fiancé's in the scholastic profession and of course we've got to wait till the boys break up for the summer holidays.

BRADLEY: Almost the first thing Sheppey said when he knew he'd won a prize was, now I shall be able to give my daughter a slap-up wedding.

FLORRIE: My fiancé's father was on the Stock Exchange, you know, and sometimes my fiancé says he wonders if he didn't make a mistake not going into the City, on account of the money, you know, but I say to him, money isn't everything, if you're in the scholastic profession you do have decent hols.

MRS. MILLER: [*To* BRADLEY.] 'Olidays, you know. Well, if it wasn't for the money your Dad's getting for the Sweep I don't know when you'd 'ave married. In them County Council schools the pay's terrible.

BRADLEY: Oh? Teacher in a board school, is he?

FLORRIE: Of course, if you're a professional man you don't expect to make the money you do in trade.

MRS. MILLER: How they expect a fellow to keep a wife and two or three children on it, I don't know, especially when you consider the position they have to keep up.

> [*There is a tat-tat-tat on the door.*

FLORRIE: There's Ernie.

> [*She bolts out of the room.*

BRADLEY: Bit of luck Sheppey winning all that money, Mrs. Miller.

MRS. MILLER: I know. Florrie was crazy to get married. She was in the City, you know, typewriting. She didn't take long to give in her notice, I can tell you.

BRADLEY: It'll make a difference to you too.

MRS. MILLER: I expect it will. I shan't be sorry to 'ave a girl to do the rough work for me. Funny thing, you know, I never 'ave liked washing-up, and God knows I've done enough of it. But when you've been in the 'ouses I 'ave, with always a kitchen-maid to do the rough work, it goes against the grain to do it yourself, and that nobody can deny.

> [FLORRIE *comes in with* ERNEST TURNER. *He is a very young man, twenty-two or twenty-three, and extremely good-looking in a somewhat romantic way, with long wavy hair, fine eyes and the profile of a film-star. He is dressed in grey flannel trousers and a brown tweed coat, loose, easy and shabby, because it is his pose not to pay any attention to the minor matter of clothes. He is alert, vibrant, as they say, and charming.*

ERNIE: Hulloa, Mrs. Miller.

MRS. MILLER: Come in, Ernie. This is Mr. Bradley, Dad's employer.

ERNIE: [*Shaking hands with him cordially.*] I'm very glad to meet you.

BRADLEY: Same here. I hear I've got to congratulate you on being engaged to this young lady.

ERNIE: We've been engaged for two years. What you can

congratulate me on is that I'm going to make a blushing
bride of her now.

BRADLEY: Send me an invite and I'll roll up with a wedding
present.

MRS. MILLER: Of course we'll send you an invite, Mr.
Bradley. It'll be an honour to 'ave you come.

BRADLEY: Well, Sheppey's been in my employment for
fifteen years and I look upon him as a friend. I really
do. You know we all call him Sheppey at the shop?

ERNIE: Yes, I know. I call him Sheppey too. Seems to
suit him somehow.

MRS. MILLER: I've got in the 'abit of it meself now.

BRADLEY: He's wonderfully popular with my customers.
Lot of them won't let anybody touch them but him, and
if he's busy they'll wait or come another day.

MRS. MILLER: I never asked you if you'd like a cup of tea,
Mr. Bradley.

BRADLEY: No, thank you. I wouldn't trouble you.

MRS. MILLER: It's no trouble. I've got to go into the
kitchen anyway to get my supper going.

FLORRIE: If you want to please mum you'll ask her to show
you the kitchen. She's as proud of that.

MRS. MILLER: Sheppey give me one of them new Eagle
stoves for my birthday. You wouldn't believe the
difference it makes.

BRADLEY: I know. He was talking about it in the shop. I
should like to see that, I must admit. If all I hear is
true, I've half a mind to buy one myself.

MRS. MILLER: I'll show it you with pleasure.

BRADLEY: [To FLORRIE.] You'll excuse me, won't you?
    [They go out. FLORRIE turns and faces ERNIE, smiling.

ERNIE: You've got a nerve, shooing him off like that.

FLORRIE: I saw at a glance that he was that sort of man, interested in contraptions.

ERNIE: Wonderful eye for character you've got.

> [*He goes up to her and leans his face forward. She leans hers forward too and gradually their lips meet. Then he takes her in his arms and a long kiss is exchanged. She breaks away with a sigh.*

FLORRIE: Oh! I feel all the better for that.

ERNIE: I don't think it's done me any harm either.

FLORRIE: Did you win your match?

ERNIE: What do you think? With me umpiring. As a matter of fact I had a few words with their umpire. But I wasn't going to let my boys be licked by any Cricklewood chaps. You can't blame me.

FLORRIE: I don't. You'd do anything for your boys, wouldn't you?

ERNIE: Well, I like them, I don't deny that, and they like me. They're getting up a subscription, a penny each, to give me a wedding present.

FLORRIE: That is nice of them.

ERNIE: It's voluntary, of course, but I shouldn't like to be in any boy's shoes who didn't subscribe. It's a grand thing, teaching. Getting a hold on all those young minds and training them. I mean, it must mean something to a man when he sees the way they look up to him.

FLORRIE: I should be very much surprised if they didn't look up to you.

ERNIE: That's as it may be, but it does give one a sort of sense of responsibility. After all, they're the citizens of the future. And what sort of citizens they'll be depends on me. You might almost say that what I think to-day Camberwell'll think to-morrow.

FLORRIE: It is a responsibility, I see that.

ERNIE: Kiss me.

[*They kiss again.*

FLORRIE: Oh, Ernie, I do love you so.

ERNIE: I'm not going to blame you for that.

FLORRIE: I wish you loved me as much as I love you.

ERNIE: I love you more than anyone in the world. I can't say more than that. But you mustn't forget that man's love is of man's life a thing apart; 'tis woman's whole existence.

FLORRIE: You're so ambitious.

ERNIE: Well, don't you want me to be?

FLORRIE: Yes. I won't stand in your way, Ernie. I know you want to get on.

ERNIE: There's no reason why I shouldn't, that I can see. I mean, think of the advantages I've got. And this money you'll have now. That'll make a difference. I don't see why I shouldn't stand for Parliament.

FLORRIE: Oh, Ernie, that would be lovely.

ERNIE: It's a chance in a lifetime. The old men are finished. Youth is the only thing that counts now. The world's in a mess and who's going to put it right? Youth. It's people like you and me who've got to get busy if we don't want to see civilisation crumbling under our feet. What the people want is a leader.

FLORRIE: You couldn't expect to be a leader right away, Ernie.

ERNIE: Perhaps not, but just as a matter of historical information I don't mind telling you that Pitt was Prime Minister at twenty-four. You wouldn't mind living in Downing Street, would you? Convenient, you know.

FLORRIE: Ernie.

ERNIE: Well, why not? Look at Snowden and Ramsay MacDonald. If they could do it, why can't I? With my brains and your beauty we can do anything.

FLORRIE: With the light behind you're not bad-looking yourself, Ernie.

ERNIE: Looks don't matter for a man. What a man wants is personality. That's one of the reasons I'd like to go to Paris for our honeymoon. One's got to develop one's personality.

FLORRIE: I was telling mum just now. She doesn't like the idea much. I think Dad's going to give us a hundred pounds, and I don't see why we shouldn't do what we like with it.

ERNIE: We could go to Switzerland on that.

FLORRIE: Oh, Ernie, I'd simply love to climb Mont Blanc.

ERNIE: I wouldn't mind myself. And Switzerland does seem the right place for a schoolmaster to go to in August. We'd meet lots of my colleagues.

FLORRIE: And then there's lovely Lucerne.

ERNIE: There's only one thing; it seems a bit thick doing all that on your money.

FLORRIE: That's silly. It won't be my money, it'll be our money.

ERNIE: Of course it's really an investment. It's not as if we were going just for pleasure. We're going to enlarge our minds. What can they know of England that only England know?

FLORRIE: That's right.

ERNIE: We've got to train ourselves so that when the opportunity comes we shall be ready to take it. We don't want to live for ourselves. We want to live for others. A life of service, that's what I look forward to.

FLORRIE: Well, I'll do all I can, Ernie.

ERNIE: I know you will. But look here, I think we ought to begin as we mean to go on. It's struck me, when we're in a big position, it'll sound silly you calling me Ernie and me calling you Florrie. I think we ought

to stop it before it gets so much of a habit we can't
break it.

FLORRIE: Whatever do you mean, Ernie?

ERNIE: Well, I think I ought to call you Florence and you
ought to call me Ernest.

FLORRIE: It would make me laugh.

ERNIE: Well, try. To oblige me. You couldn't call a Prime
Minister Ernie. People wouldn't have any respect
for him.

FLORRIE: All right. I don't mind trying. But not till after
the honeymoon. As long as we're on our honeymoon
I want you to be just Ernie.

ERNIE: Have it your own way.

FLORRIE: Oh, isn't life lovely?

ERNIE: Of course it's lovely. I'm an optimist, I am. I
mean, what's the good of taking a gloomy view of
things? I know the world isn't perfect. But you can't
have everything all at once. I believe in life and I
believe in my fellow-men. You must believe.

FLORRIE: Kiss me.

[*Just as he is about to kiss her* BRADLEY *comes in.*

BRADLEY: Your ma wants you a minute, Miss Florrie.

FLORRIE: Oh, does she? All right.

[*She goes out.*

BRADLEY: Well, aren't you going to say thank you?

ERNIE: What for?

BRADLEY: Leaving you alone with your young lady. I saw
you couldn't get rid of me fast enough. I've been a
young fellow myself, you know.

ERNIE: I see you've got tact.

BRADLEY: You want it in my business. A hairdresser that
hasn't got tact is no more use than a canary that can't
sing. I just wanted to have a word or two with you.

ERNIE: Fire away.

BRADLEY: I flatter myself I'm not a bad judge of character, and the moment I saw you I said to myself, that young fellow's got his head screwed on his shoulders all right.

ERNIE: I know how many beans make five, if that's what you mean.

BRADLEY: You'll never guess why I've come here to-day. Now Sheppey's got all this money it's all wrong that he should only be an assistant. [*Impressively.*] I've come here to-day to offer him a partnership in my business.

ERNIE: You haven't?

BRADLEY: I have. And mind you, it's a fine business. The accounts are in apple-pie order, and anyone can see them who wants to. I'll give him ten per cent on his money and a share of the profits.

ERNIE: That sounds pretty good to me.

BRADLEY: I expect he'll jump at it, but he's a funny fellow, Sheppey; he may not like the idea of the responsibility. I want you to back me up.

ERNIE: I certainly will. I don't think anyone can call me a snob, but there is a difference between having a father-in-law who's a hairdresser and a father-in-law who runs a high-class saloon in Jermyn Street.

BRADLEY: All the difference in the world. Then that's settled. But there's something else I wanted to say to you.

ERNIE: Yes?

BRADLEY: Sheppey was up in the West End last night. He left a letter at my place. There's a pub just opposite. The Bunch of Keys it's called. He always has his dinner there.

ERNIE: I know. A cut off the joint, veg. and half a pint of bitter. Every day of his life as regular as clockwork.

BRADLEY: And every night after shutting up he goes there
and has another half-pint. A creature of habit, that's
what he is. You can always depend on him. Well, I
just happened to hear that he was in there last night.

ERNIE: Nothing strange in that.

BRADLEY: No. Only he's got to know a tart there. He
brought her in to my place to have a drink the evening
he heard about the Sweep. Well, to cut a long story
short, he went off with her last night.

ERNIE: You don't mean to tell me that.

BRADLEY: Of course it's no business of mine. All I mean
to say is, if he's coming into partnership with me, he
can't go about with common tarts, can he? It would
be a pity if just because he's got a bit of money he went
off the rails.

ERNIE: You do surprise me. That's the last thing I should
ever have thought he'd do.

BRADLEY: You know what these women are.

ERNIE: He's so steady.

BRADLEY: I know he is. Mind you, I'm not accusing him.
I only say it looks fishy.

ERNIE: What do you expect me to do about it?

BRADLEY: I thought if you gave your young lady a hint—
girls know a lot nowadays—she'll understand, and if
she gave her ma a hint to keep an eye on him . . . A
good woman's influence can do a lot, and my experience
is, if a fellow's wife once gets suspicious he has to be
pretty smart to put anything over on her.

> [SHEPPEY *comes in. His cheeks are flushed and his eyes
> are shining, but otherwise he looks just as he did when
> we last saw him. Of course he does not wear the
> official wig of his business hours.*

SHEPPEY: Good evening, gentlemen.

BRADLEY: There you are.

SHEPPEY: Mrs. Miller told me you was 'ere, sir. Sorry I've kept you waiting.

BRADLEY: That's all right. I'm glad to see you looking so fit.

SHEPPEY: I'm fine. The doctor says I've made a wonderful recovery.

ERNIE: You'd better not let him find out you've been out and about when he said you were to stay in and keep quiet.

BRADLEY: Now, young fellow, if you wouldn't mind. I'd just like to have a talk with Sheppey.

ERNIE: I'll hop it. See you later.

[He goes out.

BRADLEY: I wasn't a bit surprised to get your letter, Sheppey.

SHEPPEY: Won't you sit down, sir?

BRADLEY: No, I'll stand if you don't mind. You sit down.

SHEPPEY: I think I will. I'm a bit tired. I been doing a lot to-day.

BRADLEY: Naturally it was a bit of a shock to me when you said you were leaving. After fifteen years. But in a manner of speaking I was expecting it. I said to myself at once, now Sheppey's got all this money he won't want to go on being an assistant. I mean, it's not in human nature.

SHEPPEY: I've always been very 'appy with you, sir. You've been a good master. And I know I've tried to give satisfaction.

BRADLEY: You're the best assistant I've ever had, Sheppey, and I don't mind who knows it. No one's got the way you have with a customer. And they like you. You've got a sense of humour.

SHEPPEY: I suppose I 'ave. Sometimes the things I say almost make me laugh myself.

BRADLEY: I suppose it's no good offering you more wages?

SHEPPEY: No, sir, it isn't. When I wrote that letter resigning my position it wasn't because I wanted a rise. I've always been satisfied with what I got.

BRADLEY: It's no good beating about the bush. Fair and square's my motto. I'm prepared to put my cards on the table. I don't want to lose you, Sheppey.

SHEPPEY: They say the best of friends must part.

BRADLEY: I know what you want, Sheppey, and I'm prepared to give it to you.

SHEPPEY: What do you mean by that, sir?

BRADLEY: Oh, go on. I wasn't born yesterday. And look here, you needn't go on calling me sir. From now on I'm Jim to you. The moment I read your letter I saw what the game was. Well, all right. I'm on.

SHEPPEY: I give you my word I don't know what you're talking about.

BRADLEY: Oh, yes, you do. And I'm quite agreeable. I'll take you in. Of course we shall have to discuss terms. We must keep the old name. The public's used to it and it's worth something.

SHEPPEY: You're not offering me a partnership in Bradley's?

BRADLEY: Yes, I am.

> [SHEPPEY *gives him a little startled look, hesitates for a moment, and then speaks in a low, harsh voice.*

SHEPPEY: Get thee behind me, Satan.

BRADLEY: [*Startled.*] Sheppey! What d'you mean?

SHEPPEY: You know there's nothing I wanted more than to be a partner at Bradley's. It's been the ambition of my life. I never shut up the shop, not a night, without saying to meself, I'd give a lot to be Jim Bradley's partner.

BRADLEY: Well, now you can be.

R

SHEPPEY: No, I can't. It's come too late. I've got other fish to fry.

BRADLEY: You haven't fixed up with another firm? Sheppey, you wouldn't play me a dirty trick like that, without saying a word to me about it? Not after fifteen years. Look here, Sheppey, I tell you what I'll do. I'll put your name up beside mine. Bradley and Miller it'll be. What do you say to that? It'll be a wonderful moment for you when you see it over the window.

SHEPPEY: It's not that, Mr. Bradley. I'm giving up the 'airdressing.

BRADLEY: You're not going to lead an evil life, Sheppey?

SHEPPEY: [Smiling.] I 'ope not. It would be rather late in the day for that.

BRADLEY: They say there's no fool like an old fool. You've got money now, I know. But it won't last for ever. Wine, women and song, and you'll run through it in no time.

SHEPPEY: I'm going to invest it.

BRADLEY: You'll never find a better investment than what I offer you.

SHEPPEY: That's a matter of opinion.

BRADLEY: A man that's got a real gift for hairdressing. I mean, it's such a waste. What do you expect to get for your money?

SHEPPEY: [Casually.] Treasure in 'eaven.

BRADLEY: Now, my boy, don't you go into any wild-cat schemes. You talk to your wife about it. She's a sensible woman. I know this offer of mine comes sudden. I'm not going to take no for an answer now. You think it over.

SHEPPEY: Thanks. But I've quite made up my mind.

BRADLEY: My experience is that no married man's ever made up his mind till he's heard what his wife has got to

say about it. I'll tell you what I'll do. I'll be off now.
You'll be working next week, I suppose?

SHEPPEY: Yes. I must work out my notice.

BRADLEY: I'll give you the week to think it over. Say
good-bye to Mrs. Miller for me, won't you?

SHEPPEY: I will. I'll just see you to the door.

BRADLEY: I'll find my way out all right. Don't trouble.

SHEPPEY: O.K. Good evening, sir. Thank you for coming.

> [BRADLEY *goes out.* SHEPPEY *goes over to the window and
> looks out into the street.* MRS. MILLER, FLORRIE
> *and* ERNIE *come in.*

ERNIE: We heard him go.

SHEPPEY: Nice-looking car, that is. My word, the governor's
proud of it.

FLORRIE: You'll be having one just as good yourself now,
dad.

MRS. MILLER: Ernie's told us, dad.

SHEPPEY: Told you what?

FLORRIE: Oh, dad, don't try and make a secret of it.

MRS. MILLER: I'm so glad for your sake, dear. I know
there's nothing you wanted so much. I almost feel like
crying.

SHEPPEY: Now what are you all talking about?

ERNIE: It's like this, Sheppey, Bradley gave me a hint. In
fact he told me in so many words that he was going to
offer you a partnership.

SHEPPEY: Oh, that?

FLORRIE: Don't take it so calm, dad. Aren't you excited?

MRS. MILLER: It'll be a grand day for me when I walk up
Jermyn Street and see your name in great big letters
alongside of Mr. Bradley's.

FLORRIE: Whoops, dearie.

MRS. MILLER: And of course there's the position too. I must 'ave a girl to do the rough work now.

FLORRIE: You don't want a girl. You must have a general and a char in twice a week to do the scrubbing.

MRS. MILLER: [*With a happy little grin.*] I shall be quite the lady before I'm finished.

ERNIE: And why not?

SHEPPEY: [*Quietly.*] I'll tell you why not. Because I've declined the governor's invitation with thanks.

FLORRIE: Dad.

MRS. MILLER: Whatever for? Your 'eart's been set on being your own master.

SHEPPEY: I know it 'as.

ERNIE: You haven't turned it down flat?

SHEPPEY: I 'ave.

ERNIE: Naturally he wasn't going to make his final offer straight away. He said to me terms would have to be discussed.

MRS. MILLER: It's not the responsibility you're afraid of, Sheppey?

SHEPPEY: No.

ERNIE: But it's a chance in a thousand.

FLORRIE: You don't want to be ordered about when you can order other people about, surely.

SHEPPEY: I gave in my notice last night. Of course I shall 'ave to work out the week. Then I'm through.

MRS. MILLER: D'you mean you're giving up work altogether? You'd never be 'appy without something to do, dad.

ERNIE: You can't get more than three and a half per cent on your money now, you know. What with income tax and one thing and another you won't find you'll have so much. I mean, it'll be a tight squeeze to make both ends meet.

FLORRIE: Especially with me and Ernie getting married so soon. We counted on your being able to help us a bit at first.

SHEPPEY: I'm not going to invest my money at three and a half per cent. I'm not going to invest it to bring that sort of return at all.

ERNIE: What's the idea?

SHEPPEY: Well, you know, I been worried lately. You know that day I had to go to the police court. The prisoners, you know, they was just the same as you and me, I mean, if you'd passed them in the street you'd 'ave thought them exactly like anybody else, and d'you know what put them in the dock, three out of four? Just that they 'adn't enough to eat. It give me quite a turn.

ERNIE: The Government's to blame.

MRS. MILLER: Quiet, Ernie.

SHEPPEY: And that same evening I met a woman I know up west, and I discovered accidentally that she 'adn't 'ad a bite of food in twenty-four hours.

ERNIE: Times are bad, of course.

SHEPPEY: Now, this money I've got. I could do with it, of course, but I don't really need it, not in comparison, I mean, with the people 'as 'aven't got enough to eat and no coal to put in their grates.

ERNIE: Perhaps not. But you've got it and they haven't. That's the luck of the game. You were born lucky. I've heard you say that dozens of times.

SHEPPEY: I know it. And perhaps the luckiest thing that's ever 'appened to me is 'aving the chance I've got now.

MRS. MILLER: What d'you mean exactly, dad?

SHEPPEY: Well, I don't feel justified some'ow in keeping this money.

FLORRIE: Then give it to Ernie and me. We'll be glad to take it.

SHEPPEY: [*With a smile.*] You don't want it either.

ERNIE: What are you going to do with it then?

SHEPPEY: Ever read the Gospel, Ernie?

ERNIE: Of course I have. It's got some damned good lines in it. And the style's fine. Of course you wouldn't want to write like that now.

SHEPPEY: I been reading it a lot this last week. Not being able to go to the shop, you know. But I'm not an educated man like you, Ernie. I read it for the story.

ERNIE: It's a good story. I don't think anyone would deny that.

SHEPPEY: I came across one bit that knocked me all of a heap. It seemed as if it 'ad been written for me.

ERNIE: What was that?

SHEPPEY: Sell all that thou 'ast, and distribute it to the poor, and thou shalt 'ave treasure in 'eaven: and come and follow me.

ERNIE: I know. And it goes on: it's easier for a camel to go through the eye of a needle than for a rich man to enter the Kingdom of Heaven. The rich have been trying to get round that for the last two thousand years.

SHEPPEY: It was like a great white light. I saw my way plain before me. I'm going to give this money of mine away to them as needs it more than I do.

[*They are thunderstruck. They speak on each other's words.*

MRS. MILLER: Sheppey, what do you mean?

ERNIE: You're crazy. You can't do a thing like that.

FLORRIE: I should think mum would have something to say to that.

MRS. MILLER: You don't mean it, dad?

SHEPPEY: Yes, I do.

ERNIE: It's ridiculous.

FLORRIE: Criminal, I call it.

ERNIE: After all, what's eight thousand pounds? A drop in the ocean. You might as well throw the money down a drain-pipe for all the good it will do.

MRS. MILLER: But, Sheppey, you can't afford to do a thing like that. It would be all very well for some of them rich people in the West End.

SHEPPEY: They can't do anything. They 'aven't got more money than they know what to do with.

ERNIE: Never heard that before.

SHEPPEY: That's why I'm telling you. Now I do know what I'm talking about. We've always 'ad a tip-top trade at Bradley's. Some of the most important men in the country. Why, only the other day I 'ad a gentleman in as said if things didn't look up soon 'e'd 'ave to give up either his yacht or 'is racing stable.

ERNIE: He isn't obliged to have a racing stable, is he?

SHEPPEY: It's not for 'imself 'e 'as it. 'E's told me over and over again. It's for the good of the country.

ERNIE: And do you believe that?

SHEPPEY: 'E's a gentleman. There's no reason for 'im to tell me a lie, is there? And you wouldn't believe 'ow much it costs to run a pack of 'ounds. I was shaving Lord Mereston one day last week and 'e said to me, Sheppey, 'e said, you wouldn't believe 'ow expensive life is, my daughter's coming out and I've got to give a ball, seven 'undred people and champagne at eighteen bob a bottle. My boy's nursing a constituency and it's costing me fifteen 'undred a year, and to put the lid on, Sheppey, 'e says, I've 'ad to fork out a couple of thousand quid for a diamond bracelet to give my wife for our silver wedding. I tell you what, Sheppey, 'e says, if things don't take a turn for the better soon I'll 'ave to give up being shaved and damned well shave meself. The rich ain't got more money than they can spend on themselves.

I know that for a fact. And besides, they don't know about the poor.

ERNIE: They can find out, can't they? They can read the papers.

SHEPPEY: Well, by the time they've read the court and society news, the divorces and the sporting intelligence, they've read enough. They don't want to be depressed by reading about unpleasant things. You can't 'ardly blame them. It's the poor as must 'elp the poor.

ERNIE: And they do, don't they? Everyone knows that the poor are splendid to one another. Everyone who writes about them says that. But when all's said and done charity begins at home.

FLORRIE: That's right. I mean, one must think of those who are near and dear to one first.

ERNIE: Mind you, I don't deny that things are pretty rotten in the state of Denmark. But it's no job for an individual. It's a problem and a very grave one, but it's a problem for the community. And the community's tackling it. I don't say charity doesn't want organising. It does. But there's one thing I'm quite sure about, that the indiscriminate charity of private individuals does more harm than good. That's been proved over and over again. I mean, there's not a charity organisation in England that won't tell you that to give a penny to a beggar in the street is a crime.

SHEPPEY: You may be right. But when you see an old fellow with one leg selling matches in the bitter cold it seems almost against 'uman nature not to give 'im a copper.

ERNIE: Well, one ought not to. One's only encouraging them. One's got to take a broad view of things. The law of life is simple as A B C. Get on or get under. If a man can't earn his own living he's no good, to the state or anybody else, and he must be eliminated. That's natural selection. If you molly-coddle the unfit you only make it harder for the rest of us.

SHEPPEY: I'm not an educated man, but I 'ave got two eyes in my 'ead. And I can't see much difference between the fit and the unfit. It seems to me that good and bad are pretty much alike. I think it's just a toss up which you are. You remember that story about the seed that was thrown on stony ground and the seed that was thrown on good rich ground.

ERNIE: You've got that all wrong, Sheppey. That seed never did any good because it couldn't adapt itself to its surroundings. That's the struggle for life and the survival of the fittest. It just proves what I say.

SHEPPEY: I read it different. I thought perhaps if it'd been watered a bit and given a bit of shade it might 'ave been all right. You see, these organisations are all very well, but there's a lot of red-tape about them, you know that, and they don't realise a lot of people are proud and don't like asking, and some of them ain't got the nerve to, and there's a lot as are downright stupid, you can't deny that.

ERNIE: Well, what can you do about it?

SHEPPEY: I'll tell you. I'll just keep my eyes open and talk to people, and I'll give 'alf a crown 'ere and five bob there, just as man to man, you know, and a sack of coals to someone as 'asn't got any, and if I see a kid wants a pair of boots I'll buy him a pair.

ERNIE: Of course you know you'll have every rotter and sponger after you. And those half crowns and five bobs, where do you think they'll go? On drink.

SHEPPEY: I dare say I shall make mistakes sometimes. I don't think that matters. Besides, if a chap's down and out and thinks he'd rather spend 'alf a crown on beer than on food and lodging, that's 'is look out.

ERNIE: And what do you expect to get out of it for yourself?

SHEPPEY: Oh, I don't know. Peace of mind. The Kingdom of Heaven, perhaps.

ERNIE: And what'll be the result? In a year or two your money'll be gone. D'you think anything'll be different?

SHEPPEY: You never can tell. Perhaps someone'll come and take my place. If I can only get people to see what I mean. I might be an example to others. Someone's got to start a thing like this.

ERNIE: D'you think a hairdresser's the right man to start it?

SHEPPEY: I don't know why not. Jesus was only a carpenter, wasn't he?

FLORRIE: I think it's awful comparing yourself to Jesus, dad. I wonder you're not afraid a thunderbolt'll come down from Heaven and smite you.

ERNIE: [Sulkily.] Well, it's not my money, and it's no business of mine what you do with it, but if you'll take my advice you'll look before you leap.

SHEPPEY: [With a twinkle in his eye.] I'm always glad to take advice from those younger than myself.

FLORRIE: What about me and Ernie getting married? We were going to wait, but when you won that Sweep, we settled to marry now. I've given notice at the office and everything.

SHEPPEY: There's no reason I can see why you shouldn't get married. You'll 'ave as much as mum and me 'ad when we married.

FLORRIE: Things are different now. And besides, Ernie's got to keep up a position that you didn't have to. We were counting on your paying the rent of our flat.

SHEPPEY: You can live here.

FLORRIE: Can I? Well, I'm marrying to have a home of my own. Say something, mum, do. You can't let him play ducks and drakes with our money like that.

MRS. MILLER: I don't know if I'm standing on me 'ead or me 'eels.

ERNIE: [*Crossly.*] Well, it's not the first time a man has loved the human race so much he's left his own family to starve.

FLORRIE: Don't blame me, Ernie.

SHEPPEY: I knew it would be a sort of disappointment to you.

ERNIE: The mistake you make, Sheppey, is taking things too literally. The New Testament must be looked upon as fiction, a beautiful fiction if you like, but a fiction. No educated man accepts the Gospel narrative as sober fact. In fact a great many people believe that Jesus never existed at all.

SHEPPEY: I don't know that that matters so much.

ERNIE: Just now, when I asked you what you expected to get out of it, you said the Kingdom of Heaven.

SHEPPEY: I know I did. But sometimes I think the Kingdom of 'Eaven's in me own 'eart.

FLORRIE: You're barmy.

SHEPPEY: [*Smiling.*] Because I want to live like Jesus?

FLORRIE: Well, who ever heard of anyone wanting to live like Jesus at this time of day? I think it's just blasphemous.

ERNIE: And there's another thing you must remember. Everyone knows the Gospels were written by ignorant men. I mean they were just ordinary working chaps. And the parables and all that were addressed to the same sort of crowd you might see at Woolworth's of a Saturday night.

SHEPPEY: Well, perhaps that's why it all come 'ome to me so much, because I'm an ignorant working man meself.

ERNIE: Yes, but don't you see, they've got to be explained. Why do you suppose they have professors of theology and doctors of divinity? They're there to explain to people that whatever Jesus said he didn't really mean it, but something quite different.

SHEPPEY: You may be right, of course. But I don't see why 'e shouldn't 'ave.

ERNIE: It stands to reason. Those precepts, the sermon on the Mount and all that, may have been very well for a small peasant community, but they're just not applicable to our great world states. They're impracticable.

SHEPPEY: I don't know so much about that. Personally I don't know anyone as 'as tried to put them in practice.

FLORRIE: Well, that's a proof they're impracticable, dad. I mean, if they were, clergymen and ministers and that like, would do them.

SHEPPEY: Perhaps they don't believe in them.

FLORRIE: I don't know why they shouldn't. I believe in them. But there's all the difference in believing a thing just as a thing you believe . . .

ERNIE: Theoretically, she means.

FLORRIE: Yes, and believing it so that you act on it. I mean, when you believe a horse can't lose, you don't believe it in the same way as you believe that if you go out in the rain you'll get wet.

ERNIE: [To SHEPPEY.] I see what you mean, of course. It's an ideal. But you've always got to remember this, an ideal's something you aim at; as soon as you reach it, it stops being an ideal.

SHEPPEY: It don't seem like an ideal to me. It seems to me like plain commonsense.

ERNIE: Well, I think it's the damnedest nonsense I ever heard.

SHEPPEY: I'm not quite sure that what you think is gospel truth either.

FLORRIE: Ernie's an educated man, dad, and you're not.

[*A knock at the door is heard.*

MRS. MILLER: See who that is, Florrie. Who ever can be coming here at this hour?

[FLORRIE *goes to the window.*

FLORRIE: Oh, mum, it's a lady. She's got a silk dress on. Her shoes don't look none too good.

SHEPPEY: I know who it is. It's someone I was expecting. I'll go.

[*He goes out.*

FLORRIE: Did you know anything about this, mum?

MRS. MILLER: Not a word. It's come as a complete surprise to me.

ERNIE: [*To* FLORRIE.] You got it in one, Florrie. You hit the nail on the head.

FLORRIE: How do you mean?

ERNIE: He's barmy.

MRS. MILLER: Oh, Ernie, that's a horrible thing to say.

ERNIE: I don't say it's permanent. But he's barmy. I mean, that's obvious. Look here, what do you say to me running for the doctor?

FLORRIE: That's a good idea, Ernie.

MRS. MILLER: I don't know what to say. I mean it's so unlike him.

FLORRIE: Go on, Ernie. Here's my key.

ERNIE: [*Taking it.*] I shan't be two ticks.

[*He goes out.*

MRS. MILLER: And him that's always been so sensible. He's never been near, that's not in 'is nature, but 'e's never been one to throw money about neither.

FLORRIE: Ernie's upset.

MRS. MILLER: I don't know what he's got to be upset for.

FLORRIE: Oh, don't you? Mum, this has got to be stopped. I won't lose Ernie. I won't.

Mrs. Miller: Oh, don't be so silly, Florrie. Why should you lose Ernie?

Florrie: You don't know men like I do.

Mrs. Miller: I like that. I suppose I didn't know men before you were born.

Florrie: When a woman's been married a year or two she forgets. I can see Ernie's upset.

[Sheppey *comes in with* Bessie Legros.

Sheppey: Come in, my dear. Mum, I've brought a friend to see you. This is my wife and that's my daughter Florrie.

Mrs. Miller: Oh, Sheppey, and me not dressed or anything. [*To* Bessie.] Good evening. Won't you sit down?

Bessie: Pleased to meet you. [*To* Florrie *with a smile.*] Good evening.

Florrie: Good evening. [*She looks her up and down and with her cockney sharpness sums her up and purses her lips.*]

Sheppey: She's going to stay and 'ave a bit of supper with us.

Mrs. Miller: Oh, dad, you might 'ave warned me.

Sheppey: You don't mind pot-luck, do you?

Bessie: Me? A pleasure, I'm sure.

Sheppey: There's always plenty and my wife's a wonderful good cook. You'd be surprised 'ow tasty she makes things.

Florrie: [*To* Bessie.] You known dad long?

Bessie: Well, in a manner of speaking I have and in a manner of speaking I haven't.

Sheppey: I knew 'er by sight first. She was always at the Bunch of Keys when I went in to 'ave my beer after I'd shut up. And so we got talking, see? And then last week when I fainted she brought me round. She came in the taxi with me as far as the door.

BESSIE: I thought he wasn't fit to take a taxi by himself.

MRS. MILLER: That was very kind of you, I'm sure. I'll give you a nice supper. I'm very glad Sheppey asked you to drop in.

FLORRIE: [*Suspiciously.*] But I thought you fainted *after* the shop shut.

SHEPPEY: So I did. We'd just been 'aving a bottle of fizz to celebrate the occasion and the others 'ad gone.

FLORRIE: [*Acidly.*] Oh, I see.

SHEPPEY: Now look 'ere, Florrie, I want you and 'er to be friends. I want you to be a sister to 'er. And I want mum to be a mother to 'er.

FLORRIE: The acquaintance is a bit short for that, isn't it?

SHEPPEY: She's in trouble, mum, and I want you to 'elp 'er. That evening when I fainted she 'adn't 'ad a bit of food all day and I don't believe she's 'ad much to-day either. She ain't got a place to sleep to-night, so I said we'd give 'er a shake-down here.

MRS. MILLER: Sheppey, we 'aven't got room.

SHEPPEY: Yes, we 'ave. There's the attic and we can rig up that old bed you said you was going to sell.

MRS. MILLER: I wouldn't like to ask anybody to sleep in that.

BESSIE: Didn't I tell you? I knew they wouldn't like it. It's all right. I'll manage somehow.

SHEPPEY: [*To his wife.*] To oblige me, my dear. If you say no, it means the Embankment or the streets.

FLORRIE: Well, she'd be at home there, wouldn't she?

SHEPPEY: You speak when you're spoken to, Florrie. [*To his wife.*] She's a nice woman and a good woman. You can't deceive me. It's not often I ask you to do me a favour.

MRS. MILLER: [*Giving in.*] I'll be glad to 'ave you to stay the night, Miss.

BESSIE: That is kind of you. It's a relief to me. I tell you that straight. I didn't know which way to turn.

> [ERNIE *comes in. He gives* FLORRIE *a little nod to indicate that he has executed his commission.*]

SHEPPEY: 'Ullo, Ernie, where 'ave you been?

ERNIE: I just went out to get a packet of fags.

SHEPPEY: There are some in the snuff-box.

ERNIE: I thought they were only for show. [*Seeing* BESSIE.] Got a visitor?

SHEPPEY: This is Ernie, our Florrie's intended. And this is Bessie.

ERNIE: Bessie what?

BESSIE: Legros.

SHEPPEY: She ain't really French.

BESSIE: No, it's the name I go by for business purposes.

FLORRIE: Dad met her at the Bunch of Keys.

ERNIE: [*Remembering what* BRADLEY *had said to him.*] Oh, did he? I see.

MRS. MILLER: Well, I'll just go and 'ave a look and see 'ow my supper's getting on.

> [*She goes out.*

FLORRIE: I'll be getting the table laid.

BESSIE: If I can lend a hand I'll be glad to, I'm sure.

FLORRIE: [*With a little sniff.*] I can manage.

SHEPPEY: [*To* BESSIE.] I'd like to show you my snuff-box. [*He goes over to the chimney-piece and takes it up.*] One of my customers left it me in 'is will. A very nice gentleman 'e was. I shaved 'im when 'e was dead.

BESSIE: It's lovely.

SHEPPEY: 'E told me it was given to 'is grandfather by King George the Fourth.

BESSIE: It must be worth a packet.

SHEPPEY: It's not that so much. It's the sentiment. I mean, 'aving it left me, see? I wouldn't sell it for a thousand pounds.

FLORRIE: [*Getting out the tablecloth.*] I suppose you haven't asked anyone else to drop in, dad?

SHEPPEY: Well, now you come to mention it, I 'ave.

FLORRIE: Oh, you haven't, dad?

SHEPPEY: Yes, you know that chap what I caught sneaking the doctor's overcoat. I told 'im to come round.

FLORRIE: Dad!

ERNIE: Isn't he in gaol?

SHEPPEY: No, the magistrate said 'e'd give 'im another chance this time, 'im 'aving been out of work so long, and not 'aving 'ad anything to eat for two days.

ERNIE: But the copper told you he'd been in jug two or three times before.

SHEPPEY: Yes, 'e's 'ad bad luck. That's right. 'E's never 'ad a chance really.

FLORRIE: Oh, and are you going to give him one?

SHEPPEY: That's the idea.

[*The door is opened and the* DOCTOR *comes in. He is a middle-aged, red-faced man, and very hearty.*

DOCTOR: May I come in?

SHEPPEY: Why, doctor, where 'ave you sprung from?

DOCTOR: I was just passing and I thought I'd look in and see how you were getting along.

SHEPPEY: I've never been better in my life. I'm going back to work next Monday.

DOCTOR: You mustn't try and do too much. When are they going to pay you your Sweep money?

SHEPPEY: In a week or two, I believe.

DOCTOR: Why don't you go down to the Isle of Sheppey for

a bit, and have another look at that cottage you've had your eye on?

SHEPPEY: I'm not going to buy that now.

DOCTOR: Oh, why not? I thought your heart was set on it.

SHEPPEY: [*With a sigh.*] I know. I can't. Not now. I should never 'ave a moment's peace.

DOCTOR: You'll have to be looking out for a nice safe investment then. Don't put too many eggs in one basket, that's all.

SHEPPEY: I've just been talking about that to my family. I'd be very much obliged if you'd tell them I'm in full possession of my senses.

DOCTOR: Why? What's the trouble?

SHEPPEY: Well, you see, it's my money, isn't it? I don't see why I shouldn't do what I like with it.

DOCTOR: And what do you want to do with it?

SHEPPEY: Clothe the naked and visit the sick, give food to 'im that is a'ungered and drink to 'im that is athirst.

DOCTOR: Very praiseworthy of course, within reason. What put the idea into your head?

SHEPPEY: It came. A great white light.

DOCTOR: Oh, yes. I see. Of course it's a thing to think over. What we've got to do before we go any further is to get you fit and strong. At your age one can't take liberties with one's constitution. I don't mind telling you I don't like this high blood pressure of yours. Often has funny effects. D'you see things?

SHEPPEY: I see you.

DOCTOR: Yes, of course. I mean, do you see things other people don't see?

SHEPPEY: I see wickedness and vice beating the land with their wings.

[*The* DOCTOR *looks at him meditatively, wondering what he shall ask him next, when* MRS. MILLER *comes in.*

MRS. MILLER: Sheppey, there's a man at the door says you told him to come here.

SHEPPEY: That's right.

> [COOPER *appears at the open door. He is a ragged-looking fellow in a cap, with a scarf round his neck.*

SHEPPEY: Come in, old man. Pleased to see you. Found your way all right?

COOPER: I 'ave good reason to remember.

SHEPPEY: You'll stay to supper, won't you?

COOPER: I don't mind if I do.

MRS. MILLER: Who is 'e, dad?

SHEPPEY: He's your brother.

MRS. MILLER: That! That's no brother of mine. I 'aven't got a brother and no one knows that better than what you do.

SHEPPEY: 'E's your brother and my brother.

MRS. MILLER: I never 'ad but one brother. 'Is name was Percy, and 'e died of meningitis when 'e was seven years of age. [*To* COOPER.] What's your name?

COOPER: Cooper, mum. Jim Cooper.

MRS. MILLER: I never even known a Cooper. [*To* SHEPPEY.] What are you going to do with him?

SHEPPEY: 'E's 'ungry and I'm going to give 'im food. 'E's 'omeless and I'm going to give 'im shelter.

MRS. MILLER: Shelter? Where?

SHEPPEY: 'Ere. In my 'ouse. In my bed.

MRS. MILLER: In my bed? And where am I to sleep, then?

SHEPPEY: You can sleep with Florrie.

FLORRIE: I can tell you who he is, mum. He's the chap dad caught sneaking the doctor's coat and he's been in and out of prison half a dozen times. He's a thief.

COOPER: 'Ere, who are you a'calling a thief?

FLORRIE: Well, you are, aren't you?

COOPER: I may be. But if you was a man I'd like to see you say it.

FLORRIE: [*To* BESSIE.] And as for you. You're a tart.

BESSIE: You can call me that if you like, but when I had my little flat in Kennington I described myself as an actress.

MRS. MILLER: Supper's ready. If you don't want it to spoil you'd better finish laying the cloth, Florrie.

[FLORRIE *sinks down on a chair and gives a sob.*

FLORRIE: What a humiliation! What a humiliation for people in our position!

MRS. MILLER: I thought this Sweep money was going to bring us all peace and 'appiness. It don't look much like that now.

SHEPPEY: Peace and 'appiness, that's what we're all looking for, but where are we going to find it?

END OF ACT TWO

ACT THREE

The Scene is the same as in the preceding Act.

Florrie *is at the window, looking out.* Bessie *comes in. She has an exercise book in her hand.*

Bessie: Your ma says, what's this doing in the kitchen? She very nearly throwed it away.

Florrie: I shouldn't have cared if she had. It's my exercise book. Fat chance I've got of going to France now.

Bessie: It's a long lane that has no turning.

Florrie: What's the time? [*She looks out of window again.*]

Bessie: Getting on for six. Expecting somebody?

Florrie: Yes and no.

Bessie: Dead-and-alive street this. You never see anything going on.

Florrie: It's a very good class of street, that's why.

Bessie: I don't say it isn't.

Florrie: How much longer are you going to stay here?

Bessie: It depends on your pa. I mean, as far as I'm concerned, I'm sure I don't want to stay where I'm not wanted. You don't like me, do you?

Florrie: Oh, I don't mind you. After the first shock, I mean you being an immoral woman and me being virtuous, I can't see you're any different from anybody else.

Bessie: I don't feel different.

Florrie: Of course at first I thought you were after dad.

Bessie: Me? I like your pa as a friend. But that's all.

FLORRIE: Ernie says he wouldn't be surprised if it hadn't been going on ever so long.

BESSIE: He doesn't know what he's talking about.

FLORRIE: Ernie's very respectable. And when you're very respectable you always believe the worst of people.

BESSIE: You're worried about Ernie, aren't you?

FLORRIE: Well, all this has been an upset to him.

BESSIE: I can quite understand that. Men don't like surprises. They always want things to go on in the same old way. They're not like women. Anything for a change. Men are awfully conventional, you know.

FLORRIE: You see, we were going to be married next month, and now I don't know when it'll be.

BESSIE: Oh, I say. I know what it is when you've made all your plans and then something happens.

FLORRIE: He wants to break it off.

BESSIE: He hasn't said so?

FLORRIE: No. But I know he's got it in his mind. Only he's got his self-respect to think of, he's got to find an excuse. Mum says if he wants to break it off it shows he doesn't really love me. But she doesn't know men like I do.

BESSIE: They want knowing. There's no mistake about that.

FLORRIE: I wish you'd give me some advice. You ought to know more about men than most people.

BESSIE: Well, I'll tell you. They're near, they'll spend money if they can make a splash, but if they think no one'll know, they're as mean as cat's meat. They're timid, you know, make a scene in public and they'll just go all to pieces. Some of them don't like to see a woman cry. But you have to be careful not to cry too much, you may drive them away, and my experience is, if a man once goes, he don't come back.

It'd be a tough job dealing with them if they didn't like flattery. You can't lay it on too thick, my dear, they can never have enough of it. Flattery's meat and drink to them. They'll listen to it for hours. You get sick and tired, but there they are, as fresh as a daisy, just eating it.

FLORRIE: It's easy for you. I'm so much in love with Ernie. I'd forgive him anything.

BESSIE: It's bad when it takes you like that. It makes you so helpless.

FLORRIE: When you're in love with a man like I am with Ernie he does aggravate you so.

BESSIE: I know. It does seem as if they've got no sense sometimes.

FLORRIE: Ernie's stuck on politics for some reason.

BESSIE: You have to put up with a man's ideas. My experience is they don't amount to anything, really, but you must never let on you think that.

> [*There is a knock at the door.*

FLORRIE: That's his knock. Oh, my heart. It's thumping so I can hardly bear it.

BESSIE: I'll go and open the door for him. You stay here.

FLORRIE: Thanks. My knees are wobbling so I'd have a job to get to the door.

BESSIE: Pull yourself together, dear. If you let a man see he means all that to you, he'll lead you a dog's life.

> [*She goes out. In a moment* ERNIE *comes in. He has an evening paper in his hand.*

FLORRIE: [*Bright and eager.*] Ernie! I never recognised your knock. This is a surprise.

ERNIE: [*On the surly side.*] I told you I was coming along about now.

FLORRIE: I didn't know it was so late. Time slips by so quickly when you're busy.

ERNIE: I see that woman's here still. What about the fellow?

FLORRIE: Cooper? Oh, he's here. I wonder we haven't all been murdered in our beds by now.

ERNIE: Where's your dad?

FLORRIE: Out somewhere. I don't know. [*She can't keep it up any longer.*] Haven't you forgotten something, Ernie?

ERNIE: Me?

FLORRIE: You haven't kissed me.

ERNIE: Sorry. [*He goes towards her.*]

FLORRIE: You need not if you don't want to.

ERNIE: Don't be so silly. [*He kisses her.*]

FLORRIE: [*Clinging to him.*] Oh, Ernie, I'm so miserable.

ERNIE: Of course you're worried. That's only natural. You can't expect anyone to like seeing their father make a damned fool of himself.

FLORRIE: I wish he'd never won that beastly money. We were all as happy as could be.

ERNIE: I should have thought your mum could have done something.

FLORRIE: That's what I tell her. She says he won't listen.

ERNIE: It seems almost a pity you should have given up your job.

FLORRIE: [*With a quick look at him.*] I suppose the best thing I can do is to look out for another.

ERNIE: It's no good not looking facts in the face. I don't see how we can marry just yet, Florrie.

FLORRIE: Of course it's for you to say.

ERNIE: Naturally it's a disappointment. But we were prepared to wait before and I suppose we can wait now.

FLORRIE: [*Clutching her hands in her wretchedness.*] If you want to break it off you've only got to say so.

ERNIE: Me? Whatever put an idea like that in your head?

FLORRIE: Only that I saw it was in yours.

ERNIE: I wouldn't let you down, Florrie. Not for anything in the world.

FLORRIE: It's not much good being engaged if nothing's ever going to come of it.

ERNIE: Who says nothing's ever going to come of it?

FLORRIE: You don't love me like you did a month ago.

ERNIE: That's a lie.

FLORRIE: Listen, Ernie, I love you so much, I've got to know one way or the other. This uncertainty's killing me.

ERNIE: My dear, you must be reasonable. We decided we wouldn't be married till I was in a position to provide for you. I didn't want you to have to work. You'd have enough to do looking after the home. And you ought to have a kid or two.

FLORRIE: Oh, don't, Ernie. It makes me feel awful, hearing you talk like that.

ERNIE: You must look at my side of it too.

FLORRIE: What d'you mean?

ERNIE: Well, I'm ambitious. I know I've got ability. I've got a good brain.

FLORRIE: No one's ever denied that, Ernie.

ERNIE: If I've got exceptional powers I ought to use them. I don't want to stick in the common rut. They say you can't keep a good man down, but it's no use hanging a millstone round your neck.

FLORRIE: Meaning me?

ERNIE: Of course not. I wasn't thinking of you. I love you no end, Florrie. I've never seen a girl I could think of marrying except you and my firm conviction is that I never shall.

FLORRIE: You're not just saying that to please me?

ERNIE: No, I swear I'm not. And you mustn't think that what I'm going to say now doesn't mean I don't love you as much as ever I did. If things come right and we could be married to-morrow there wouldn't be a happier chap in London.

FLORRIE: Well, what is it you're going to say?

ERNIE: It's just this: what your father does is his business, and he can do what he likes with his own money. But I'm not going to be made to look a fool by any man.

FLORRIE: What's going to make you look a fool?

ERNIE: If I have a father-in-law who lives like Jesus of course I shall look a fool. How do you expect me to keep my authority over the boys I teach when they know my father-in-law's a funny old buffer mixing with the lowest of the low, and giving his money away? They'd rot the life out of me.

FLORRIE: It's not very nice for mum or me.

ERNIE: I think it's awful for your poor mother. Of course it won't really be so bad for you, having your work in the City, and naturally, people there won't know anything about it.

FLORRIE: All the same, I don't see how I can help feeling the disgrace of it.

ERNIE: There you are, you see. Now, put yourself in my place.

FLORRIE: What do you propose?

ERNIE: Well, I'd rather leave it to you.

FLORRIE: I see.

[MRS. MILLER *comes in.*

FLORRIE: Here's mum.

ERNIE: Oh, good evening.

MRS. MILLER: Why, Ernie, you're quite a stranger.

ERNIE: I've had a lot of school work to do yesterday and the day before.

MRS. MILLER: The place 'as been all upside-down with Bessie and that there Cooper being 'ere.

ERNIE: A shame, I call it.

MRS. MILLER: The extra work keeps me from thinking and that's something.

FLORRIE: It isn't our house any more. It's a home for waifs and strays.

ERNIE: Where's Sheppey, now?

MRS. MILLER: 'E 'ad an appointment to see the doctor at four. I'm surprised 'e's not back. It's gone six.

FLORRIE: You never told me he was going to the doctor's, mum.

MRS. MILLER: I thought I'd better not say anything about it. It's not very pleasant.

ERNIE: Why, what's up?

MRS. MILLER: I'd rather not speak about it.

FLORRIE: Oh, go on, mum. We shall have to know sooner or later.

MRS. MILLER: Well, the fact is, Dr. Jervis is making an examination as to the state of his mind. I didn't like the idea myself, but 'e said 'e thought 'e ought to. It seems so under'and somehow.

ERNIE: How do you mean?

MRS. MILLER: Well, Dr. Jervis got Sheppey up there pretending 'e wanted to make a thorough examination of 'is 'eart. Said 'e could do it better in 'is consulting-room, where 'e 'ad all 'is instruments, than what he could 'ere.

ERNIE: Well, Sheppey's got a high blood pressure, we know that, I mean I shouldn't be surprised if his heart wasn't a bit wonky.

MRS. MILLER: Dr. Jervis 'as got a friend of 'is to come up. 'E's a specialist it seems, and 'e's coming as a great favour to Dr. Jervis. 'E's one of the 'eads at Bethlehem.

ERNIE: The lunatic asylum!

[FLORRIE *with clasped hands begins to move her lips, speaking with soundless words.*

MRS. MILLER: 'E's going to pretend 'e's just dropped in for a cup of tea, and then Dr. Jervis is going to ask Sheppey to stay and 'ave a cup. And they're going to get 'im in conversation. Dr. Jervis said it might take an hour or more before they come to a decision. I tell you I can't bear it. I can't bear the idea of letting my poor old man walk into a trap like that.

ERNIE: It's for his own good, isn't it?

MRS. MILLER: [*Noticing* FLORRIE.] Florrie, whatever are you doing of?

FLORRIE: Praying to God.

MRS. MILLER: Not in the sitting-room, Florrie. I'm sure that's not right.

FLORRIE: O God, make them say he's potty. O God, make them say he's potty. O God, make them say he's potty.

MRS. MILLER: Oh, Florrie, how can you ask God to do a thing like that?

FLORRIE: If God makes them say he's potty he'll be shut up. Then he can't throw all that money away and he can't make an exhibition of himself. [*Going on in a whisper.*] O God, make them say he's potty. O God, make them say he's potty.

MRS. MILLER: They won't shut him up. I shouldn't like them to do that. Oh, do stop it, Florrie.

FLORRIE: I won't stop it. It means life and happiness to me. O God, make them say he's potty, and I'll give up sugar in my tea all through Lent.

MRS. MILLER: That's not giving up very much. You're trying to break yourself of sugar as it is because you think it's fattening.

FLORRIE: Well, it's giving up something you like, isn't it? O God, make them say he's potty, and I promise I won't go to the pictures all next month. [*She goes on muttering to herself with her hands clasped and her eyes turned to the ceiling.*]

MRS. MILLER: I wish I 'adn't let Dr. Jervis persuade me. I never thought they might want to shut 'im up.

ERNIE: It's quite evident he can't manage his own affairs.

MRS. MILLER: 'Ow do you know?

ERNIE: Well, it's obvious, isn't it? Wanting to give his money away.

FLORRIE: [*Interrupting herself for a moment.*] And filling the house with riff-raff. O God, make them say he's . . . [*Her voice dwindles away, but her lips keep on moving.*]

ERNIE: It's not the behaviour of a sane man. Nobody can deny that.

MRS. MILLER: 'Ow do you know 'e's not sane, and it ain't all the rest of us as are potty?

ERNIE: That's absurd. Sanity means doing what everybody else does, and thinking what everybody else thinks. That's the whole foundation of democracy. If the individual isn't prepared to act the same way as everybody else there's only one place for him and that's the lunatic asylum.

FLORRIE: Don't argue with her, Ernie. O God, make them say . . .

MRS. MILLER: Jesus didn't do what everybody else did.

FLORRIE: Oh, mum, don't talk about Jesus. It's blasphemous, it really is. Can't you see I'm praying?

ERNIE: All that was a long time ago. As I was saying to Sheppey only the other day, circumstances alter cases. We're civilised now. Besides—mind you, I don't want to say anything offensive, live and let live is my motto, and I'm all for toleration—but looking at the facts impartially I can't help seeing there was a lot to be said on the other side and if I'd been in Pontius Pilate's position I dare say I'd have done just what he did.

MRS. MILLER: I was brought up different from you. Living in the country and all, I never 'ad the opportunity to get the education girls get now. I began to earn my own living when I was fifteen.

FLORRIE: [Sharply.] Mum. We don't want to go into ancient history. [Her lips go on moving as she repeats and repeats her prayer.]

MRS. MILLER: But we was church-going people, and I used to go to Sunday school. Nothing of what Sheppey says was new to me, as you might say.

FLORRIE: [Aghast.] Whatever do you mean by that, mum?

MRS. MILLER: Well, I knew it all, I mean. I'd 'eard it all over and over again when I was a girl. I never paid any attention to it of course, but when Sheppey brought it up again it all come back to me.

ERNIE: I may be dense, but really I don't follow.

MRS. MILLER: Sheppey's right about what Jesus said. About giving to the poor and all that. And loving your neighbour as yourself. I remember all that.

ERNIE: I dare say you do. But you never knew anyone that acted on it, did you?

MRS. MILLER: They was young ladies as took Sunday school at 'ome, and I don't think they'd 'ave liked it if one acted on it. They'd 'ave thought it presuming.

ERNIE: And so it is presuming. It's always presumption to think you know better than other people.

MRS. MILLER: I'm sure Sheppey doesn't mean it like that. No one knows 'is place better than what he does. Why, I've 'eard 'im say twenty times, I like a joke as well as any man, but I wouldn't take a liberty with one of my customers any more than I'd like 'im to take a liberty with me.

FLORRIE: [*Almost with agony.*] You're not going to take dad's side? You can't do that, mum. I mean, think of Ernie and me.

MRS. MILLER: It's not a matter of taking sides. I want to do what's best for everybody. But it's like this, if the doctors say 'e's not quite right in 'is 'ead, well, that settles it. But if they say 'e is, then I don't feel justified in preventing 'im from doing what 'e thinks is right.

FLORRIE: Mum. Mum. I think that's awful. [*Almost in tears.*] O God, make them say he's potty. O God, make them say he's potty.

MRS. MILLER: I don't say that I don't think the idea's peculiar. And I know it won't be very pleasant for any of us. But 'ow do I know 'e's not right?

ERNIE: I should have thought your common sense would have told you that.

MRS. MILLER: I'm not clever like you, Ernie. I feel a lot that I can't exactly say. There's something in my 'eart that says, dear old Sheppey, 'e always was a character.

ERNIE: D'you mean to say you're going to sit there twiddling your thumbs and watch him throwing all that money down the drain?

MRS. MILLER: I shan't like it, of course. I mean, I should 'ave liked to own this 'ouse and it would 'ave been a 'elp to 'ave a girl in to do the rough work. But there's something inside me that says, all that don't matter really; if Sheppey wants to do what Jesus said—well, that's only what you was taught when you was a girl.

FLORRIE: And what's to happen to you when the money's gone? You don't suppose they'd have dad back at the shop after making such an exhibition of himself?

ERNIE: And jobs aren't easy to get these days. Especially for a man of Sheppey's age.

MRS. MILLER: Well, 'e's been a good 'usband to me. Never a 'arsh word. 'E's worked for me a good many years. I can earn my own living and 'is too.

ERNIE: Easier said than done.

MRS. MILLER: When one's as good a cook as what I am, and honest, it's not 'ard to get a job. Why, there's not one of these girls that's a patch on me. I'm not one for praising myself, God knows, but I do know my own value. Put me in front of a decent stove and give me the materials and not even the Queen of England can turn out a better dinner than me. And now, my girl, you'd better come and peel the potatoes.

FLORRIE: All right, mum. Are you coming, Ernie?

ERNIE: Yes, I will in a minute. I just want to take a look at the paper.

> [FLORRIE *quickly bites her finger to choke down the tears that have sprung to her eyes. The two women go out. *ERNIE* opens the paper, but he does not read it, he looks sullenly in front of him. *BESSIE* comes in. He gives her a look, but does not speak. He starts reading.*

BESSIE: Anything in the paper?

ERNIE: No.

BESSIE: What are you reading then?

ERNIE: The news.

BESSIE: Racing?

ERNIE: No, political.

BESSIE: Florrie tells me you want to be a Member of Parliament.

ERNIE: Fat chance I have now.

BESSIE: I suppose you was counting on Sheppey doing something for you.

ERNIE: Wouldn't you have in my place?

BESSIE: Well, whatever happens you're lucky to have got Florrie. She's a nice girl. And with her looks she could marry almost anybody.

ERNIE: I suppose you think she's throwing herself away on me?

BESSIE: There's no accounting for tastes. Working in the City like she does I wonder she hasn't been snapped up by one of them rich men long ago.

ERNIE: I'll thank you not to put ideas in Florrie's head. Her future's settled and if I hear of another fellow running after her I shall have something to say to him.

[BESSIE *smiles quietly to herself. The door is opened softly and* COOPER *slinks in.*

COOPER: 'Afternoon all.

BESSIE: Hulloa! How did you get in? I never heard you knock.

COOPER: The lock's got one of them safety catches. I don't 'ave to 'ave anybody open a door like that for me.

BESSIE: That's good news, I must say.

COOPER: Any fags around?

BESSIE: I haven't got any.

COOPER: Suppose I shall 'ave to smoke me own then.

[*He takes a packet out of his pocket and lights a cigarette.*]

BESSIE: You aren't going to offer me one, I suppose?

COOPER: No, I don't approve of ladies smoking.

ERNIE: [*Taking out a packet and offering it to* BESSIE.] Here's one if you want it.

BESSIE: Thanks.

COOPER: What won the three-thirty?

ERNIE: I haven't looked.

COOPER: What'd you buy a paper for then? Wanton waste, I call that.

ERNIE: If you two are going to have a little chat I'll ask you to excuse me.

BESSIE: [*Mincing.*] Oh, don't mention it.

[ERNIE *goes out.*

COOPER: Quite the gentleman, eh?

BESSIE: He's all right. He's only a kid. Swallowed the multiplication table when he was at school and it won't go up or down. Makes him kind of uneasy like.

COOPER: Where's Sheppey?

BESSIE: Out somewhere.

COOPER: What's he after? I can't make 'im out.

BESSIE: He's a puzzle to me too.

COOPER: Religion, I suppose it is, at the back of it.

BESSIE: I'm not so sure. I know a lot about religion. When I had my little flat in Kennington one of my regulars was a religious man. He was a draper in a very good way of business. A prominent Baptist he was. Used to come every Tuesday and Friday. After he'd had his little bit of fun he used to love a good old talk about religion. But he didn't give much away. He used to say there wasn't a draper in the South of London as could squeeze more profit out of a reel of cotton than what he could.

COOPER: You have to be pretty smart with all the competition there is nowadays.

BESSIE: D'you find that in your business?

COOPER: There's always room at the top.

BESSIE: Swank.

COOPER: Besides, what is my business?

BESSIE: Petty thieving, ain't it?

COOPER: Oh, and who do you think you are? You've got no cause to despise me.

BESSIE: I don't despise you. I shouldn't have thought it was worth it, that's all. I mean, in and out of quod all the time. It can't be pleasant.

COOPER: Well, I'll tell you, it's the excitement. And then again, when you've done a job you feel all keyed up, if you know what I mean. You can't hardly help laughing when you think how blasted clever you are. But it's the excitement that's the chief thing.

BESSIE: I can understand that. You'd think after all I've been through, turned out of my room and everything, now I've got a good bed to sleep in and plenty to eat, I'd be satisfied. But if the truth was only known, when it gets about time for me to get all dolled up and go up West—oh, I feel simply terrible.

COOPER: Do you really?

BESSIE: D'you know what I did last night? I put my dress on and I made up the old face and I put on my usual perfume, and I just stood in my room and fancied myself walking down Jermyn Street.

COOPER: Why didn't you go?

BESSIE: Oh, well, on account of poor old Sheppey, I suppose.

COOPER: It don't look as if he was going to show up.

BESSIE: What d'you want to see him about?

COOPER: Well, if you must know, I get sort of restless when the pubs open. I could do with a bob to get a drop of beer.

BESSIE: Oh, well, I don't blame you.

COOPER: [*Going.*] If he asks for me, say I've gone up the street. I'll be back presently.

> [BESSIE *gives a quick look round and sees the snuff-box is missing. She gets between* COOPER *and the door.*

BESSIE: Where's that snuff-box?

COOPER: What snuff-box?

BESSIE: You know. The one Sheppey had left him.

COOPER: How should I know?

BESSIE: Sheppey sets a rare store on that. He wouldn't lose it for the world.

COOPER: Perhaps the old girl put it away when you come 'ere. Thought it safer.

BESSIE: It was here a minute ago. I saw it.

COOPER: I can't 'elp that. I don't even know what you're talking about.

BESSIE: Yes, you do. You give it up now.

COOPER: 'Ere, who are you talking to?

BESSIE: I thought you was in a great hurry to get out all of a sudden.

COOPER: Look 'ere, my girl. You mind your own business or something unpleasant will 'appen to you.

BESSIE: I'm not frightened of a dirty little tyke like you.

COOPER: Get out of my way. D'you think I'm going to demean myself by arguing with a common prostitute?

BESSIE: You give up that snuff-box.

COOPER: I tell you I 'aven't got it.

BESSIE: Yes, you have. It's in your pocket. Why, I can see it.

COOPER: [*With an instinctive gesture of his hand towards his hip pocket.*] That's a lie.

BESSIE: [*With a hoarse chuckle of triumph.*] Ah. I've caught you. I knew you had it.

COOPER: [*Trying to push past her.*] Oh, shut your mug.

BESSIE: You're not going out of this room till you give that back.

COOPER: What's it got to do with you, anyway?

BESSIE: He may be a silly old fathead, but he means well, and I'm not going to stand by and see you sneak his bits and pieces.

COOPER: I tell you I've got to 'ave a drink.

BESSIE: What you do outside's got nothing to do with me. But not here you don't do anything.

COOPER: If you don't get out of my way I'll give you such a swipe over the jaw.

BESSIE: [*Peering right into his face.*] You dare to hit me. You filthy little sneak-thief. You snivelling little mongrel cur. You dirty son of a . . . [*With a quick movement she tries to snatch the snuff-box out of his pocket.*]

COOPER: No, you don't.

BESSIE: Damn you.

[*There is a short struggle in the middle of which* SHEPPEY *comes in.*

SHEPPEY: Hulloa, what's this?

[*They separate. They are both a trifle out of breath.*

BESSIE: He's got that snuff-box of yours.

SHEPPEY: What about it?

BESSIE: He was just going out to pawn it.

SHEPPEY: What d'you want to do that for, Jim?

COOPER: It's a bleeding lie.

SHEPPEY: It ain't in its usual place.

COOPER: If anyone took it she did. You know what them women are. Just trying to put the blame on me.

BESSIE: You look in his hip-pocket.

SHEPPEY: Empty out your pockets, old man.

COOPER: I won't. I won't be treated like this by any man. D'you think you've got the right to insult me just because I'm your guest?

BESSIE: Oh, dear, 'ark at you.

SHEPPEY: It's no good, old man, I'm afraid you've got to empty them pockets of yours.

COOPER: Who says so?

SHEPPEY: I do and if necessary I can make you.

COOPER: I've 'ad enough of this. I'm going.

> [*He tries to brush past* SHEPPEY, *but* SHEPPEY, *with surprising quickness, seizes him and trips him up, and with his knee on his chest to hold him down gets the snuff-box out of his pocket.*

SHEPPEY: Get up now. Why didn't you give it quietly?

COOPER: 'Ere, you nearly broke my arm.

BESSIE: Why, Sheppey, I am surprised. I didn't know you was as nippy as that.

SHEPPEY: I was a bit of a wrestler when I was a young feller.

BESSIE: Shall I get a cop?

COOPER: [*Springing to his feet.*] You ain't going to give me in charge, Governor? I didn't really mean to take it. It was a sudden temptation. I didn't know what I was doing really.

BESSIE: Whine. Go on. Whine.

SHEPPEY: No, I'm not going to give you in charge. The judge said 'e'd give you the maximum if you ever come before 'im again.

BESSIE: You ain't going to let him go? After all you done for him.

SHEPPEY: I ain't done anything for 'im. What I done I done for meself. Sorry if I 'urt you, old man. I'm stronger than you'd think for, and sometimes I put more strength into a thing than I should.

COOPER: No one's got a right to leave things like that about.

SHEPPEY: It's not gold, you know, it's only silver-gilt. It's not the worth I value it for, it's the sentiment. It was left me by a gentleman I'd attended for years and all through 'is last illness 'e would 'ave me go to his 'ouse and shave 'im every day. 'E said to 'is daughter only the day before 'e died, if I appear before my Maker looking like a gentleman it'll be to Sheppey I owe it. 'Ere take it. [*He hands the snuff-box to* COOPER.]

COOPER: What d'you mean?

SHEPPEY: I'm giving it you.

COOPER: Why?

SHEPPEY: You want it, don't you?

COOPER: No.

SHEPPEY: Why did you pinch it, then?

COOPER: That's quite another matter. I didn't mind pinching it. I'm not going to take it as a present. I only pinched it because I wanted a bob or two for a few beers. I'd 'ave give you back the ticket. Straight, I would.

SHEPPEY: If you wanted a bob why didn't you say so? [*Putting his hand in his pocket and taking out a shilling.*] 'Ere you are.

[COOPER *looks at the shilling in his hand and then at* SHEPPEY. *He is full of suspicion.*

COOPER: 'Ere, what's the meaning of this?

SHEPPEY: If a chap can only see God in a pint of beer 'e may as well look there as not see 'im at all.

COOPER: Is it a trap?

SHEPPEY: Don't talk so silly.

[COOPER *is puzzled and uneasy. He looks at the shilling, and he looks at* SHEPPEY.

COOPER: I don't like this. There's something funny about it all. What are you getting at? What's the idea? 'Ere, take your bob. I won't 'ave it. It'll bring me bad luck.

I'm off. I've 'ad enough of this place. I like to know
where I am with people. This gives me the creeps. I
wish I'd never come 'ere.

[*He goes out quickly.*

BESSIE: Well, that's a good riddance to bad rubbish.

SHEPPEY: Whoever would 'a thought it'd 'ave taken 'im like
that?

BESSIE: What did you want to give him that there box for?

SHEPPEY: Well, I just couldn't 'elp meself.

BESSIE: You know, you ought to be a bit more careful.
You're going to get a nasty knock one of these days if
you go on treating good and bad alike.

SHEPPEY: The fact is, I can't see there's much to choose
between them.

BESSIE: Come off it, Sheppey. Why, that Cooper, he's just a
dirty tyke.

SHEPPEY: I know 'e is. Some'ow I don't mind.

BESSIE: Fact is, Sheppey, you've got no moral sense.

SHEPPEY: I suppose that's it. Lucky I was born lucky.

BESSIE: You're a caution and no mistake.

SHEPPEY: Sorry 'e's gone. I'd got quite used to seeing 'im
about the 'ouse.

BESSIE: I'm going too, Sheppey.

SHEPPEY: Why? Ain't you getting on with mum and Florrie?

BESSIE: It's not that, I want to get back to the West End.
I've been glad to have a bit of a rest here. It's done me
no end of good. I miss the girls and I miss the street.
When you've been used to meeting a lot of people you do
come to depend on it somehow. And then, you never
know what's going to happen to you. It's not the going
with men I like, it's the getting off. I mean, you can't
help feeling, well, that's one up to me. And besides—
oh, well, I don't know, it's the whole thing. It's got its

ups and downs, I don't say it hasn't, but it's exciting;
even if you don't get off it's exciting. That's what I mean,
see?

SHEPPEY: I thought you was fed up with it.

BESSIE: So I was. I was run down and out of sorts. But
now it's different somehow. I know it's a disappointment to you. I'm sorry. Thank you for all you've done
for me.

SHEPPEY: All right. 'Ave it your own way. There'll always
be a 'ome for you 'ere when you want one.

BESSIE: D'you mean to say you'd take me back?

SHEPPEY: Of course I would. I don't blame you. I only
want people to be 'appy.

BESSIE: I think I know a thing or two about men, but I
don't mind saying you've got me beat. Well, so long.

SHEPPEY: You're not going now?

BESSIE: Yes, I am. I can't stand it another minute. I'll just
get myself dressed and then I'll slip away without saying
anything to nobody.

SHEPPEY: All right. And don't forget when you feel like
coming you're welcome.

BESSIE: It's a strange world and no mistake.

[*She goes out. In a moment* MRS. MILLER *comes in.*

MRS. MILLER: I 'eard you come in. I couldn't leave my
kitchen. I was just making a nice calves-foot jelly for
Mrs. Robinson.

SHEPPEY: That's right, my dear. She'll enjoy that.

MRS. MILLER: I told you they was twins, didn't I?

SHEPPEY: Yes.

MRS. MILLER: What did the doctor say about you?

SHEPPEY: Oh, we 'ad a rare set to. 'E 'ad a friend there,
another doctor, Ennismore 'is name was, a tip-top swell,
it appears, and Dr. Jervis said as 'e was there we might

just as well profit by it and 'e examined me too.

MRS. MILLER: I see.

SHEPPEY: A very nice gentleman, he was. Intelligent. He
was very interested in my plan. He got me to tell him
all about it. My word, he did ask me some funny
questions. I couldn't 'ardly 'elp laughing. Asked me
if I'd ever seen my dad 'ave 'is bath. Yes, I said, every
Saturday night, 'e used to make me scrub 'is back
for 'im.

MRS. MILLER: You *were* gone a time.

SHEPPEY: I know I was. We must 'ave talked for nearly
two hours. I left them at it. Dr. Jervis said they'd 'ave
a little chat and 'e'd come 'ere later. [*There is a knock at
the front door.*] That might be 'im now.

MRS. MILLER: Oh, I do hate doctors.

SHEPPEY: Why, you're not anxious, are you?

MRS. MILLER: Yes.

SHEPPEY: That's silly. There's nothing the matter with me.
I never felt better in my life.

[FLORRIE *opens the door.*

FLORRIE: Mum, will you come a minute?

SHEPPEY: Is it the doctor? [*He goes to the door.*] Come in,
doctor.

[DR. JERVIS *comes in followed by* ERNIE.

DR. JERVIS: Good afternoon, Mrs. Miller.

MRS. MILLER: Good afternoon, sir.

DR. JERVIS: Your husband told you? By a piece of good
luck a friend of mine, a West End specialist, happened
to be there when Sheppey came.

SHEPPEY: I was just telling about 'im. 'E made quite an
impression on me.

DR. JERVIS: We've had a talk about you. Heart a bit weak,
you know. We think a rest would do you good.

SHEPPEY: Me?

DR. JERVIS: We want you to go into a home for a while where you'll be comfortable and looked after properly.

> [MRS. MILLER, FLORRIE *and* ERNIE *at once see what this means*. MRS. MILLER *can hardly restrain a start of dismay.*

SHEPPEY: I'm not going to no 'ome. Can't spare the time. I'm a busy man.

MRS. MILLER: Couldn't we look after 'im 'ere?

DR. JERVIS: It's not the same thing. My doctor friend is at the head of a very good hospital. You'll be under his direct care. I don't say you're seriously ill, but you're ill, and you want proper attention.

SHEPPEY: You know, doctors don't know everything.

DR. JERVIS: They don't pretend to.

FLORRIE: It's silly to talk like that, dad. If Dr. Jervis says you're ill, you are ill.

SHEPPEY: I know more about me own 'ealth than 'e does.

DR. JERVIS: Why do you say that? I'd never pretend to know as much as you do about the care of the hair.

SHEPPEY: Sit down, and just let me 'ave a look at your 'air.

DR. JERVIS: Oh, my hair's all right.

SHEPPEY: That's what people say. There's many a man walking about London now with a bald 'ead who'd 'ave a good 'ead of 'air if he'd taken my advice in time.

DR. JERVIS: [*Humouring him.*] All right, you have a look at it.

> [*He sits down and* SHEPPEY *steps over to him. He takes a glass out of his pocket and inspects the doctor's hair.*

SHEPPEY: Been falling out a bit lately?

DR. JERVIS: A bit, you know. I'm getting on.

SHEPPEY: It's just as I thought. If you don't do something

about it you'll be as bald as I am in six months.

DR. JERVIS: Oh, I can't believe that.

SHEPPEY: It's true. And it's a pity. You've got beautiful 'air. I mean, it's not often one comes across a gentleman with 'air of this texture.

DR. JERVIS: Funny you should say that. My wife always says I have nice hair.

SHEPPEY: She won't be able to say it much longer.

DR. JERVIS: Well, I don't know what can be done about it.

SHEPPEY: I do. If you'll massage your 'ead for five minutes night and morning with our number three I guarantee that in six months you'll 'ave as fine a 'ead of 'air as you've ever 'ad in your life.

DR. JERVIS: D'you expect me to believe that?

SHEPPEY: No.

DR. JERVIS: [*Good-naturedly.*] Well, I'll tell you what I'll do: when I'm passing down Jermyn Street I'll drop in and buy myself a bottle.

SHEPPEY: You needn't do that. I always keep a small stock 'ere, in case any of my friends want any. I'll just pop along and put you up a little. Eight and six or thirteen and four?

DR. JERVIS: Thirteen and four. I may as well be hanged for a sheep as a lamb.

SHEPPEY: You'll never regret it. It won't take me more than five minutes.

[*He goes out.*

DR. JERVIS: Of course I only did that to humour him, you know.

MRS. MILLER: Oh, doctor, whatever do you mean?

DR. JERVIS: My friend, Dr. Ennismore, is one of the greatest authorities in England on diseases of the mind and he's made a thorough examination of your husband. He has no doubt at all that he's suffering from acute mania.

MRS. MILLER: Oh, dear.

DR. JERVIS: We want you to persuade him that it's for his own good to go into a home. I'll have another talk with him to-morrow myself. If he won't consent we're prepared to certify him.

MRS. MILLER: Is that really necessary? I mean, I can't bear the thought of 'im being put away.

DR. JERVIS: I must tell you that the prognosis in these cases is not favourable. It's much better that he should be put under restraint before he commits some act that may have unfortunate consequences to himself or to others.

ERNIE: I don't want to say I told you so, but the fact remains, I said he was crazy from the beginning.

DR. JERVIS: It's quite obvious that a sane man is not going to give all his money away to the poor. A sane man takes money from the poor. He runs chain stores, founds building societies, or engages in municipal work.

MRS. MILLER: Sheppey always 'as liked people. I mean, you might almost say 'e loved 'is fellow-men.

DR. JERVIS: That's not a healthy sign, you know. The normal man is selfish, grasping, destructive, vain and sensual. What is generally termed morality is forced upon him by the herd, and the obligation he is under to repress his natural instincts is undoubtedly the cause of many of the disorders of the mind. Dr. Ennismore said to me just now that he had little doubt that philanthropy in general could always be ascribed to repressed homosexuality.

ERNIE: Is it really? I call that very interesting.

DR. JERVIS: He is of opinion that with rational education of the young, philanthropy could be entirely stamped out of this country.

ERNIE: I should like to meet him. He sounds clever.

DR. JERVIS: He asked Sheppey some very searching questions and it looks very much as if there was a distinct father-complex at the bottom of his trouble.

ERNIE: Œdipus and all that. I know.

DR. JERVIS: [*To* MRS. MILLER.] He was asking me when you first noticed anything peculiar.

MRS. MILLER: I never noticed anything peculiar, not till all of a sudden 'e said 'e wanted to live like Jesus.

DR. JERVIS: Has he always been a religious man?

MRS. MILLER: No, that's just it. I mean, 'e never went to church or anything like that. 'E liked to spend 'is Sunday mornings doing odd jobs about the 'ouse. If 'e'd been a bad man it would be different. It seems so funny for a good man to become religious.

DR. JERVIS: Didn't you suspect something was wrong when you saw him reading the Bible?

MRS. MILLER: I'll tell you exactly what 'appened. 'E always reads the *Morning Post*, on account of the Society news, you know. 'E finds it useful with 'is customers to know who's engaged to be married and all that.

DR. JERVIS: I see.

MRS. MILLER: Well, when 'e was ill I went out and got it for 'im. And on the Monday morning when I took it in to 'im, 'e said, mum, 'ave we got a Bible in the 'ouse? Yes, I said, and I give it 'im. I meant no 'arm. Naturally I thought 'e wanted it for a cross-word puzzle.

DR. JERVIS: That's the peculiar cunning of the insane. It's often very difficult indeed to get them to say what you want them to. Now I don't know if you remember, last week when I saw him I asked him if he saw things. He said he saw sin and wickedness beating with their wings. It struck me at the time. That beating with the wings—very suggestive. And then he talked of a great white light. Dr. Ennismore is convinced he has visual hallucinations, but will he admit it? He's as obstinate as a mule.

MRS. MILLER: 'E never 'as been. 'E was a man as would always listen to reason.

DR. JERVIS: His general state is typical. The bright eyes and flushed cheeks. The restlessness and insomnia. Ennismore is a very careful man and he wouldn't say what wasn't a fact. He says he's never seen a prettier case of religious paranoia in all his practice.

MRS. MILLER: I've never 'eard of there being any madness in 'is family. It's like a stigma on all of us.

DR. JERVIS: Get that idea out of your head at once, Mrs. Miller. Ennismore's opinion is that everybody's mad. He says we couldn't live in this world if we weren't.

[SHEPPEY *comes in with a bottle neatly made up into a paper parcel.*

SHEPPEY: 'Ere you are, doctor. I've made it into a nice little package for you.

DR. JERVIS: Would you like cash?

SHEPPEY: No, take it off my bill. I know our number three. After you've once used it you'll never be able to do without it.

DR. JERVIS: Well, I must be getting along.

SHEPPEY: I'll just show you out.

DR. JERVIS: Good-bye, Mrs. Miller. [*He nods to the others.*] Good evening.

MRS. MILLER: Good evening, sir.

[DR. JERVIS *goes out accompanied by* SHEPPEY.

ERNIE: I sympathise with you, Mrs. Miller. I do indeed. But you must say it's the best that could have happened for all parties.

FLORRIE: It would have been a shame to throw all that good money away.

ERNIE: What d'you say to going to the pictures, Florrie? Early show.

FLORRIE: Right ho. You don't want me, mum, do you?

MRS. MILLER: [*A little doubtfully.*] No, dear.

FLORRIE: Why, what's the matter?

MRS. MILLER: Well, I shouldn't 'ave thought you'd want to go to the pictures to-night, when your poor old dad . . .

FLORRIE: I can't do him any good by staying at home. And I want to go all I can these next few days, as I shan't be able to go all next month.

ERNIE: Why not?

FLORRIE: I promised God I wouldn't, not if he made the doctors say poor dad was potty.

ERNIE: You're not going to pay any attention to that? That's only superstition.

FLORRIE: I don't care what it is. I've promised and I'm going to keep my promise. I may want something else one of these days, and then where should I be if I hadn't kept it.

ERNIE: You don't suppose it had any effect really?

FLORRIE: No one can say that, Ernie. I promised I'd do something for God if he'd do something for me. Well, he has, and I'm going to keep my word.

ERNIE: Oh, well, darling, have it your own way.

FLORRIE: Besides, what with getting ready for the wedding and poor dad being in an asylum, we shan't have much chance of going to the pictures next month anyway.

ERNIE: You're a grand girl, Florrie. I don't know what I should do without you.

FLORRIE: You wouldn't have liked breaking it off, would you?

ERNIE: Me? Why, the thought never entered my head.

FLORRIE: Oh, yes it did. And I don't blame you.

ERNIE: Well, I don't mind telling you now that I was having a bit of a struggle between my inclinations and my duty to myself. And when I say my duty to myself, of course I mean my duty to the community.

MRS. MILLER: [*With a sigh, tolerantly.*] Oh, go on with you. After all one's only young once.

FLORRIE: Come on, Ernie. We don't want to get there when it's half over.

[*As they are going out* SHEPPEY *comes in.*

SHEPPEY: 'Ulloa, where are you two off to?

FLORRIE: Going to the pictures. See you later.

[*They go out.*

MRS. MILLER: You look a bit tired, dear. Why don't you go to our room and 'ave a lay down?

SHEPPEY: No, I don't fancy that. I'll just sit in my chair and perhaps I'll 'ave forty winks. I don't feel very grand, really. I've 'ad a busy day.

MRS. MILLER: You won't be going out again, will you? Let me take off your boots.

[*She goes down on her knees and begins to take them off.*

SHEPPEY: You've been a good wife to me, Ada.

MRS. MILLER: Oh, don't be so silly. If you talk like that I shall think you're ill and I shall put you right to bed with a 'ot-water bottle.

SHEPPEY: You 'ave, you know. I expect I've often been aggravating and unreasonable like.

MRS. MILLER: Oh, go on. If you want me to 'ave a good cry, say so.

SHEPPEY: I expect this 'as been a disappointment to you, about the money, I mean. I know you wanted to finish paying for the 'ouse and a girl to do the rough work.

MRS. MILLER: Don't let's talk about that, Sheppey.

U

SHEPPEY: We must, my dear. It'll be all right for Florrie. She's got Ernie. 'E's a bit conceited, but that's because 'e's young. 'E's a good boy really. Florrie 'll lick 'im into shape all right. She'll turn 'im round 'er little finger like you 'ave me, dear.

MRS. MILLER: I like that.

SHEPPEY: But it's going to be different for you. I know that. That's why I want you to look at it like I do. It's the pain of the world that gets me.

MRS. MILLER: Oh, Sheppey, don't you think that's just because you're run down?

SHEPPEY: I tell you I never felt better in me life. I feel so light in myself if it wasn't for me 'eavy boots I believe I'd float right away.

MRS. MILLER: You would look funny, Sheppey, flying around like a butterfly.

SHEPPEY: I'm going to 'ave a grand time, Ada.

MRS. MILLER: Are you, dear?

SHEPPEY: Don't think I'm not grateful for all you done for me, Ada. Don't think I'm not sorry to disappoint you. But I've got to do this.

MRS. MILLER: I know you wouldn't do anything but what you thought was right, Sheppey.

SHEPPEY: You won't 'old it up against me, dear?

MRS. MILLER: As if I'd ever 'old anything up against you, Sheppey. Aggravating as you may be.

SHEPPEY: It's many a day since you kissed me, Ada.

MRS. MILLER: Go on with you. What would anyone want an old woman like me kissing them for?

SHEPPEY: First time I kissed you, you slapped my face good and proper.

MRS. MILLER: I thought you was a bit too free and easy.

SHEPPEY: Come on, Ada. To show there's no ill feeling.

> [*He leans forward and she puts up her face. They kiss one another gently on the lips.*

MRS. MILLER: It makes me feel quite foolish.

SHEPPEY: What 'ave you got for supper to-night?

MRS. MILLER: Well, I've made a cottage pie.

SHEPPEY: D'you know what I'd fancy?

MRS. MILLER: No.

SHEPPEY: I'd fancy a couple of kippers. You know I always 'ave liked kippers.

MRS. MILLER: I know you 'ave. I'll tell you what I'll do. I'll run out in a little while and get them for you.

SHEPPEY: You're sure it's not too much trouble?

MRS. MILLER: It's no trouble at all. Now you just sit down in your chair. See if you can 'ave forty winks.

SHEPPEY: All right.

MRS. MILLER: I won't disturb you till supper's ready. We'll 'ave it the moment Florrie and Ernie come back.

SHEPPEY: I don't mind telling you that I shall enjoy a bit of a rest.

MRS. MILLER: I'll draw the blind.

> [*She goes to the window and does this. She goes out. SHEPPEY sits down in the winged grandfather's chair, so that he is hidden from sight. The stage is darkened to show the passage of a couple of hours.*

> [*When the scene grows a little lighter, night has fallen. Through the blind is seen the light of an arc lamp in the street. The chair in which SHEPPEY is sleeping is vaguely discernible. There is a knock at the door. No answer comes from SHEPPEY and the knock is repeated.*

SHEPPEY: Come in. [*The door is not opened.*] Come in. [*He gets up.*] I thought I 'eard a knock.

[*The door is opened wide, silently; and as it opens it gives the impression that it has not been pushed but has swung open of its own accord.* BESSIE *stands in the door. She wears a long black cloak, but no hat.*

SHEPPEY: Oh, it's you, is it? I thought I 'eard a knock.

BESSIE: I didn't knock.

SHEPPEY: Didn't you? I suppose I was dreaming. Come in, dear.

[*She comes in and the door closes behind her.*

SHEPPEY: Got somebody with you?

BESSIE: No.

SHEPPEY: Who shut the door then? It's funny. I must be half asleep. [*He goes to the door, opens it and looks out.*] There's nobody there.

BESSIE: [*With the shadow of a smile.*] No.

SHEPPEY: You 'aven't been gone long.

BESSIE: Have you been expecting me?

SHEPPEY: Thought better of it, I suppose. Well, I can't say I'm sorry. I'll put on some light. [*He switches on a standard lamp. The room is now dimly lit.* BESSIE *stands near the door, motionless.*] What are you standing like that for? Come in.

BESSIE: Thanks.

[*She enters into the room. There is something about her that seems strange to him. He cannot quite make it out. It makes him vaguely uneasy.*

SHEPPEY: Did my old woman let you in?

BESSIE: The house is empty.

SHEPPEY: I suppose she's popped out to get them kippers. We wasn't expecting you in to supper.

BESSIE: I generally come before I'm wanted.

SHEPPEY: No, you don't, not 'ere. I said you was always welcome and I meant it.

BESSIE: It's pleasant to hear that for once.

SHEPPEY: I say, why are you speaking so funny all of a sudden?

BESSIE: Am I? I didn't know.

> [*The cockney accent with which* BESSIE *spoke has in fact disappeared, and this woman speaks now in ordinary English.*]

SHEPPEY: All posh. [*Imitating her.*] The house is empty. It's pleasant to hear that for once. No good trying to be the perfect lady with me, you know.

BESSIE: I'm afraid you must take me as I am.

SHEPPEY: Oh, go on, speak natural. 'Ave you been drinking? [*She does not answer and he gives her a quick suspicious look.*] What's the matter with you to-night? You are Bessie Legros, aren't you? You're just like 'er. [*He goes up to her.*] And yet there's something different. [*Puzzled and astonished.*] You're not Bessie Legros.

WOMAN: No.

SHEPPEY: Who are you?

WOMAN: Death.

SHEPPEY: [*With his usual friendly good humour.*] Well, I'm glad you've told me. I shouldn't have known otherwise. Sit down, won't you?

DEATH: No, I won't do that.

SHEPPEY: In a hurry?

DEATH: I have no time to waste.

SHEPPEY: Are you on your way to Mrs. Robinson's? My wife was making her some calves-foot jelly only this afternoon. If it's the twins I don't suppose they'll be sorry. They've got four already and Robinson's been out of work for eight months.

DEATH: Has he? No, I wasn't thinking of going there.

SHEPPEY: Well, you know your own business best.

DEATH: I have my whims and fancies.

SHEPPEY: Being a woman.

DEATH: You like your little joke, don't you?

SHEPPEY: I always 'ave. 'Aving a sense of 'umour 'as been
an asset to me. I've often 'eard my customers say to
the governor, No, I'll wait for Sheppey. 'E always gives
me a good laugh.

DEATH: That's more than my customers can say of me.

SHEPPEY: [*Gently chaffing her.*] I suppose on the whole people
would just as soon 'ave your room as your company.

DEATH: I'm not often welcome. And yet sometimes you'd
think they'd be glad to see me.

SHEPPEY: Well, I don't know. It's not a very nice thing
to say to a lady, but I think your looks are a bit against
you.

DEATH: I felt there must be something.

SHEPPEY: Funny me taking you for Bessie Legros. Now I
come to talk to you you're not a bit like her. Of course
she's what they call a common prostitute, but there's
something you can't 'ardly 'elp liking about 'er. [*He
pinches his arm.*]

DEATH: Why do you do that?

SHEPPEY: I was only pinching my arm. I wanted to see if
I was awake. I'm dreaming, but I know I'm dreaming.
That's funny, isn't it?

DEATH: What makes you think you're dreaming?

SHEPPEY: Well, I know I am. I'm sitting in my chair 'aving
a nap really. I've been 'aving the most extraordinary
dreams lately. I was telling the doctor about them only
this afternoon. Our own doctor thought I was potty.
[*With glee.*] I got back on 'im all right. Sold 'im a bottle
of our number three.

DEATH: That was clever of you.

SHEPPEY: I know it was. 'E tried to pretend 'e was only buying it to 'umour me. My eye and Betty Martin. He bought it because I 'ypnotised 'im. And 'e'll use it night and morning like I told 'im to. There's no one I couldn't sell our number three to. I could sell you a bottle if I wanted to.

DEATH: I don't think it would do me much good.

SHEPPEY: Now don't say that. When people say a thing like that it puts me on my mettle. Just let me 'ave a look at your 'air.

DEATH: I haven't got time just now.

SHEPPEY: I don't say you 'aven't got a good 'ead of 'air, but 'ow d'you know you're going to keep it? 'Ulloa, who's this?

[*The door opens and* COOPER *slinks in.*

COOPER: It's me, governor.

SHEPPEY: You've come back then?

COOPER: Been waiting on the opposite side of the street till the coast was clear. They're all out.

SHEPPEY: Yes, I know they are.

COOPER: As I was going out I 'eard them talking. I was 'iding just outside the kitchen and I 'eard every word they said. They're going to shut you up, governor.

SHEPPEY: Me? What for?

COOPER: 'Cause you're barmy.

SHEPPEY: Don't be so silly.

COOPER: God's truth, governor. I swear it is. Florrie and that bloke of 'ers. They're going to shut you up so they can get 'old of your money. Your old woman's in it too.

SHEPPEY: You make me laugh. Why, my old woman wouldn't let them touch a 'air of my 'ead.

COOPER: They're going to try and make you go to the asylum peaceful, but if you won't they're going to sign you up.

SHEPPEY: Oh, is that what you think? And what are you going to do about it?

COOPER: Well, I've come to warn you.

SHEPPEY: That's very kind of you, I'm sure.

COOPER: When I thought you was in your right mind you give me the creeps. That's why I skipped. Now I know you're barmy—well, that's another story altogether. I'm used to people like that. My mother's uncle was barmy. Used to live with us. Thought 'e was a loaf of sugar. Wouldn't wash, because 'e thought 'e'd melt.

SHEPPEY: That's a funny idea.

COOPER: You've been a good sport to me. Saved me from a stretch. One good turn deserves another. You slip out of the 'ouse now with me when there's nobody about. I'll take care of you, see? Never mind about the money.

SHEPPEY: [*To the woman.*] What do you think about that? I knew 'e was no worse than anybody else, really.

COOPER: [*Startled.*] Who are you talking to?

SHEPPEY: That lady there.

COOPER: Where? I don't see no lady.

SHEPPEY: Look again.

COOPER: There's no one there.

SHEPPEY: That's a good one. Looking straight at you and says there's no one there.

DEATH: I'm not surprised.

SHEPPEY: [*To* COOPER.] Hear that?

COOPER: What?

SHEPPEY: She says she's not surprised.

COOPER: Nobody's spoke but you and me.

SHEPPEY: 'E don't seem to 'ear either.

DEATH: Why should he? I have nothing to say to him yet.

SHEPPEY: I was just going to sell her a bottle of our number three when you come in. Women think they're artful. They're just as easy as men really.

COOPER: Look 'ere, governor, if you want to get away you'd better look nippy. They'll be back in 'alf a mo'.

SHEPPEY: Not me. I ain't going to trust myself to a fellow that's as blind as a bat and as deaf as a post.

COOPER: Don't I tell you if you stay 'ere they'll shut you up?

SHEPPEY: Maybe you mean well and maybe you don't. Maybe you're the devil in disguise. I'm a respectable member of society and I'm not going on any 'arum-scarum adventures.

COOPER: Don't say the gipsy never warned you.

SHEPPEY: That's all right. I'm in the middle of an interesting conversation with this lady. I don't want to be disturbed.

COOPER: Oh, all right, 'ave it your own way.

[*He slips out of the room.* SHEPPEY *turns to* DEATH *with a smile.*

SHEPPEY: Funny 'im not being able to see you.

DEATH: The hemp's not picked yet to make the rope that's waiting for him.

SHEPPEY: That's not a very nice thing to say about anybody.

DEATH: It all comes to the same thing in the end, you know.

SHEPPEY: But I say, if you ain't there really, 'ow is it *I* see you?

DEATH: Can't you guess?

SHEPPEY: [*With a sudden movement of dismay.*] Look 'ere, you ain't come 'ere on my account?

DEATH: Yes.

SHEPPEY: You're joking. I thought you'd just come to 'ave a little chat. I'm sorry, my dear, there's nothing doing to-day. You must call again some other time.

DEATH: I'm too busy for that.

SHEPPEY: I don't think that's treating me right. Coming in all friendly and pleasant. If I'd known what you was after I'd 'ave nipped off with Cooper when 'e asked me.

DEATH: That wouldn't have helped you much.

SHEPPEY: I wish now I'd gone down to the Isle of Sheppey when the doctor advised it. You wouldn't 'ave thought of looking for me there.

DEATH: There was a merchant in Bagdad who sent his servant to market to buy provisions and in a little while the servant came back, white and trembling, and said, Master, just now when I was in the market-place I was jostled by a woman in the crowd and when I turned I saw it was death that jostled me. She looked at me and made a threatening gesture; now, lend me your horse, and I will ride away from this city and avoid my fate. I will go to Samarra and there death will not find me. The merchant lent him his horse, and the servant mounted it, and he dug his spurs in its flanks and as fast as the horse could gallop he went. Then the merchant went down to the market-place and he saw me standing in the crowd and he came to me and said, Why did you make a threatening gesture to my servant when you saw him this morning? That was not a threatening gesture, I said, it was only a start of surprise. I was astonished to see him in Bagdad, for I had an appointment with him to-night in Samarra.

SHEPPEY: [*With a little shudder.*] D'you mean there's no escaping you?

DEATH: No.

SHEPPEY: [*Trying to wheedle her*.] I don't fancy the idea of leaving this world. I know my way about and I'm at 'ome 'ere. Seems silly at my age to go on a wild-goose chase like this.

DEATH: Are you afraid?

SHEPPEY: What of? The Judgment Day? [*With a little smile*.] No, not really. You see, the way I look at it is this: I've 'ad dozens of apprentices under me, and often they was silly and inattentive and broke things, you know what boys are, fond of a lark; well, of course I told 'em off, but I never 'eld it up against them. I'm not going to believe in a God that's not got as much common sense and as much sense of 'umour as I 'ave.

DEATH: Are you ready then?

SHEPPEY: What for?

DEATH: To start.

SHEPPEY: Now? This minute? I never knew you meant that. Why, what's the 'urry? I must talk it over with my wife first. I never do a thing without consulting 'er.

DEATH: She can't help you now.

SHEPPEY: Besides, she's giving me kippers for my supper. She'd be terribly upset if I wasn't 'ere to eat them after she's taken all that trouble.

DEATH: Others will eat them in your place.

SHEPPEY: To tell you the truth, I'm feeling rather tired. I don't feel like making a journey to-night.

DEATH: It's an easy one.

SHEPPEY: And then there's another thing. I daresay you don't read the papers and 'aven't 'eard about it. I won over eight thousand pounds in the Irish Sweep and I've made up my mind to use it in a particular way. It would be ridiculous for me to pop off just when I'm going to do a bit of good in the world.

DEATH: It does happen like that sometimes. The world will get on quite well without you. You men, you find it hard to realise that.

[*There is the sound of the street door being closed.*]

SHEPPEY: There's my wife just come in. I'll call her, shall I?

DEATH: She wouldn't hear you if you did.

SHEPPEY: You know, we've never been separated since we married. I don't think she'll like me going off like this without 'er.

DEATH: She can't come with you on this journey.

SHEPPEY: She'll be quite lost in the 'ouse without 'aving me to look after. Of course I suppose in a way it'll be a rest for 'er. Cooking my dinner and washing my clothes. It won't 'urt 'er to take things a bit easy for the rest of 'er life. It'll seem strange to 'er just at first.

DEATH: People get used to it, you know.

SHEPPEY: Especially widows, I've noticed. Seems funny me talking of Ada as a widow. She'll take it terrible 'ard, you know.

DEATH: She'll get over it in time.

SHEPPEY: That's not much consolation to me. Look 'ere, I'll tell you what I'll do, I'll give you a thousand pounds of my Sweep money and you go out the way you came.

DEATH: Money's no use to me.

SHEPPEY: You know, I don't feel at all well. I think I ought to see the doctor.

DEATH: You'll feel better presently.

SHEPPEY: You seem to 'ave an answer to everything. Seems a pity, when you come to think of it, me not being able to do what I'd set me 'eart on. Of course, they kep' on telling me I'd do more 'arm than good. What was that other thing 'e said? Thy will be done. [*With a sigh.*] Fact is, I'm so tired, I don't seem to mind any more.

DEATH: I know. It's often surprised me. People are so frightened beforehand, and the older they are the more frightened, but when it comes to the point they don't really mind.

SHEPPEY: There's just one thing I'd like to ask you before we go. What's on the other side really?

DEATH: I've often wondered.

SHEPPEY: Do you mean to say you don't know? [*She shakes her head.*] Are you going to tell me you go about taking people away, one after the other, young and old, whether they like it or not, and you don't know where it is they're going?

DEATH: It's no business of mine.

SHEPPEY: I don't think you're justified for a minute. I mean, you 'aven't got the right to take a responsibility like that.

DEATH: To tell you the truth, I've sometimes wondered if it isn't all a terrible misunderstanding.

SHEPPEY: [*Indignantly.*] All right, then. I'll just go and see for myself. Which way do we go?

DEATH: Out of the door.

SHEPPEY: That seems rather tame. I thought we'd fly out of the window or pop up the chimney. Something spectacular, you know.

DEATH: No.

SHEPPEY: Well, I'll just put on my boots. [*He looks round for them.*] There now. That artful old woman, she was afraid I'd go out and she's taken them away and 'id them.

DEATH: You'll have to come without.

SHEPPEY: I shall look funny walking about without my boots on.

DEATH: Nobody will notice.

SHEPPEY: I'll just put out the light. No good running up an electric light bill.

> [*He switches off the electric light at the door. The door is opened and they pass out. In the empty room a rattle, the death rattle, is heard. It seems to come from the chair in which* SHEPPEY *was sleeping.*

> [*The door is opened again and* FLORRIE *and* ERNIE *come in. He switches on the light.* ERNIE *turns back and speaks to* MRS. MILLER *in the passage.*

ERNIE: No, he's not here.

FLORRIE: Perhaps he's gone out.

MRS. MILLER: [*In the door.*] No, 'is 'at's in the 'all. I expect 'e's 'aving a lay down in our room. I'll let 'im be till supper's ready. You lay the table, Florrie.

FLORRIE: Right you are, mum.

> [MRS. MILLER *disappears from sight.* FLORRIE *gets the tablecloth and the knives and forks from the sideboard.* ERNIE *helps her to lay the cloth.*

ERNIE: No lodgers to-night, it appears.

FLORRIE: Thank goodness.

ERNIE: What's happened to them?

FLORRIE: I don't know and I don't care. Though I don't mind Bessie really.

ERNIE: Sorry I didn't have a talk to her. Oldest profession in the world, they say. It would have been interesting to clarify my views on the subject.

> [MRS. MILLER *comes in with the tray on which are glasses, a loaf of bread and a jug of water.*

MRS. MILLER: What was the picture like?

FLORRIE: Lovely.

ERNIE: Bit sloppy for me. I hate all this sentiment.

FLORRIE: I saw you crying all right.

ERNIE: What a lie.

MRS. MILLER: It's nothing to be ashamed of. I like a good cry myself.

> [*She goes out.*

ERNIE: Good-looking chap, the gangster. I'll admit that.

FLORRIE: He wasn't as good-looking as you.

ERNIE: The rot you talk, Florrie.

FLORRIE: I mean it.

ERNIE: Oh, do you?

> [*They are standing together, close to the gramophone. He puts his arms round her and kisses her. Their lips linger.*

FLORRIE: Love me, Ernie?

ERNIE: I couldn't love anyone like I love you.

> [*With his disengaged hand he switches on the gramophone. They begin to dance cheek to cheek.*

FLORRIE: Mum's a bit low to-night.

ERNIE: Worried about your dad, I suppose.

FLORRIE: Naturally she's anxious. The doctor told her the other day he might pop off any minute.

ERNIE: Don't you believe it. They live for ever in asylums. He's good for another twenty years.

FLORRIE: Isn't it lovely to think of everything coming out all right?

ERNIE: Must you talk?

> [*He kisses her on the lips as they dance on.* MRS. MILLER *comes in again with the tray. There is a cottage pie on it, and on a plate* SHEPPEY'S *two kippers.*

MRS. MILLER: Really you're a disgrace, you two. Is that what you call laying the table?

> [*They stop and* ERNIE *turns off the music.*

ERNIE: The woman tempted me and I fell.

FLORRIE: That's right, blame me.

ERNIE: I don't know what it is, but there's something about her I can't help liking.

MRS. MILLER: Oh, dear, don't be so silly. One of you's just as bad as the other. D'you think nobody's ever been in love before? Run up and tell your dad supper's ready, my girl.

> [ERNIE's *glance falls on the grandfather's chair.*

ERNIE: You needn't do that. Here he is ready and waiting.

> [*He swings round the chair sideways so that an arm and a hand are seen to fall over the arm of the chair.*

FLORRIE: Why, he's asleep.

> [MRS. MILLER *takes a step forward and stops suddenly.*

MRS. MILLER: That's not sleep. [*She looks at him for a moment.*] He always said 'e was born lucky. He's died lucky too.

THE END